D0190448

EARLY CHILDHOOD EDUCATION SERIES
Sharon Ryan, Editor

ADVISORY BOARD: Barbara T. Bowman, Harriet K. Cuffaro, Stephanie Feeney, Doris Pronin Fromberg, Celia Genishi, Stacie G. Goffin, Dominic F. Gullo, Alice Sterling Honig, Elizabeth Jones, Gwen Morgan

Young English Language Learners

CURRENT RESEARCH AND EMERGING
DIRECTIONS FOR PRACTICE AND POLICY

Edited by

Eugene E. García
Ellen C. Frede

Teachers College, Columbia University
New York and London

Published by Teachers College Press, 1234 Amsterdam Avenue, New York, NY 10027

Library of Congress Cataloging-in-Publication Data

Young English language learners : current research and emerging directions for practice and policy / edited by Eugene E. García, Ellen C. Frede.
    p. cm. — (Early childhood education series)
Includes bibliographical references and index.
ISBN 978-0-8077-5111-4 (pbk. : alk. paper)
ISBN 978-0-8077-5112-1 (hardcover : alk. paper)
    1. English language—Study and teaching (Preschool)—United States—Foreign speakers. 2. Linguistic minorities—Education (Preschool)—United States. I. García, Eugene E., 1946– II. Frede, Ellen C.
PE1128.A2Y68   2010
428.2′4—dc22   2010014218

ISBN 978-0-8077-5111-4 (paper)
ISBN 978-0-8077-5112-1 (hardcover)

Printed on acid-free paper
Manufactured in the United States of America

17   16   15   14   13   12   11   10   8   7   6   5   4   3   2   1

Contents

Acknowledgments

The chapters in this volume were initially presented as papers at the Enhancing the Knowledge Base for Serving Young English Language Learners Invitational Research Symposium, co-sponsored by the National Institute for Early Education Research (NIEER) at Rutgers University and the Education Research Section of the Woodrow Wilson School of Public Policy at Princeton University. Additional funding was provided by the Pew Charitable Trusts and the Packard Foundation. We are grateful for this generous support. Dr. Lisa Markman-Pithers of Princeton University and Ms. Alexandra Figueras-Daniel of NIEER were instrumental in ensuring the success of the symposium. Alex continued to offer invaluable assistance in communicating with the authors and initially helping to organize the chapters. We also appreciate the help given by Dr. Delis Cuellar and Dr. Bryant Jensen at Arizona State University.

Chapter authors and the few other invited attendees at the symposium provided useful comments and critiques for each chapter, and we especially appreciate the suggestions provided by Dr. Diane August, Ms. Yasmine Daniel, Ms. Danielle Gonzales, and Mr. Albert Wat. Dr. Steve Barnett not only offered useful critiques at the symposium, but continued to advise us on some of the more technical methodological questions. This design of shared expertise across authors and attendees greatly enhanced the content and clarity of the volume.

Preparing the volume for final submission was a huge task and in this we were ably assisted. Terri Manzo of NIEER was invaluable with her attention to detail, speedy turnaround, incredible knowledge of APA guidelines, and superb word-processing skills. We are overwhelmingly grateful for her work.

Finally, we cannot express our gratitude and appreciation in strong enough terms for the unimaginable grace and patience combined with astounding insight and expertise offered by Marie Ellen Larcarda of Teachers College Press. What an exceptional editor she is.

Young English Language Learners

CURRENT RESEARCH AND EMERGING DIRECTIONS FOR PRACTICE AND POLICY

CHAPTER 1

Overview and Introduction

Eugene E. García
Ellen C. Frede

One of the nation's most important and long-standing educational challenges is to develop a set of proven strategies for making more rapid, sustained progress in raising the level of academic achievement of students who come to U.S. schools speaking a home language other than English.

At every level of the education system, these English Language Learners (ELLs) continue to lag well behind other students in critical academic areas (reading, science, history, mathematics, etc.) by all traditional measures, including standardized test scores, grade point averages, and class rankings. Moreover, little progress has been made in closing these gaps over the past 2 decades, despite extensive efforts by educators and policymakers (August & Shanahan, 2006). This lack of significant progress is increasingly problematic because ELL students now constitute nearly one-fifth of the nation's young children, and the Hispanic share is growing rapidly. In 2006, 24.2% of the babies born in the United States had a mother who reported a primary home language other than English (Miller & García, 2008).

In response to these circumstances, this volume presents a collection of research, policy, and practice reviews in critical areas relevant to this population. The focus is on the early years, because the achievement patterns in language and reading of racial/ethnic groups are largely established in the period from birth through the end of the primary grades (age 8 or 9 for most children). The emphasis is on language and reading, owing to the importance of having strong academic language and literacy capabilities and repertoires, especially by the start of 4th grade. At that point, students need solid reading comprehension skills to master most areas of the curriculum.

THE ELL STUDENT ACHIEVEMENT GAP

The volume is designed to address several aspects of the ELL achievement gap. First, ELL students continue to be heavily overrepresented among low-achieving students—students within the bottom 5% to 25% of the achievement distribution; and they are severely underrepresented among high achievers—those in the top 5% to 25% of the distribution at all grade levels (Lee, Grigg, & Donahue, 2007).

Second, the academic achievement of ELL students lags behind that of their non-ELL student counterparts at all socioeconomic levels, whether social class is measured by parent education, family income, parent occupation, or a combination of the three. Moreover, some of the largest of these "within-class" achievement gaps are at high socioeconomic status (SES) levels (García & Miller, 2008).

Third, children from immigrant families who are English language learners tend to achieve at much lower levels than youngsters who are English speakers when they enter school (Reardon & Galindo, 2006a). As indicated earlier, there is evidence that this is a problem to some extent for ELL students at all social-class levels; it is most acute for children from low-SES families. Because a large percentage of Hispanic children are ELL students from low-SES circumstances, improving the reading readiness and reading achievement of these children will be essential if ELL students are to reach achievement parity.

Let us turn briefly to an important longitudinal analysis of ELL student achievement and related achievement gaps early in a student's schooling experience. These data are available in recent analyses of K–5 reading and math achievement trajectories that used data from the Early Childhood Longitudinal Study–Kindergarten Cohort (ECLS-K), which is following a national sample of children who started kindergarten in 1998 (Miller & García, 2008).

The number of students in the ECLS-K of Hispanic descent allows inspection of these students by immigration status and ELL status. This analysis is revealing, since the substantial majority of ELL students are Hispanic (Hernandez, this volume). Table 1.1 provides a look at 5th-grade achievement as measured in ECLS-K for ethnic groups and SES levels, as well as a comparison of ELL students who were identified at the beginning of kindergarten for this sample. The data in Table 1.1 show that the reading situation had changed considerably by the end of 5th grade. Importantly, the 70% of Hispanics who had been assessed in English at the start of kindergarten demonstrated stronger reading skills than the African American youngsters at the end of 5th grade, even though the Hispanics continued to lag well behind the White and Asian American children. For instance, among the 70% of Hispanics, 41% were proficient at

TABLE 1.1. Percentages of Hispanics, Whites, Blacks, and Asian Americans Scoring at or Above Levels 6, 7, 8, and 9 in Reading at the End of 5th Grade, Overall and by SES Quintile

Group	Level 6	Level 7	Level 8	Level 9
30% of Hispanics that were not English Proficient, Fall K	72	41	23	1
70% of Hispanics that were English Proficient, Fall K	86	69	41	5
First (Lowest) SES Quintile	77	51	29	1
Second SES Quintile	89	74	44	6
Third SES Quintile	86	66	38	2
Fourth SES Quintile	92	81	51	9
Fifth (Highest) SES Quintile	95	87	59	13
All Third Generation Whites	91	79	52	10
First (Lowest) SES Quintile	73	51	30	3
Second SES Quintile	86	68	40	4
Third SES Quintile	91	77	48	7
Fourth SES Quintile	94	86	55	9
Fifth (Highest) SES	96	91	64	20
All Third Generation Blacks	78	53	31	2
First (Lowest) SES Quintile	70	39	23	2
Second SES Quintile	76	52	30	2
Third SES Quintile	83	59	33	2
Fourth SES Quintile	88	72	44	7
Fifth (Highest) SES Quintile	85	66	39	4
81% of Asian Americans that were English Proficient, Fall K	93	84	54	10

Source: Reardon & Galindo (2006b)

evaluating and interpreting beyond text (Level 8), while this was the case for 31% of Blacks, 52% of Whites, and 54% of Asians.

Table 1.1 also includes 5th-grade reading data for the 30% of Hispanic children who were identified as ELLs at the start of kindergarten. That large group of Hispanic children had about the same English-reading-proficiency pattern at the end of 5th grade as the lowest-SES-quintile African American youngsters. Thus, at the end of 5th grade, both of these segments were doing more poorly in reading, not only lower than the low-SES Whites, but also worse than the low-SES Hispanics who were among the 70% of Latinos who did have sufficiently strong oral English skills at the start of kindergarten to be assessed in it.

THE PROMISE AND CHALLENGE OF ELLs AND EARLY EDUCATION

One potential remedy for this troubling data of low achievement for ELLs is early educational intervention and, specifically, preschool. The number of 3- and 4-year-old children attending some form of center-based education has been increasing each year, with more than 1.1 million children served in state-funded pre-kindergarten programs and slightly more than 900,000 served in Head Start in 2007–2008 (Barnett, Epstein, Friedman, Stevenson-Boyd, & Hustedt, 2008). Twenty-four percent of all 4-year-olds are served in 50 state pre-K programs in 38 states. State funding for pre-K is almost $4.6 billion, with average per-child spending at $4,609. In addition to children participating in state-funded pre-K and Head Start, 3- and 4-year-olds also participate in a patchwork of other care and education settings, including locally funded pre-kindergarten, special education (IDEA), and private preschools and child care programs (both funded privately by parents and government subsidized).

Head Start

Founded in the 1960s, Head Start has a long history of providing preschool education to disadvantaged children. The program also offers family supports, such as employment counseling for parents and medical referrals for children, and requires that each Head Start agency establish transition plans with the local public schools in their catchment area. The program is funded by the U.S. Department of Health and Human Services, which provides grants to local entities. Eligibility for the program is primarily determined by the family's poverty status, and children can remain eligible for program participation for multiple years even when their family circumstances change. In the 2007–2008 program year, Head Start served 906,922 children (Barnett et al., 2008). Head Start spent $7,909 per child in the 2007–2008 school year for an estimated cost of more than $6.2 billion per year. In 2007–2008, only 40% of Head Start children were served in full-day programs. In addition, teachers with college degrees were not paid on par with public school teachers, making it difficult to prevent turnover. Measures of the classroom quality and outcomes for children of Head Start programs vary, but studies generally find that Head Start offers a good quality educational program (Zill et al., 2006).

State Programs

State-funded pre-K, primarily targeted toward select groups of 3- and 4-year-olds, is available in 48 distinct programs in 39 states. States use a variety of mechanisms to fund pre-kindergarten—for example, Georgia uses proceeds from the lottery, California uses money from tobacco taxes, and many states combine multiple funding streams including federal child care dollars, Title I, and local property taxes. Presently, Florida, Georgia, Illinois, Iowa, New York, Oklahoma, and West Virginia have enacted policies to eventually offer pre-K services to all children regardless of their family income. However, only Oklahoma currently approaches universal service, with 92% of 4-year-olds enrolled in state pre-K, Head Start, or preschool special education. Most states offer *targeted* programs that are designed to serve children who are eligible because of their family's low income status.

ELLs and Preschool

The historical increase in funding and provision of preschool reflects a growing awareness of the results of research on preschool's educational and financial benefits. Hundreds of studies have documented the educational advantages conferred by attendance in high-quality preschool, and many of these studies have shown that the benefits continue into school-age and even adulthood. The educational benefits include higher grades and scores on other measures of achievement, reduction in grade retention and special education placement, greater graduation rates, and increased enrollment in higher education. Adults who attended preschool as children were less likely to engage in crime, more likely to own a home, and earned more when compared to control groups of adults who did not attend preschool. These differences also result in savings to taxpayers over and above the cost of the preschool program.

Given the achievement gap documented above for children who do not speak English when they enter kindergarten, it is not surprising that policymakers and advocates have begun calling for greater attention to enrolling young ELLs in preschool (National Task Force on Early Childhood Education for Hispanics, 2007). Starting in the 2007 State Preschool *Yearbook*, NIEER researchers collected data on provision of services for English language learners. In the 2008 *Yearbook* (Barnett et al., 2008), states reported the number of ELL children served. Of the 24 states that collect this information, the percentage of enrolled children who were ELLs ranged from a high of approximately 43% in Nevada and Texas to less than 1% in West Virginia. Many of the states that serve a larger proportion of their total 4-year-old population are also states with large Hispanic or other language-minority populations. For example, Oklahoma, Florida, Texas, New York, Illinois, and New Jersey are all in the top 15 states for access to preschool. However, other high language-minority states, such as Nevada, Oregon, and Arizona, serve less than 10% of their 4-year-old population in state-funded pre-K. Since all Head Start programs and 30 of the state-funded preschool programs are targeted to low-income families, a relatively large proportion of the children served are likely from homes where English is not the primary language. This is especially likely given that 16 states use home language as a criterion for enrollment beyond income. Another seven states allow local districts to determine additional risk factors for enrollment, and it is likely that districts use language spoken in the home as one criterion. How to best educate this important and growing population is a concern for policymakers and practitioners.

Three studies of early care and education in states provide some information about the experiences ELL children have in these programs. In a study of state-funded center-based care in California, researchers found that close to 60% of children have teachers with no training in bilingual education and that most of the teachers do not speak Spanish (Karoly, Ghosh-Dastidar, Zellman, Perlman, & Fernyhough, 2008). In a study of New Jersey's largest state-funded preschool program, nearly 54% of the children are Hispanic and 24% come from homes where only Spanish is spoken. In these classrooms, where all of the teachers are required to be college graduates with certification in early childhood education (ECE), 50% of the teachers who have Spanish-speaking children speak Spanish themselves, and the majority of classrooms have at least one adult who speaks Spanish. In the early years of the program, classroom observations revealed that teachers who spoke Spanish mostly used it to give directions or reprimands to children when they did not understand English. As the program matured and professional development focused more on the value of dual language support for classroom practice, utilization of bilingual interactions and materials became the norm (Frede, 2005; Frede, Jung, Barnett, Lamy, & Figueras, 2007). In the state-funded Tulsa, Oklahoma, preschool program, 61% of Hispanic preschoolers attend the program, but only a small number of the teachers are Hispanic. The researchers conclude that "clearly, teachers have managed to connect with Hispanic children despite the absence of an ethnic bond. [This may be due to the fact that] their classroom quality is higher than average and their time devoted to academic subjects is much higher than average" (Gormley, 2007, p. 17). Results of the research show that, as a result of pre-K attendance, Hispanic students improved in early literacy and mathematics. Children of Mexican immigrants or from Spanish-only homes made the most gains; being in a classroom with a Spanish-speaking teacher enhanced gains, and gains were greater in English language tests—but children gained in both languages.

As Gormley concluded, it may be that the content of the curriculum is important and this should be guided by whether a state has established preschool learning standards to guide curriculum and teaching. Of the 38 states that fund preschool, all but five have comprehensive standards that specify learning outcomes across subject domains, but in language learning most specifically. Few of these standards, however, have specific expectations for ELLs, but some states expressly indicate that children's language progress may be in a language other than English. In New Jersey, for example, the relevant language learning outcome states: "Children converse effectively in their home language, English, or sign language for a variety of purposes relating to real experiences and different audiences" (New Jersey State Department of Education, 2004, p. 35). California recently published specific learning standards for children whose home language is not English that address first and second language acquisition directly. States may also translate early learning standards into other languages in order to help parents and teachers who do not speak English to access them.

THIS VOLUME'S CONTRIBUTION TO ADDRESSING THE EARLY EDUCATION OF ELL CHILDREN

This volume attempts to address the present knowledge base for the growing population of young English language learners.

In our introductory comments, we tried to give a very brief overview of the major issues. The following chapters add depth to this overview by addressing the research knowledge base and related policy and instructional implications more specifically.

Chapter 2, by Donald J. Hernandez and colleagues, provides a comprehensive picture of who these children are culturally and linguistically, what types of family characteristics best describe their development circumstances, and what socioeconomic attributes help us better understand their educational prospects. Chapter 3, by Claudia Galindo, explores more specifically the educational achievement attributes of ELLs utilizing the ECLS-K database, a very well-regarded set of national longitudinal data. She provides a comprehensive portrait of the education conditions of young ELL children. In Chapter 4, Fred Genesee details the research foundations related to bilingual development and second language acquisition during the preschool years. The review is a rich and comprehensive background of fundamental language-development research and conclusions related to young ELL populations and their education. In Chapter 5, José E. Náñez addresses a relatively new area of investigation that links bilingual development to cognitive processes, revealing significant research from the neurosciences that enhances our understanding of the links between linguistic and cognitive processes.

Flora V. Rodríguez-Brown, in Chapter 6, begins to turn the volume's attention to educational variables that relate to addressing ELL early education. This contribution focuses on the importance of engaging parents and other family members in early learning endeavors. Although primarily focusing on Hispanic ELL children, the chapter provides a thorough review of research and practices significant in enhancing parent/family positive enhancement of ELL education outcomes. Chapter 7 addresses one of the most significant educational challenges in serving ELL children: language and academic assessment. In this chapter, Linda M. Espinosa provides both the challenges and the importance of getting assessment right for young ELL children utilizing a "best practices" approach. In Chapter 8, this same author turns to issues related to instruction of this population of young students. She outlines again the challenges and the best practices that come from new research in classroom-level teaching. Following closely from Espinosa's conclusion that the quality of instruction is related to the quality of the teacher, Margaret Freedson, in Chapter 9, addresses what we know about early education, ELL workforce preparation, and related policy issues that need to be considered if we are to address the particular needs of ELL early learning.

In the last chapter, we acknowledge that significant research frontiers are ahead of us as we contemplate the enhanced future educational well-being of ELL children. We are clearly making research progress as the contributions to this volume indicate. However, new research endeavors in all the areas addressed in this volume are needed if our hopes for removing educational achievement gaps for ELL students through early learning environments are to be realized.

Clearly, the educational circumstances discussed in this volume have led early childhood educators, policymakers, and parents to address the early schooling of ELL students with diverse forms of responses. We have systematically tried to address, with the best literature base available, the movement toward an up-to-date knowledge base that can guide new research, practice, and policy.

REFERENCES

August, D., & Shanahan, T. (Eds.). (2006). *Developing literacy in second language learners: Report of the national literacy panel on language minority youth and children*. Mahwah, NJ: Lawrence Erlbaum.

Barnett, W. S., Epstein, D., Friedman, A. H., Stevenson-Boyd, J., & Hustedt, J. (2008). *The state of preschool: 2007 state preschool yearbook*. New Brunswick, NJ: National Institute for Early Education Research.

Frede, E. (2005). *Assessment in a continuous improvement cycle: New Jersey's Abbott Preschool Program*. Invited paper for the National Early Childhood Accountability Task Force with support from the Pew Charitable Trusts, the Foundation for Child Development, and the Joyce Foundation.

Frede, E., Jung, K., Barnett, W. S., Lamy, C. E., & Figueras, A. (2007). *The Abbott Preschool Program longitudinal effects study: Interim report*. New Brunswick, NJ: National Institute for Early Education Research.

García, E. E., & Miller, L. S. (2008). Findings and recommendations of the National Task Force on Early Childhood Education for Hispanics. *Child Development Perspectives, 2*(2), 53–58.

Gormley, W. (2007, August). *The effects of Oklahoma's pre-K program on Hispanic children*. Paper presented at the annual meeting of the American Political Science Association, Chicago. Retrieved October 9, 2009, from http://www.crocus.georgetown.edu/reports/CROCUSworkingpaper11.pdf

Karoly, L., Ghosh-Dastidar, B., Zellman, G., Perlman, M., & Fernyhough, L. (2008). *Prepared to learn: The nature and quality of early care and education for preschool-age children in California*. Retrieved October 9, 2009, from http://www.rand.org/pubs/technical_reports/TR539/

Lee, J., Grigg, W., & Donahue, P. (2007). *The nation's report card: Reading 2007*. Washington, DC: U.S. Department of Education, Institute of Education Sciences, National Center for Education Statistics.

Miller, L. S., & García, E. (2008). *A reading-focused early childhood education research and strategy development agenda for African Americans and Hispanics at all social class levels who are English language speakers or English language learners*. Tempe, AZ: Arizona State University, Office of Vice President for Education Partnerships.

National Task Force on Early Childhood Education for Hispanics. (2007). *Para nuestros niños: Report of expanding and improving early education for Hispanics— Main report*. Tempe, AZ: National Task Force on Early Childhood Education for Hispanics. Retrieved August 6, 2007, from http://www.ecehispanic.org/work/expand_MainReport.pdf

New Jersey State Department of Education. (2004, July). *Preschool teaching & learning expectations: Standards of quality*. Trenton: New Jersey State Department of Education.

Reardon, S., & Galindo, C. (2006a, April). *K–3 academic achievement patterns and trajectories of Hispanics and other racial/ethnic groups*. Paper presented at the annual meeting of the American Educational Research Association, San Francisco.

Reardon, S. F., & Galindo, C. (2006b). *Patterns of Hispanic students' math and English literacy test scores. Report to the National Task Force on Early Childhood Education for Hispanics*. Tempe: Arizona State University.

Zill, N., Resnick, G., Kim, K., O'Donnell, K., Sorongon, A., Ziv, Y., et al. (2006). *Head Start performance measures center family and child experiences survey (FACES 2000)* [Technical report]. Retrieved October 9, 2009, from http://www.acf.hhs.gov/programs/opre/hs/faces/reports/technical_2000_rpt/tech2k_final2.pdf

CHAPTER 2

A Demographic Portrait of Young English Language Learners

Donald J. Hernandez
with Suzanne Macartney and Nancy A. Denton

Children learn language first from their parents. If parents speak only English or only another language at home, the children will be monolingual, at least until they spend time with peers or in a school that exposes them to a second language. If parents speak two languages at home, the children are on a path to becoming bilingual. Children in immigrant families often have parents who speak a language other than English and may be designated as English language learners (ELLs) when they enter school. The extent to which young children are fluent or limited in their English proficiency will depend on the English language skills of their parents. The aim of this chapter is to present a demographic portrait of children who are most likely to be English language learners by focusing on the circumstances of children in three groups: those living with parents who are limited English proficient only, those living with parents who are English fluent only, and those living with a mix of limited English proficient and English fluent parents.

We begin by discussing the extent to which children in immigrant and native-born families live with parents who speak English or other languages and the extent to which their parents are limited English proficient or English fluent. We then describe the circumstances of these children related to immigration, such as citizenship status. Next we discuss family strengths and challenges reflected in the children's family and household composition, in their parents' education, employment, and earnings, and in their family poverty. Focusing on children themselves, the chapter then presents results pertaining to enrollment in early education. We close by highlighting the wide distribution across the United States of children whose parents are limited in their English proficiency.

Young children ages 3 to 4 are our focus, because they are about to begin or are experiencing their earliest years of formal education. Results are calculated by the authors using data from Census 2000, specifically the Integrated Public Use Micro Data Series (IPUMS).

ENGLISH AND OTHER LANGUAGES
SPOKEN BY CHILDREN'S PARENTS

Utilizing our analysis of IPUMS, we find that one in five (21%) of young children ages 3 to 4 lives in an immigrant family with at least one foreign-born parent. But only 1% of all young children and only 5% of young children in immigrant families live with a parent who speaks no English at home. These small proportions are not surprising, insofar as most immigrants come to the United States with the hope of improving their economic situation and as English language skills are necessary to work at most jobs in the United States. Even among children in the immigrant-origin group most likely to have a parent who speaks no English at home (Mexico), fewer than one in ten (9%) of young children in immigrant families from Mexico lives with a parent speaking no English at home. (See Table 2.1 in the Appendix for a specific summary of U.S. data.)

Thus, most young children in most immigrant groups have parents who speak two languages (including English) at home. Overall, 82% of young children in immigrant families have parents who speak English and another language at home, and the range is 80 to 98% for 21 of the 30 countries/regions of origin/racial groups for which results are presented here. The results are similar for only one native-born group, island-origin Puerto Ricans, that is, young children who were born in Puerto Rico or have at least one parent born in Puerto Rico. For immigrant groups among whom fewer than 80% have parents speaking two languages in the home, the proportion with parents who speak only English at home ranges from 22% to 27% (young children with origins in Korea, China, and the former Soviet Union and Whites from Africa); to 39% (children with origins in Other Europe and Canada); to 86 to 87% (children with origins in Jamaica or the English-speaking Caribbean.

Thus, very few young children in immigrant families live in homes where the parents speak no English, and most live in immigrant groups within which at least four out of five have parents speaking two languages at home. These children, as well as island-origin Puerto Rican children, are positioned to become bilingual speakers—if schools provide them with the opportunity to build on their oral language skills—and to develop literacy (reading and writing) in both languages.

These levels of exposure to English may not be surprising, but results for children in native-born families with both parents U.S. born may not be what many people would expect. The vast majority (95%–96%) of young children in native-born families who are White or Black live with parents who speak only English at home. But the proportion is substantially lower (73%–78%) for young children who are Asian American, Hawaiian/ Pacific Islander, or Native American. Thus, 18 to 27% of young children in these three native-born groups live in families in which parents speak two languages at home. This rises to a majority (57%–63%) among young children in native-born families who are Mexican American, Other Hispanic/Latino, or mainland-origin Puerto Rican (with both parents born in the continental United States, Hawaii, or Alaska). Thus, many children in most native-born groups also are exposed by their parents at home to a second language in addition to English.

Just as there is great diversity across groups in the proportion with parents who speak English only or both English and another language at home, there is great diversity in the number of languages spoken. Among children ages 0 to 17, for example, sample data from Census 2000 identify 93 distinct languages spoken in the home. Insofar as children can be provided with the opportunity to maintain or develop bilingual speaking and literacy skills, children living with parents speaking two languages are well positioned to become language emissaries connecting the United States to nations throughout the world, including regions where the United States has important economic and geopolitical interests such as Latin America, China, and the nations of West Asia where Arabic and Persian are spoken. Education policies and programs fostering bilingualism among children in immigrant families could provide a valuable competitive edge as the United States seeks success in the increasingly competitive global economy.

MEASUREMENT AND IMPLICATIONS
OF PARENTAL ENGLISH LANGUAGE FLUENCY

Beyond the enormous diversity across groups in languages spoken in the homes of young children, there also is considerable diversity in the English language fluency of parents. Although Census 2000 does not ask about English fluency for young children under age 5, it does, for parents who speak a language other than English at home, ask how well the parents speak English. Parents are classified in results presented here as either English fluent (speak English exclusively or very well) or limited English proficient (speak English well, not well, or do not speak English). Based on this classification, children are distinguished in this study by whether all the parents in the home are English fluent, or all are limited English proficient, or there is one who is English fluent and one who is limited English proficient.

It is likely that, on average, young children living only with parents who are limited English proficient will themselves have limited English skills and will be classified by schools as English language learners, while young children living only with English fluent parents will be less likely to be classified as English language learners. It also seems likely that young children living with one parent who is English fluent and a second parent who is limited English proficient will be intermediate, on average, in their English language skills and will be less likely to be classified as English language learners in school.

The English language skills of parents have important implications beyond the language skills they impart to their young children. Parents with limited English proficiency are less likely than fluent English speakers to find well-paying, full-time, year-round jobs. These parents also may be less able to help their children study for subjects taught in English. Insofar as education, health, and social service institutions do not provide outreach in the country-of-origin language spoken by parents, they and their children may also be cut off from access to important public and private services and benefits.

LEVELS AND GROUP DIFFERENCES
IN PARENTAL ENGLISH LANGUAGE FLUENCY

Although only 1% of all young children and 5% of young children in immigrant families live with parents who speak no English at home, the proportion with parents in the home who all are limited English proficient reaches 9% of all young children and 40% of young children in immigrant families (as seen in Table 2.1 in the Appendix).

The proportion in native-born families with parents in the home who all are limited English proficient is no more than 4% for most groups, although this is slightly higher (6%) for various Hispanic groups and even higher (27%) for island-origin Puerto Ricans. Thus, although large proportions of young children in most native-born groups (except Whites and Blacks) have parents who speak both English and another language at home, the overwhelming majority (89%–99%) in all native-born groups (except island-origin Puerto Ricans) live with parents who all are English fluent, and even larger proportions (94%–100%) live with at least one parent who is English fluent.

The variation across immigrant groups is, not surprisingly, much larger. At one extreme, among Hmong in immigrant families (63%) and those with origins in Mexico (57%), about six in ten live with parents who all are limited English proficient; the proportion is about one-half for young children with origins in Central America, Dominican Republic, Cambodia,

Laos, and Vietnam (50%–54%). For 11 other groups, the proportion is within a much lower range (25%–40%) and is lower still (13%–19%) for young children in immigrant families with origins in the Philippines, India, Iran, Israel/Palestine, Other West Asia, and Other Europe and Canada and for Whites and Blacks from Africa. Thus, substantial to large proportions of children in most immigrant groups live with parents who all are limited English proficient.

Nevertheless, it is important to highlight that for all immigrant groups reported here except Hmong, at least 43% have at least one English fluent parent in the home. But even among these groups there is considerable diversity in the proportion with only English fluent parents, although there is little variation in the proportion having in the home both an English fluent and a limited English proficient parent. Between 12% and 26% of children in 27 of the 30 immigrant groups studied here have two parents in the home, where one is English fluent and the other is limited English proficient. The only exceptions are Other Europe and Canada (11%) and Jamaica and English-speaking Caribbean (2%–3%).

But the proportion of young children in immigrant families with all parents in the home being English fluent ranges from 21 to 31% for young children with origins in Mexico, Central America, the Dominican Republic, Cambodia, Laos, and Vietnam or who are Hmong; to a majority (63%–77%) for young children with origins in Philippines, India, Iran, Israel/Palestine, and Other Europe and Canada and Whites and Blacks from Africa; to nearly all (96%–97%) for children with origins in Jamaica and the English-speaking Caribbean.

Overall, then, there is enormous diversity across immigrant groups with respect to parental English language fluency. Nevertheless, at least 20% of most groups have only English fluent parents in the home and at least 20% of most groups have only limited English proficient parents in the home. Looking at the whole group of young children in immigrant families, 20% live with both an English fluent and a limited English proficient parent, while 40% live with parents who only are limited English proficient and a nearly identical 42% live with parents who only are English fluent.

Immigrant and U.S.-Born Parents

One reason that some immigrant groups have comparatively high proportions of children with parents who all are English fluent and comparatively low proportions with parents who all are limited English proficient is that, in those cases, English is commonly spoken in the country of origin, for example, in Jamaica, English-speaking Caribbean countries, the Philippines, India, and African immigrant countries. A second reason is that some groups with high levels of English proficiency also have a high proportion with a U.S.-born parent, namely, those from Cuba (39%), South America (35%), Japan (50%), Thailand (36%), Iran (34%), and Israel/Palestine (46%).

For several other countries of origin, it is the case both that English is commonly spoken there and that the proportion with a U.S.-born parent is high. Examples (with proportion of children having a U.S.-born parent given in parentheses) are Philippines (36%) and Other Europe and Canada (59%). This is also true for Whites from Africa (43%). In other countries/regions/groups studied here, the proportions with nonimmigrant parents are in a much lower range (11%–22%) or even lower (4%–8%) for China, Pakistan/Bangladesh, and the Hmong.

It is not surprising for children in immigrant families of various origins that, among those with all parents limited English proficient, the proportions with only immigrant parents in the home are in the range of 95 to 100%. This drops to 60 to 85% for a majority of origin groups among children with both an English fluent parent and a limited proficient English parent; for nearly all origin groups, the proportion with a U.S.-born parent is somewhat lower among children with all English fluent parents than among children with both an English fluent and a limited English proficient parent.

Citizenship of Children

Children who are American citizens have the same rights under the laws and Constitution of the United States, regardless of where their parents were born. Because children in native-born families were all born in the United States, it is taken for granted that they are U.S. citizens. But it is less well known that the vast majority of young children in immigrant families (80%–97% for the origin groups discussed here) are U.S. citizens because they were born in the United States, with only five exceptions (see Table 2.2 in the Appendix). Even among these young children, a large majority were born in the United States (72%–76% for those with parental origins in Japan, Korea, China, and Thailand and 62% for those with origins in the former Soviet Union).

Perhaps not surprisingly, among young children with all parents English fluent at least 80% were born in the United States, except for those with origins in the former Soviet Union (53%) and China (49%). It is likewise true for children who have parents who are both English fluent and limited English proficient—except for those with origins in Japan (76%) and Pakistan/Bangladesh (73%)—that most were born in the United States. Although this holds true for only about half of the immigrant origin groups studied here among children with all parents limited English proficient, it is the case that even among these groups, the proportion falls below 60% for only two groups: Other Europe and Canada (56%) and Japan (30%).

Overall, among young children in immigrant families, the vast majority are U.S.-born American citizens, regardless of their parents' English language skills (90%–92% for those with one or all parents English fluent and 84% for those with all parents limited English proficient). Thus, most children in immigrant families, regardless of parental language skills, share with children in native-born families the same rights as U.S. citizens, including eligibility for publicly funded services and benefits.

Parents in the Homes of Young Children

Parents bear the most immediate and direct responsibility for nurturing and caring for their children, and children living with two parents tend, on average, to be somewhat advantaged in their educational success (Cherlin, 1999; McLanahan & Sandefur, 1994). Immigrant families with many children benefit from this strength across all English fluency groups. All together, 87% of young children in immigrant families live with two parents, compared to 75% for children in native-born families. Among children in native-born families, the proportion living with two parents ranges from 85% for Whites and 76% for Asians, to 63 to 70% for Native Americans, Hawaiian/Pacific Islanders, and most Hispanic groups, to 54% for mainland-origin Puerto Ricans, and to 42% for Blacks.

Every young child in an immigrant family with both an English fluent and a limited English proficient parent has, by definition, two parents in the home. The proportions living with two parents are at the level of Whites in native-born families (83%–85%) for young children overall with all English fluent parents in the home and for young children overall with all limited English proficiency parents in the home. The proportions are below 80% for both the English fluent and limited English proficient immigrant origins groups only for children with origins in Central America (76%–79%), the Dominican Republic (57%–61%), Haiti (64%–72%), and Cambodia (71%–77%). The proportions also are below 80% for children with all English fluent parents from Laos (88%) and for children with all limited English proficient parents from Cuba (77%), South America (79%), and Philippines (77%) and for Blacks from Africa (70%).

Thus, the vast majority of children in immigrant families, regardless of origin or parental English fluency, live with two parents. However, a noteworthy 10 to 25% have only one in the home, usually the mother. While in the minority, these children are more likely to be in need of services or programs that ease the difficulties that confront one-parent families.

Siblings in the Homes of Young Children

Brothers and sisters can be both a liability and an asset. The amounts of income and time that parents have available to devote to their children are limited and must be spread more thinly in families with a large number of siblings. As a result, children in larger families tend, other things being equal, to experience less educational success and to complete fewer years of school than children with few siblings (Blake, 1985, 1989; Hernandez, 1986). But siblings can also provide child care for younger children in the family and peer companionship if they are close in age, and they can act as a critical mutual support network throughout life. Children with immigrant origins differ greatly with respect to the size of their families and, consequently, differ substantially in the constraints and benefits they experience because of this.

The proportion of young children in native-born families with four or more siblings ages 0 to 17 is in the range of 8 to 11% for Whites and Asians and in the range of 12 to 20% for other race-ethnic groups. For young children in immigrant families, the proportions are below these ranges if their origin is Korea, China, Hong Kong, or Taiwan (3%–4%), and the range is generally similar (1%–5%) regardless of parental English language skill. Only among young children in immigrant families from Jamaica, English-speaking Caribbean, South America, Japan, Philippines, Iran, and Other Europe and Canada and among Whites from Africa is the range similar to Whites and Asians in native-born families. For these immigrant groups, too, there usually is little variation across parental English skill groups.

Family size among many other immigrant groups is similar to or slightly larger than family size for native-born groups of the same country of origin, with the exception of Whites and Asians. The proportions for having four or more siblings is notably larger, however, for young children in immigrant families from Laos, Thailand, and Israel/Palestine (26%–33%) and, especially, for the Hmong (70%). Thus, service providers with a family focus can expect to find great variability in the number of siblings in the home across various immigrant origin groups.

Grandparents, Other Relatives, and Nonrelatives in the Homes of Young Children

Besides parents and older siblings, grandparents, other relatives, and nonrelatives living with young children can provide child care, nurturing, and economic resources. Young children in immigrant families are about twice as likely as Whites in native-born families (13% versus 6%) to have a grandparent in the home, but this is less than the proportion for children in other native-born, race-ethnic groups (14%–22%), except for island-origin Puerto Ricans (13%). There is little difference in this proportion (13%–14%) for young children in immigrant families across parental English language skill levels (see Table 2.3 in the Appendix).

The proportions do differ substantially, however, across immigrant origin groups. Among children with origins in Japan, Israel/Palestine, and Other Europe and Canada, as well as Whites from Africa, only 3 to 5% live with a grandparent. Most likely to have a grandparent in the home are young children with immigrant origins in Philippines, Cambodia, Laos, Thailand, Vietnam, and India, as well as the Hmong (20%–23%). Only for young children with immigrant origins in China are there large differences between those with parents speaking English fluently (10%), those with a parent speaking English fluently and a parent limited English proficient (17%), and those with only limited English proficient parents (29%). Thus, most native-born and immigrant groups are two to four times more likely than Whites in native-born families to have a grandparent in the home, but there is usually little difference in parental English language skills across children in specific race-ethnic or immigrant origin groups.

Only 5% of children in White native-born families have another adult relative 18 years or older (including older siblings) in the home, compared to 10 to 19% for other native-born race-ethnic groups. Among immigrant groups, the proportion is about the same as Whites only for children with origins in Japan, Taiwan, Israel/Palestine, the former Soviet Union, and Other Europe and Canada, as well as Whites from Africa (3%–8%). The proportions reach or exceed 20% for immigrant children with origins in Latin America and the Caribbean (Mexico, Central America, the Dominican Republic, Haiti, and English-speaking Caribbean; 22%–32%), Indochina (Cambodia, Laos, Thailand, and Vietnam; 21%–27%), and Pakistan/Bangladesh (20%) (see Table 2.4 in the Appendix).

For five of these countries/regions (Mexico, Central America, Dominican Republic, Haiti, and Vietnam), as well as South America and Philippines, young children whose parents are limited English proficient are more likely than young children with at least one English fluent parent to have other adult relatives in the home, with differences usually in the range of 8 to 21%. Thus, some immigrant origin groups, especially from Latin America and the Caribbean and Asia are especially likely to experience the benefits (and disadvantages) of having additional adult relatives in the home.

Nonrelatives in the home also can serve to enhance resources available to children. Two immigrant origin groups are notably more likely to have nonrelatives in the home than are other immigrant or native-born groups—those with origins in Mexico and Central America. Most of the high proportion for these groups is due to children living with parents who both are limited English proficient (15% for Mexico and 20% for

Central America). Some groups with large numbers of siblings also are among those most likely to have in the home grandparents (Indochinese countries) or other relatives or nonrelatives (Mexico, Central America, Haiti) who provide nurturing and child care, as well as share economic resources with immigrant children and families.

Parents Not Graduating from High School

Sociological studies found more than 4 decades ago that children whose parents completed fewer years of school tend, on average, to themselves complete fewer years of school and to have lower paying jobs when they enter the adult workforce (Blau & Duncan, 1967; Featherman & Hauser, 1978; Sewell & Hauser, 1975; Sewell, Hauser, & Wolf, 1980). Parents with educational levels reaching only the high school or elementary level may be especially limited in the knowledge and experience needed to help their children in school. Immigrant parents often have high educational aspirations for their children (Hernandez & Charney, 1998; Kao, 1999; Rumbaut, 1999) but may know little about the U.S. education system, particularly if they have completed only a few years of school in the United States.

Children in native-born families are least likely to have a father who has not graduated from a U.S. high school if they are Asian (8%), White (10%), or Hawaiian/Pacific Islander (11%). The proportions for other native-born groups are much higher—17% for Blacks, 21 to 25% for Native Americans and various Hispanic groups—and still higher for island-origin Puerto Ricans (34%). Among 14 of the 30 immigrant groups studied here, the proportion with a father not graduating from high school is in the range of 3 to 15%, similar to Asians, Whites, and Hawaiian/Pacific Islanders in native-born families. But for many of these immigrant groups, the proportion with fathers not graduating from a U.S. high school reaches a much higher range—26 to 32% for children with parents who all are limited English proficient (from China, Hong Kong, India, Pakistan/Bangladesh, Other West Asia, or Other Europe and Canada and Blacks from Africa).

Among another set of immigrants, 18 to 23% have a father not graduating from a U.S. high school, but, among children with only parents limited English proficient, the proportion jumps to 30% (from South America) and 50% (from Cuba). For children with various Indochinese origins, the overall proportions are 24 to 40%, but the proportions with fathers not graduating from high school range from 11 to 17% (children with only English fluent parents) to 38 to 54% (children with only limited English proficient parents).

The pattern across English language fluency groups is also quite pronounced for children with origins in the four remaining immigrant origin countries/regions. Among young children in immigrant families from

Haiti, 23% have a father who did not graduate from a U.S. high school. This rises from 17% for those with only English fluent parents to 43% for those with only limited English proficient parents. Similarly for young children with immigrant origins in the Dominican Republic, the overall proportion is 42%. However, the proportions increase from 25% for children with only English fluent parents, to 42% for children with both English fluent and limited English proficient parents, to 51% for children with only limited English proficient parents. Finally, for children with immigrant origins in Central America and Mexico, the overall proportions with a father not graduating from high school are 54% and 67%. But this increases across the only English fluent group (29%), the both English fluent and limited English proficient group (50%), and the only limited English proficient group (71%) for children with origins in Central America and from 47% to 61% to 76%, respectively, for children with origins in Mexico (though not discussed here, results are similar for mothers not graduating from high school).

Educational attainment is, however, especially limited among fathers from nine of these origin groups (Mexico, Central America, Dominican Republic, Hmong, Cambodia, Laos, Thailand, Vietnam, and Iraq) because, not only have many not graduated from high school, but also they have completed no more than 8 years of school. One in 10 young children from immigrant families from Thailand have fathers who have completed 8 years or fewer of school in the United States. This reaches 15 to 18% for the Dominican Republic, Thailand, and Iraq; 21% for Cambodia and Laos; 27 to 30% for Central America and the Hmong; and 39% for Mexico.

But the proportions are much lower among children with these origins with only English fluent parents and much higher among those with only limited English proficient parents. For example, among young children living with only limited English proficient parents, the proportion with a father completing 8 years of school or less is 22% for the Dominican Republic, 31 to 32% for Cambodia and Laos, 39% for the Hmong, 43% for Central America, and 49% for Mexico. In fact, among young children with origins in Mexico and Central America, 15 to 16% have fathers who completed no more than 4 years of school; this reaches 25 to 27% for Cambodia and Laos and 34% for the Hmong.

Among several additional immigrant origin groups, the overall proportions with fathers completing no more than 8 years of school is comparatively low (2%–8%), but among those with only limited English proficient parents, the proportions are in a much higher range of 12 to 17% (Other West Asia, Blacks and Whites from Africa, and Other Europe and Canada).

Parents who have not graduated from high school, and especially parents who have no more than 8, or even 4, years of schooling may be less able to effectively work with educators on behalf of their children, particularly if the English proficiency of the parents is limited. Thus, young children who are most likely to be classified as English language learners often have parents who, not only are all limited English proficient, but also have very low educational attainments. This can pose special challenges for the schools and teachers of these children.

It should also be noted, however, that the situation is quite different with young children in immigrant families with other origins. The proportion with a father graduating from college is 12 to 16% for most native-born race-ethnic groups, but this reaches 33% for Whites and 46% for Asians. The proportion is higher than for Whites in native-born families among young children in immigrant families with origins in the Philippines and Other Europe and Canada (40%–41%) and higher than for the Asians in native-born families among children in immigrant families with origins in the former Soviet Union (48%), for Blacks from Africa (53%), for children who have origins in Japan, Korea, China, Hong Kong, Pakistan/Bangladesh and for Whites from Africa (57%–62%), and for those with origins in India or Iran (74%–76%). Although the proportions with fathers who graduated from college tend to be substantially lower among children with these origins who have one or all limited English proficient parents, it is nevertheless the case that many children from these groups with only limited English proficient parents (18%–84%) also have fathers who graduated from college. Thus, schools teaching young English language learners with these origins often will be working with parents who are highly educated (see Table 2.5 in the Appendix).

POVERTY

Young children in poverty-level homes often go without decent housing, food, clothing, books and other educational resources, child care/early education, and health care. They also tend to experience a variety of negative developmental outcomes, including less success in school and lower educational attainments, and earn lower incomes as adults (Duncan & Brooks-Gunn, 1997; McLoyd, 1998). Poverty rates merit considerable attention because extensive research documents that poverty has greater negative consequences than either limited mother's education or living in a one-parent family (Duncan & Brooks-Gunn, 1997; McLoyd, 1998).

The official poverty rate for children in immigrant families is as low or lower than the rates for Whites and for Asians in native-born families among only seven immigrant groups—children with origins in Japan (7%), Hong Kong (5%), Taiwan (5%), Philippines (5%), India (6%), Iran (8%), and Other Europe and Canada (9%). Among immigrant groups with all English fluent parents, however, most have official poverty rates of no more than

15%. Among those for whom reliable results can be calculated—that is, excluding the Hmong and those with origins in Afghanistan and Iraq— the poverty rates are higher only for children with origins in Pakistan/ Bangladesh (17%), Cambodia (19%), Dominican Republic (24%), and Mexico (24%). Among children with all limited English parents, the official poverty rate is at least 29% for 13 of the 23 origin groups for which reliable estimates can be calculated, with the highest levels (36%–45%) for those with origins in Mexico, Dominican Republic, Pakistan/Bangladesh, and the former Soviet Union and for the Hmong and Blacks from Africa.

The official poverty rate is most commonly used to assess economic need, but it has come under increasing criticism because it has not been updated since 1965 for increases in the real standard of living (Citro & Michael, 1995; Hernandez, Denton, & Macartney, 2007). To provide a more complete picture of economic need for children, results are presented here for two alternatives that take into account the local cost of various goods and services (Bernstein, Brocht, & Spade-Aguilar, 2000; Boushey, Brocht, Gundersen, & Bernstein, 2001; Hernandez et al., 2007).

The first alternative measure of economic need presented here is the Baseline Basic Budget Poverty rate, which takes into account the local cost of food, housing, transportation for parents to commute to work, and "other necessities" such as clothing, personal care items, household supplies, telephone, television, school supplies, reading materials, music, and toys. The second, more comprehensive Basic Budget Poverty rate takes into account, in addition, the local cost of child care/early education and health care, although it may somewhat overestimate the effect of the cost of child care/early education and underestimate the effect of health care costs (Hernandez et al., 2007).

The Baseline Basic Budget Poverty rate is only slightly higher than the official rate for children in native families who are White (12% vs. 9%) or Asian (14% vs. 8%), but the difference is much larger for immigrant and other native groups with official poverty rates of 15% or more. Among children with parents who all are English fluent, the Baseline Basic Budget Poverty rate is typically about 10% lower, if the overall Baseline Basic Budget Poverty rate is 30% or more. But the rates are much higher for children living with all limited English proficient parents. For groups with overall Baseline Basic Budget Poverty rates of 25% or more, the rates for children with all limited English proficient parents are usually in the range of 50 to 62% (9 of 14 countries for which reliable estimates can be calculated).

But the Baseline Basic Budget Poverty measure does not take into account the cost of child care/early childhood education, which is essential for many working parents and which can have important beneficial consequences for the educational success of children in elementary school and beyond. The measure also does not take into account the cost of health insurance, which can ensure timely access to preventive health care and to medical care for acute and chronic conditions, which in turn can affect the capacity of children to function effectively in school.

A more comprehensive Basic Budget Poverty measure including these costs classifies about three in ten (31%–32%) White and Asian children in native families as poor, compared to about one-half to seven-tenths (54%–71%) of children in other native race-ethnic groups. The comprehensive Basic Budget Poverty rate is 44% or more for children with 18 of the 30 immigrant origins studied here, including the Latin American and Caribbean countries/regions except Cuba (42%), all of the Indochinese groups, all of the Southwest Asian groups except India (24%) and Iran (23%), and the former Soviet Union, as well as Blacks from Africa.

Even among children with all English fluent parents, this poverty rate is 44% or more for all the Latin American and Caribbean countries/regions except Cuba (30%) and South America (32%), as well as for Cambodia and Pakistan/Bangladesh and for Blacks from Africa. These poverty rates are typically much higher for children with all limited English parents, at more than 50% for all countries with reliable estimates except Korea, Hong Kong, Taiwan, Philippines, and India, and it reaches the extraordinary levels of 70% to 71% for South America, Cambodia, Laos, and Other West Asia, 74% to 80% for Central America, Haiti, Pakistan/Bangladesh, and the former Soviet Union, as well as for Whites from Africa, 83% to 84% for Mexico and the Dominican Republic, as well as for Blacks from Africa, and 93% for the Hmong.

In European countries, children have access to nearly universal pre-school and national health insurance programs, but this is not the case in the United States. Comparable child poverty rates are 2 to 10% in six European countries: Belgium, Denmark, Finland, France, Germany, and Sweden (Hernandez et al., 2007; UNICEF, 2005). Thus, taking into account the full range of needs of children and families, including child care/early education and health care, no more than one in ten children in several major European countries lives in poverty, compared to as many as three in ten White and Asian children in native families, and as many as one-half to nine-tenths of children in many immigrant and native race-ethnic groups, with rates that are 74% or more for nine groups with all parents who are limited English proficient.

ENROLLMENT IN EARLY EDUCATION PROGRAMS

The pre-K/nursery school enrollment rate for Whites in native families is 37% at age 3 and 61% at age 4. Three groups of young children in native families are enrolled at rates nearly this high or higher at ages 3 and/or 4

(Blacks, mainland-origin Puerto Ricans, and Asians), as are young children in immigrant families from Haiti, Jamaica, English-speaking Caribbean Islands, South America, several (mainly East) Asian countries, the former Soviet Union, and Other Europe and Canada, as well as both Blacks and Whites from Africa (see Table 2.6 in the Appendix).

Young children who experience much lower pre-K/nursery school enrollment rates include those in native families who are Mexican, island-origin Puerto Rican, Hawaiian/Pacific Islander, or Native American and those in immigrant families from Mexico, Central America, Dominican Republic, Indochina, Pakistan/Bangladesh, Afghanistan, and Iraq. The pre-K/nursery school enrollment rate gap between these groups and Whites in native families ranges between 5% and 20% at age 3 and between 2% and 30% at age 4.

For the immigrant groups with origins in Mexico, Central America, Dominican Republic, and Indochina, those with all limited English proficient parents are 1 to 10% less likely than those with all English fluent parents to be enrolled in school. The differences are much larger, usually 20 to 30%, for children with origins in Pakistan/Bangladesh, Israel/Palestine, the former Soviet Union, and Other Europe and Canada and for Blacks and Whites from Africa.

What accounts for the low overall enrollment rates of some groups? One possible reason sometimes cited, particularly for Hispanic immigrants, is that more familistic cultural values within some groups lead parents to prefer that their children be cared for at home, rather than in formal educational settings by nonrelatives (Liang, Fuller, & Singer, 2000; Utall, 1999). But alternative explanations include socioeconomic or structural factors (Hernandez, Denton, & Macartney, in press; Takanishi, 2004).

First, cost can be an insurmountable barrier for poor families. Because of limited funding, most low-income families eligible for child care assistance do not receive such assistance (Mezey, Greenberg, & Schumacher, 2002). Second, parents with extremely limited educational attainment may not be aware that early education programs are important and are used by most highly educated parents to foster their children's educational success. Third, in immigrant neighborhoods with many non-English speakers, there may be too few openings in early education programs to accommodate the demand (Hill-Scott, 2005). Fourth, even if spaces are available, access may be limited for parents who are not proficient in English, because programs may not reach out to parents in their home language (Matthews & Ewen, 2006). Fifth, parents may hesitate to enroll their children in programs that are not designed and implemented in a culturally competent manner, especially if teachers lack a minimal capacity to communicate with children in the home language (Holloway, Fuller, Rambaud, & Eggers-Pierola, 1998; Shonkoff & Phillips, 2000).

Recent research indicates that socioeconomic or structural influences, especially family poverty, mother's education, and parental occupation account for most or all of the enrollment gap separating children in immigrant and native Mexican families and children in immigrant families from Central America and Indochina from White children in native families (Hernandez, et al., in press). Depending on the age and the group, socioeconomic and structural factors account for at least half, and perhaps all, of the enrollment gap, while cultural influences account for no more than 14% of the gap for the Mexican groups, no more than 39% of the gap for Central Americans, and no more than 17% for the Indochinese.

These results, especially for Hispanics, may be surprising, but it is important to note that these estimates are consistent with the strong commitment to early education in contemporary Mexico, where universal enrollment at age 3 became obligatory in 2008–2009 (Organisation for Economic Co-operation and Development, Directorate of Education, 2006). In fact, in Mexico where preschool is free, 81% of children age 4 were enrolled in 2005, compared to only 71% among whites in U.S. native-born families in 2004 and 55% for children in immigrant families in the United States in 2004 who were from Mexico (Hernandez et al., 2007; Yoshikawa et al., 2006).

In summary, familistic cultural values are sometimes cited as a plausible explanation for the lower early education enrollment rates among children in immigrant families relative to White children in native families, but recent research regarding Hispanic and Indochinese groups indicates that socioeconomic and structural influences can account for at least 50% of and, for some groups, essentially all of the gap. Early education programs have been found to promote school readiness and educational success in elementary school and beyond (Gormley, Gayer, Phillips, & Dawson, 2005; Haskins & Rouse, 2005; Lynch, 2004). Research suggests that children with low family incomes and limited English proficiency may be most likely to benefit from early education programs (Gormley & Gayer, 2005; Takanishi, 2004), but children in several groups challenged by these circumstances are less likely than Whites and the other groups noted above to be enrolled in early education programs.

Insofar as the socioeconomic and structural barriers can account for much or all of lower enrollment in early education programs for these groups, public policies could be developed and implemented to ensure access to early education for these children. Additional research is needed to assess reasons for low enrollment among children in immigrant families from Pakistan/Bangladesh, Afghanistan, and Iraq, as well as among children in immigrant families with all limited English proficient parents with origins in Africa, the former Soviet Union, and Other Europe and Canada. It should be noted that among these last groups, comprehensive

Basic Budget Poverty rates are comparatively high, at levels similar to the immigrant Hispanic and Indochinese groups, which also experience low early education enrollment rates.

CONCLUSION

Early language development is perhaps influenced by parents' language skills more than by any other factor, because most children are more likely to be spoken to by their parents (and siblings) than by any other persons. This study helps us understand the demographic picture of present-day linguistic diversity within our U.S. population for which a language other than English serves as a significant medium of communication. That portrait is one of substantial presence of this population that can be characterized by both its diversity and homogeneity (many languages with Spanish predominating), low levels of educational achievement and attainment, economic challenges, immigrant circumstances, extended family cohesiveness, and, for the youngest, limited participation in early learning opportunities. As the United States faces the educational pursuit of ensuring that all children succeed, this baseline understanding of these children, their families, and their circumstances can help set the stage for accomplishing this educational goal.

APPENDIX:
TABLES 2.1–2.6

"—" Indicates sample size is too small to produce statistically reliable results or category does not apply to the native group.

* "Vietnam" includes Indochina not specified; "Indochina, total" includes the following: Hmong people, Cambodia, Laos, Thailand, Vietnam; "Other Europe, Canada" includes Australia and New Zealand; "Africa, Whites" includes Asian Africans.

Source: Calculated from Census 2000 5% microdata (IPUMS) by Donald J. Hernandez, Center for Social and Demographic Analysis, University at Albany, State University of New York, January 2008.

TABLE 2.1. Parental Language Skill of Children Ages 3 to 4 by Immigrant Origin and/ or Race-Ethnic Origin

	Percent of Children with					
	Parents Speaking English Only at Home	*Both English & Non-English Spoken by Parents*	*No Parent Speaking English*	*Parents English Fluent*	*Both English Fluent and LEP Parents*	*Parents LEP*
Total	**73.8**	**25.2**	**1.0**	**86.1**	**4.8**	**9.2**
Children in native-born families	**17.6**	**10.4**	**0.0**	**97.6**	**1.3**	**1.1**
White	94.8	5.2	0.0	98.9	0.8	0.3
Black	95.8	4.2	0.0	98.9	0.6	0.5
Hispanic (total)	38.3	61.3	0.4	85.4	6.5	8.0
Puerto Rican, mainland origin	76.0	62.8	0.0	88.8	5.1	6.0
Puerto Rican, island origin	9.1	93.2	2.2	54.7	18.8	26.5
Mexican	86.7	57.2	0.2	88.3	5.5	6.2
Other Hispanic/Latino	85.0	57.5	0.2	89.3	4.8	5.9
Asian	82.3	17.5	0.1	96.6	1.8	1.6
Hawaiian/ Pacific Islander	73.3	26.7	0.0	94.7	1.5	3.8
Native American	77.6	22.4	0.0	94.5	3.1	2.4
Children in immigrant families	**27.5**	**81.6**	**4.6**	**41.9**	**17.9**	**40.1**
Latin America and Caribbean	**8.3**	**84.7**	**7.1**	**29.8**	**19.7**	**50.5**
Mexico	3.2	87.8	9.0	21.5	21.1	57.3
Central America	5.8	89.4	4.8	30.2	20.2	49.7
Cuba	6.0	90.2	3.8	57.2	16.2	26.6
Dominican Republic	3.7	89.8	6.5	28.1	20.2	51.7
Haiti	6.0	93.5	0.4	44.8	16.7	38.5
Jamaica	87.0	12.9	0.1	96.8	1.8	1.4
Caribbean, English Speaking	85.6	14.4	0.0	95.8	2.5	1.8
South America	6.5	92.0	1.5	43.3	20.8	35.9

	Percent of Children with				
	Parents Speaking English Only at Home	*Both English & Non-English Spoken by Parents*	*No Parent Speaking English*	*Parents English Fluent*	*Both English Fluent and LEP Parents*	*Parents LEP*
Asia	**12.2**	**87.0**	**0.7**	**51.9**	**17.9**	**30.2**
East/ Southeast Asia	**14.5**	**84.6**	**0.9**	**47.7**	**16.8**	**35.4**
Japan	19.9	80.1	0.0	51.6	23.7	24.7
Korea	23.0	76.5	0.5	44.5	20.1	35.4
China	22.8	74.6	2.6	46.3	13.4	40.2
Hong Kong	9.8	89.4	0.9	48.9	17.9	33.2
Taiwan	9.2	90.8	0.0	41.2	21.2	37.6
Philippines	15.6	84.4	0.0	71.9	15.4	12.8
Hmong	1.3	94.8	3.9	20.7	16.2	63.1
Cambodia	7.1	91.2	1.7	30.5	16.0	53.5
Laos	3.7	94.6	1.6	29.8	17.1	53.1
Thailand	15.2	82.5	2.3	43.3	20.1	36.6
Vietnam*	6.5	92.9	0.7	31.4	15.6	53.0
Indochina*	6.5	92.1	1.3	31.3	16.2	52.5
India/ Southwest Asia	**7.6**	**92.2**	**0.3**	**60.5**	**20.2**	**19.3**
India	7.7	92.3	0.0	68.1	15.9	16.1
Pakistan/Bangladesh	2.8	97.0	0.2	46.9	26.0	27.1
Afghanistan	2.6	97.4	0.0	48.4	17.1	34.5
Iran	10.4	89.6	0.0	69.3	17.3	13.4
Iraq	6.6	90.1	3.3	36.6	25.6	37.8
Israel/Palestine	12.6	87.1	0.3	62.6	19.4	18.1
Other West Asia	8.4	91.3	0.3	58.0	24.4	17.6
Africa	**18.2**	**81.4**	**0.4**	**69.7**	**13.7**	**16.6**
Africa, Blacks	13.5	86.0	0.5	68.8	13.9	17.4
Africa, Whites*	27.3	72.4	0.3	71.4	13.4	15.2
Europe/Canada	**35.9**	**63.6**	**0.5**	**72.1**	**11.5**	**16.4**
Former Soviet Union	22.2	76.5	1.3	47.0	14.6	38.4
Other Europe, Canada*	38.8	60.9	0.3	77.3	10.9	11.9
Other	**55.2**	**44.6**	**0.2**	**83.8**	**8.5**	**7.7**

TABLE 2.2. Child U.S. Citizen, Parents Not U.S. Citizens, Children Ages 3 to 4 by Immigrant Origin and/or Race-Ethnic Origin

	Percent Who Are in Immigrant Families and Are U.S. Citizens				Percent with Parents not U.S. Citizens, Among Children with			
	Total	Parents English Fluent	Both English Fluent and LEP Parents	Parents LEP	Total	Parents English Fluent	Both English Fluent and LEP Parents	Parents LEP
Total	**18.3**	**9.1**	**72.0**	**76.2**	**8.9**	**2.5**	**23.8**	**61.2**
Children in native-born families	—	—	—	—	—	—	—	—
White	—	—	—	—	—	—	—	—
Black	—	—	—	—	—	—	—	—
Hispanic (total)	—	—	—	—	—	—	—	—
Puerto Rican, mainland origin	—	—	—	—	—	—	—	—
Puerto Rican, island origin	—	—	—	—	—	—	—	—
Mexican	—	—	—	—	—	—	—	—
Other Hispanic/Latino	—	—	—	—	—	—	—	—
Asian	—	—	—	—	—	—	—	—
Hawaiian/ Pacific Islander	—	—	—	—	—	—	—	—
Native American	—	—	—	—	—	—	—	—
Children in immigrant families	**88.0**	**90.2**	**92.1**	**83.9**	**42.8**	**24.6**	**30.5**	**67.4**
Latin America and Caribbean	**90.1**	**94.1**	**94.6**	**85.9**	**51.4**	**30.1**	**31.3**	**71.9**
Mexico	89.0	93.6	94.7	85.3	56.4	35.5	32.6	73.1
Central America	93.9	92.8	97.0	93.3	52.6	29.6	36.4	73.0
Cuba	92.9	99.1	96.0	77.6	29.5	11.2	21.6	73.7
Dominican Republic	93.4	96.3	97.1	90.3	41.4	31.2	21.1	54.9
Haiti	91.4	94.8	91.5	87.5	37.1	30.6	22.3	51.2
Jamaica	95.5	95.4	—	—	28.4	28.2	—	—
Caribbean, English Speaking	95.3	95.3	—	—	28.1	27.5	—	—
South America	86.6	93.1	88.6	77.5	38.0	18.4	22.6	70.6

	Percent Who Are in Immigrant Families and Are U.S. Citizens				Percent with Parents not U.S. Citizens, Among Children with			
	Total	*Parents English Fluent*	*Both English Fluent and LEP Parents*	*Parents LEP*	*Total*	*Parents English Fluent*	*Both English Fluent and LEP Parents*	*Parents LEP*
Asia	**85.7**	**86.2**	**88.9**	**82.9**	**29.5**	**20.7**	**27.5**	**45.8**
East/ Southeast Asia	**86.1**	**84.6**	**92.8**	**85.0**	**27.5**	**16.6**	**22.6**	**44.4**
Japan	72.0	90.2	76.4	29.7	39.4	15.2	35.8	93.4
Korea	76.4	72.0	92.5	72.8	30.3	10.4	25.0	58.4
China	71.2	49.1	89.4	90.6	31.6	20.6	40.3	41.2
Hong Kong	92.6	94.8	—	86.7	13.6	9.4	—	23.9
Taiwan	95.1	97.3	98.0	91.1	26.9	15.5	17.4	44.9
Philippines	94.3	95.6	95.8	85.0	19.6	17.8	14.6	36.1
Hmong	96.9	—	—	96.2	56.6	—	—	64.6
Cambodia	96.2	91.5	—	98.1	34.3	21.7	—	45.5
Laos	94.4	99.5	—	91.5	39.7	23.9	—	47.8
Thailand	74.8	93.1	—	—	37.9	17.0	—	—
Vietnam*	91.5	91.1	94.2	90.9	22.4	13.0	9.6	31.7
Indochina*	91.3	92.0	94.4	90.0	30.2	17.3	20.2	41.0
India/ Southwest Asia	**84.8**	**88.9**	**82.1**	**74.7**	**33.8**	**27.5**	**36.0**	**51.0**
India	80.9	83.8	72.5	76.8	44.8	41.7	50.1	52.8
Pakistan/ Bangladesh	82.1	89.0	84.2	68.3	37.1	26.2	41.0	52.2
Afghanistan	96.1	—	—	—	18.0	—	—	—
Iran	95.3	98.8	—	—	11.5	4.7	—	—
Iraq	84.1	—	—	—	39.0	—	—	—
Israel/Palestine	87.2	90.7	—	—	21.7	14.3	—	—
Other West Asia	87.3	92.6	83.1	75.2	26.2	17.4	31.5	47.9
Africa	**85.4**	**90.6**	**83.9**	**64.6**	**38.8**	**31.8**	**38.1**	**68.4**
Africa, Blacks	84.8	89.5	83.8	66.9	43.4	36.8	45.1	68.1
Africa, Whites*	86.5	92.8	84.0	59.5	30.0	22.8	24.2	69.1
Europe/Canada	**82.6**	**87.7**	**84.3**	**59.1**	**26.4**	**15.7**	**29.1**	**71.4**
Former Soviet Union	62.0	53.3	84.8	64.1	38.4	12.0	37.8	71.1
Other Europe, Canada*	86.9	92.0	84.2	55.7	23.9	16.2	26.7	71.6
Other	**84.8**	**86.9**	**77.0**	**70.8**	**26.7**	**23.5**	**31.1**	**56.9**

TABLE 2.3. Grandparent in Home, Child Age 0 to 17 Other Than Sibling in Home, Children Ages 3 to 4 by Immigrant Origin and/or Race-Ethnic Origin

	Percent with Grandparent in Home Among Children with				Percent with Child 0–17 Other Than Sibling in Home, Among Children with			
	Total	Parents English Fluent	Both English Fluent and LEP Parents	Parents LEP	Total	Parents English Fluent	Both English Fluent and LEP Parents	Parents LEP
Total	**9.8**	**9.2**	**11.2**	**14.7**	**4.9**	**3.9**	**6.8**	**13.3**
Children in native-born families	**8.9**	**8.8**	**6.0**	**20.6**	**3.8**	**3.7**	**4.0**	**11.6**
White	5.9	5.9	3.3	9.8	2.1	2.1	1.6	3.3
Black	16.2	16.2	3.8	29.8	8.1	8.1	5.5	11.6
Hispanic (total)	17.6	17.9	8.5	22.0	8.7	8.4	5.8	13.8
Puerto Rican, mainland origin	15.3	15.6	6.1	19.4	7.2	7.1	5.6	9.8
Puerto Rican, island origin	13.3	14.9	6.7	14.7	7.8	7.2	4.4	11.3
Mexican	19.2	19.3	9.7	27.0	9.5	9.2	7.0	16.0
Other Hispanic/Latino	17.0	16.9	9.6	24.3	8.0	7.7	4.9	15.2
Asian	14.4	14.1	—	—	4.2	4.0	—	—
Hawaiian/ Pacific Islander	21.9	23.0	—	—	8.5	8.9	—	—
Native American	15.0	14.8	9.9	29.5	7.9	7.8	5.9	15.2
Children in immigrant families	**13.2**	**12.6**	**12.6**	**14.1**	**9.1**	**5.5**	**7.6**	**13.5**
Latin America and Caribbean	**13.4**	**15.0**	**12.1**	**12.9**	**12.8**	**9.3**	**9.8**	**16.0**
Mexico	12.5	14.6	11.6	12.1	15.0	12.8	11.2	17.2
Central America	14.6	18.1	13.1	13.2	11.6	9.3	9.2	13.9
Cuba	15.7	14.6	13.2	19.5	3.4	2.3	2.7	6.1
Dominican Republic	17.5	18.9	12.2	18.8	8.2	6.9	5.6	9.9
Haiti	15.8	14.2	22.5	14.9	6.0	4.6	5.4	7.9
Jamaica	15.7	15.8	—	—	7.4	7.3	—	—
Caribbean, English Speaking	16.0	16.2	—	—	7.1	7.0	—	—
South America	13.8	11.0	13.0	17.6	6.3	3.0	3.3	12.2

	Percent with Grandparent in Home Among Children with			Percent with Child 0–17 Other Than Sibling in Home, Among Children with			
	Total	*Parents English Fluent*	*Both English Fluent and LEP Parents*	*Parents LEP*	*Total*	*Parents English Fluent*	*Both English Fluent and LEP Parents*	*Parents LEP*
Asia	**17.3**	**15.9**	**15.9**	**20.5**	**3.9**	**3.1**	**3.2**	**5.5**
East/ Southeast Asia	**18.3**	**16.3**	**16.2**	**22.1**	**4.4**	**3.5**	**3.5**	**6.0**
Japan	3.1	3.8	3.3	1.4	0.8	0.8	0.5	1.1
Korea	11.4	9.4	10.5	14.5	1.6	0.9	0.8	2.8
China	18.8	10.1	16.5	29.4	2.9	1.9	2.9	4.0
Hong Kong	18.1	14.8	—	23.0	1.7	0.6	—	3.6
Taiwan	9.7	8.5	8.3	11.8	0.7	0.8	1.0	0.5
Philippines	23.3	22.3	22.4	30.2	5.4	4.7	5.5	9.3
Hmong	22.4	—	—	19.8	8.8	—	—	9.5
Cambodia	22.7	22.3	—	22.7	9.9	7.6	—	13.4
Laos	22.9	19.2	—	24.6	8.3	4.2	—	11.3
Thailand	22.5	20.5	—	—	10.0	11.0	—	—
Vietnam*	19.8	17.1	17.2	22.1	5.5	4.6	6.0	5.9
Indochina*	21.0	19.5	19.1	22.5	7.0	6.1	5.1	8.2
India/ Southwest Asia	**15.1**	**15.3**	**15.3**	**14.5**	**2.8**	**2.6**	**2.7**	**3.7**
India	19.5	19.5	19.6	19.5	2.6	2.2	2.7	4.1
Pakistan/ Bangladesh	18.1	21.1	16.3	14.6	5.4	7.5	3.7	3.5
Afghanistan	11.8	—	—	—	3.5	—	—	—
Iran	14.1	13.0	—	—	1.1	0.6	—	—
Iraq	11.0	—	—	—	4.8	—	—	—
Israel/Palestine	5.0	3.4	—	—	1.3	1.8	—	—
Other West Asia	10.5	10.4	10.0	11.5	2.3	1.8	3.3	2.4
Africa	**8.0**	**8.6**	**9.9**	**3.9**	**3.9**	**3.7**	**4.0**	**4.6**
Africa, Blacks	9.1	9.8	10.7	4.7	5.0	4.8	5.8	5.1
Africa, Whites*	6.1	6.5	8.4	2.0	1.8	1.7	0.4	3.6
Europe/Canada	**7.0**	**5.4**	**8.9**	**12.8**	**1.7**	**1.5**	**1.7**	**2.8**
Former Soviet Union	12.2	8.7	17.0	14.6	1.7	1.9	1.3	1.7
Other Europe, Canada*	5.9	5.0	6.7	11.5	1.7	1.4	1.8	3.5
Other	**6.4**	**4.8**	**6.6**	**23.6**	**3.2**	**2.7**	**5.2**	**7.4**

TABLE 2.4. Other Adult Relative in Home, Nonrelative in Home, Children Ages 3 to 4 by Immigrant Origin and/or Race-Ethnic Origin

	Percent with Other Adult Relative in Home Among Children with				Percent with Nonrelative in Home Among Children with			
	Total	*Parents English Fluent*	*Both English Fluent and LEP Parents*	*Parents LEP*	*Total*	*Parents English Fluent*	*Both English Fluent and LEP Parents*	*Parents LEP*
Total	**10.3**	**7.7**	**17.2**	**30.8**	**4.5**	**3.6**	**5.4**	**12.3**
Children in native-born families	**7.2**	**7.0**	**8.4**	**20.4**	**3.4**	**3.4**	**2.5**	**6.9**
White	4.8	4.7	5.2	10.5	2.8	2.8	1.4	4.4
Black	13.1	13.2	7.7	11.5	4.9	4.9	3.0	4.9
Hispanic (total)	13.9	13.3	11.0	23.7	5.8	5.7	3.6	8.0
Puerto Rican, mainland origin	12.0	12.0	9.0	15.1	5.1	4.9	3.0	8.5
Puerto Rican, island origin	14.8	13.2	12.4	20.0	5.4	5.2	4.7	6.2
Mexican	14.9	14.2	11.6	28.0	5.9	5.9	3.0	8.9
Other Hispanic/ Latino	12.4	11.8	8.1	24.4	5.8	5.8	3.6	8.6
Asian	10.3	10.0	—	—	5.1	5.2	—	—
Hawaiian/ Pacific Islander	18.9	19.4	—	—	5.0	5.3	—	—
Native American	13.7	13.1	17.6	32.2	5.3	5.4	1.7	7.5
Children in immigrant families	**22.2**	**14.1**	**19.7**	**31.8**	**8.4**	**5.0**	**6.2**	**12.9**
Latin America and Caribbean	**28.9**	**20.9**	**23.4**	**35.8**	**11.4**	**7.2**	**8.1**	**15.1**
Mexico	32.2	25.3	25.1	37.4	12.2	8.9	8.0	14.9
Central America	27.7	20.6	23.0	33.9	14.6	8.2	11.0	19.9
Cuba	10.7	8.1	10.5	16.4	5.2	3.8	3.2	9.5
Dominican Republic	23.4	19.2	19.5	27.2	8.1	7.4	5.2	9.6
Haiti	24.5	21.6	19.0	30.3	5.6	5.4	4.1	6.4
Jamaica	19.4	19.3	—	—	5.1	5.1	—	—
Caribbean, English Speaking	21.6	21.2	—	—	3.9	4.0	—	—
South America	17.9	9.1	15.3	30.1	9.2	4.5	8.5	15.3

	Percent with Other Adult Relative in Home Among Children with				Percent with Nonrelative in Home Among Children with			
	Total	*Parents English Fluent*	*Both English Fluent and LEP Parents*	*Parents LEP*	*Total*	*Parents English Fluent*	*Both English Fluent and LEP Parents*	*Parents LEP*
Asia	**14.0**	**11.1**	**12.9**	**19.6**	**4.2**	**3.6**	**2.5**	**6.1**
East/ Southeast Asia	**15.0**	**11.6**	**13.5**	**20.3**	**4.9**	**4.3**	**2.7**	**6.6**
Japan	3.4	3.7	4.5	1.9	2.3	3.5	1.6	0.3
Korea	7.9	4.6	7.5	12.1	2.5	2.3	0.3	3.9
China	12.0	8.8	9.4	16.6	3.3	2.4	1.7	4.9
Hong Kong	9.6	5.0	—	15.7	3.5	1.4	—	7.8
Taiwan	5.7	3.8	5.2	8.1	2.9	3.1	1.4	3.5
Philippines	17.5	15.8	16.6	27.7	6.3	6.0	5.2	9.1
Hmong	21.7	—	—	23.0	4.7	—	—	5.1
Cambodia	26.5	23.7	—	29.5	8.8	7.1	—	10.8
Laos	26.5	21.2	—	29.0	7.3	6.3	—	9.1
Thailand	20.6	13.7	—	—	6.5	4.5	—	—
Vietnam*	19.6	11.9	18.4	24.6	6.1	3.9	3.5	8.1
Indochina*	21.5	15.2	20.1	25.7	6.5	5.1	3.2	8.3
India/ Southwest Asia	**12.0**	**10.4**	**12.0**	**17.0**	**2.7**	**2.4**	**2.2**	**3.9**
India	10.2	8.0	12.5	17.4	3.0	2.8	2.9	4.1
Pakistan/ Bangladesh	20.3	22.2	19.6	17.9	4.2	3.8	1.3	7.9
Afghanistan	19.1	—	—	—	1.3	—	—	—
Iran	10.8	9.9	—	—	1.5	1.5	—	—
Iraq	14.0	—	—	—	1.2	—	—	—
Israel/Palestine	7.8	8.3	—	—	2.4	2.5	—	—
Other West Asia	10.1	9.6	10.0	11.8	1.9	1.7	2.2	2.5
Africa	**15.0**	**14.6**	**14.5**	**17.2**	**5.0**	**5.2**	**2.4**	**6.0**
Africa, Blacks	18.8	19.1	17.8	18.4	5.6	5.7	2.7	7.7
Africa, Whites*	7.8	6.3	8.0	14.7	3.7	4.3	1.7	2.4
Europe/Canada	**6.0**	**4.5**	**7.1**	**11.6**	**2.5**	**2.6**	**1.8**	**2.6**
Former Soviet Union	7.8	5.4	8.1	10.7	2.6	2.8	3.3	2.1
Other Europe, Canada*	5.6	4.4	6.8	12.2	2.4	2.5	1.4	2.8
Other	**9.2**	**7.0**	**17.0**	**23.7**	**3.5**	**3.2**	**3.2**	**6.7**

TABLE 2.5. Father College Graduate, Mother College Graduate, Children Ages 3 to 4 by Immigrant Origin and/or Race-Ethnic Origin

	Percent with Father College Graduate Among Children with				Percent with Mother College Graduate Among Children with			
	Total	*Parents English Fluent*	*Both English Fluent and LEP Parents*	*Parents LEP*	*Total*	*Parents English Fluent*	*Both English Fluent and LEP Parents*	*Parents LEP*
Total	**28.4**	**31.1**	**19.4**	**9.4**	**24.3**	**26.5**	**16.3**	**7.6**
Children in native-born families	**29.6**	**29.9**	**19.1**	**8.2**	**25.3**	**25.6**	**18.5**	**7.2**
White	33.1	33.2	30.6	14.3	30.3	30.4	28.9	13.1
Black	14.6	14.6	13.9	—	11.5	11.4	17.4	14.3
Hispanic (total)	13.9	15.1	9.7	5.0	10.8	11.6	9.3	4.3
Puerto Rican, mainland origin	14.2	15.1	8.1	—	10.3	10.8	10.8	2.0
Puerto Rican, island origin	11.6	15.7	9.4	4.2	9.5	12.2	8.2	4.5
Mexican	13.3	14.2	9.0	4.5	10.2	10.7	9.0	4.2
Other Hispanic/Latino	16.1	16.7	12.7	7.3	13.0	13.6	10.9	5.3
Asian	46.4	46.9	—	—	40.3	40.4	—	—
Hawaiian/ Pacific Islander	17.6	17.6	—	—	12.9	13.4	—	—
Native American	11.6	12.1	5.7	4.1	10.5	10.8	6.2	4.3
Children in immigrant families	**24.3**	**40.6**	**19.5**	**9.5**	**20.4**	**34.5**	**15.7**	**7.6**
Latin America and Caribbean	**8.4**	**17.9**	**7.2**	**3.7**	**7.7**	**15.7**	**6.4**	**3.4**
Mexico	4.1	8.4	4.5	2.3	3.7	7.3	4.1	2.2
Central America	9.1	18.7	8.2	3.9	7.9	16.6	6.3	3.3
Cuba	27.8	35.6	16.6	18.1	26.4	33.7	13.1	18.8
Dominican Republic	12.9	20.2	12.8	8.7	10.0	18.3	8.7	6.1
Haiti	16.4	25.6	12.4	6.8	12.6	20.6	9.6	4.8
Jamaica	20.6	20.9	—	—	18.7	18.8	—	—
Caribbean, English Speaking	20.6	21.2	—	—	18.5	18.5	—	—
South America	29.4	42.8	23.8	16.4	25.8	36.8	23.1	13.7

	Percent with Father College Graduate Among Children with				Percent with Mother College Graduate Among Children with			
	Total	*Parents English Fluent*	*Both English Fluent and LEP Parents*	*Parents LEP*	*Total*	*Parents English Fluent*	*Both English Fluent and LEP Parents*	*Parents LEP*
Asia	**49.5**	**61.1**	**48.2**	**30.0**	**42.5**	**55.6**	**36.5**	**23.3**
East/ Southeast Asia	**43.8**	**54.7**	**44.8**	**28.7**	**39.5**	**53.2**	**35.4**	**22.8**
Japan	61.7	53.4	56.6	84.0	44.7	46.1	36.9	49.3
Korea	56.8	59.1	54.9	55.0	48.2	54.6	40.6	44.7
China	57.4	79.2	72.6	29.3	52.4	76.0	56.5	23.5
Hong Kong	56.6	76.1	—	27.0	51.6	76.2	—	22.5
Taiwan	82.6	84.8	84.3	78.8	72.9	77.3	71.2	69.1
Philippines	39.5	44.1	28.2	28.0	47.8	50.8	40.1	40.4
Hmong	8.5	—	—	5.2	4.2	—	—	0.5
Cambodia	15.8	—	—	3.8	10.1	22.8	—	3.0
Laos	9.0	16.6	—	4.0	5.9	12.2	—	3.4
Thailand	29.0	36.7	—	—	17.6	21.4	—	—
Vietnam*	29.0	51.9	35.8	13.3	19.5	41.3	16.6	7.2
Indochina*	23.1	41.5	28.0	10.6	15.1	31.9	12.7	5.8
India/ Southwest Asia	**60.7**	**70.9**	**54.2**	**35.0**	**48.8**	**59.7**	**38.4**	**25.4**
India	75.7	84.0	72.3	43.5	65.9	75.2	56.8	35.4
Pakistan/ Bangladesh	59.3	71.0	59.5	38.9	42.2	52.5	38.9	27.2
Afghanistan	20.7	—	—	—	15.8	—	—	—
Iran	74.0	80.6	—	—	54.2	63.8	—	—
Iraq	21.2	—	—	—	18.6	—	—	—
Israel/Palestine	43.9	47.8	—	—	39.4	48.0	—	—
Other West Asia	46.6	55.8	40.1	24.8	33.4	41.8	26.9	15.2
Africa	**55.9**	**62.9**	**49.5**	**30.0**	**34.3**	**42.1**	**19.8**	**13.7**
Africa, Blacks	52.6	61.2	43.4	24.0	27.0	35.9	9.4	5.8
Africa, Whites*	61.5	65.8	61.5	41.1	48.0	53.0	40.6	30.5
Europe/Canada	**43.0**	**48.8**	**34.7**	**23.3**	**37.5**	**42.2**	**34.4**	**19.3**
Former Soviet Union	48.0	61.4	51.0	30.5	45.8	61.4	48.4	25.7
Other Europe, Canada*	41.9	47.3	30.2	18.4	35.8	39.7	30.5	15.0
Other	**48.3**	**51.9**	**37.3**	**20.2**	**40.6**	**43.4**	**33.7**	**16.6**

TABLE 2.6. Enrolled in Pre-K/Nursery School or Kindergarten at Ages 3 and 4 by Immigrant Origin and/or Race-Ethnic Origin

	Percent with Enrolled in School, Age 3 Among Children with				Percent with Enrolled in School, Age 4 Among Children with			
	Total	*Parents English Fluent*	*Both English Fluent and LEP Parents*	*Parents LEP*	*Total*	*Parents English Fluent*	*Both English Fluent and LEP Parents*	*Parents LEP*
Total	**37.2**	**39.0**	**30.2**	**23.6**	**61.6**	**63.5**	**54.2**	**47.5**
Children in native-born families	**38.6**	**38.7**	**37.0**	**29.7**	**63.2**	**63.4**	**57.9**	**54.9**
White	37.8	37.8	39.9	30.4	63.0	63.0	61.8	46.2
Black	46.3	46.2	57.6	50.4	68.7	68.7	65.9	74.0
Hispanic (total)	31.9	32.5	31.7	26.3	55.4	55.7	52.4	54.0
Puerto Rican, mainland origin	40.4	41.4	39.1	25.2	62.2	62.1	56.5	67.5
Puerto Rican, island origin	31.9	32.0	34.8	29.1	55.4	57.5	51.1	54.1
Mexican	29.4	29.7	28.2	25.6	52.4	52.7	50.8	49.4
Other Hispanic/Latino	33.6	34.2	32.1	24.1	58.6	58.9	56.0	56.3
Asian	44.1	44.2	—	—	67.2	67.0	—	—
Hawaiian/ Pacific Islander	30.7	32.1	—	—	60.8	61.3	—	—
Native American	32.5	32.5	24.7	42.4	57.4	57.3	59.2	60.6
Children in immigrant families	**32.0**	**42.0**	**28.3**	**23.0**	**55.3**	**64.5**	**53.2**	**46.7**
Latin America and Caribbean	**25.8**	**35.5**	**23.8**	**20.9**	**49.5**	**57.9**	**49.2**	**44.7**
Mexico	20.1	26.3	19.6	18.1	43.5	48.0	44.9	41.3
Central America	27.7	33.8	26.8	24.4	51.9	57.6	52.1	48.4
Cuba	38.2	44.9	33.3	26.9	66.7	74.5	63.6	51.3
Dominican Republic	36.5	39.0	38.1	34.5	61.3	63.5	54.8	62.1
Haiti	52.6	52.8	66.6	46.1	72.3	71.7	82.9	68.4
Jamaica	51.0	50.6	—	—	75.6	75.7	—	—
Caribbean, English Speaking	48.3	48.4	—	—	68.7	68.5	—	—
South America	40.5	45.7	37.9	35.5	64.2	67.0	66.6	59.5

	Percent with Enrolled in School, Age 3 Among Children with				Percent with Enrolled in School, Age 4 Among Children with			
	Total	Parents English Fluent	Both English Fluent and LEP Parents	Parents LEP	Total	Parents English Fluent	Both English Fluent and LEP Parents	Parents LEP
Asia	**38.7**	**43.3**	**35.9**	**32.1**	**61.7**	**65.9**	**59.8**	**55.8**
East/ Southeast Asia	**36.9**	**40.0**	**34.0**	**34.0**	**59.8**	**62.4**	**59.6**	**56.5**
Japan	48.7	45.3	42.6	64.0	70.6	65.7	74.7	76.0
Korea	46.3	49.9	41.1	44.7	70.1	72.6	69.2	67.6
China	49.5	57.5	42.8	42.4	73.9	78.4	76.0	68.2
Hong Kong	53.6	55.4	—	50.8	78.3	81.6	—	68.5
Taiwan	55.1	53.5	52.6	58.1	78.9	75.9	81.6	81.0
Philippines	28.1	30.2	23.5	22.0	50.9	52.9	44.5	46.7
Hmong	22.3	—	—	30.6	33.1	—	—	26.0
Cambodia	20.1	20.5	—	17.7	37.7	50.0	—	36.9
Laos	17.4	18.8	—	16.7	38.2	30.9	—	39.7
Thailand	38.0	32.3	—	—	51.9	53.5	—	—
Vietnam*	27.5	35.6	26.1	23.0	55.4	62.0	50.3	52.9
Indochina*	26.0	30.0	25.8	23.5	48.8	54.8	46.9	45.9
India/ Southwest Asia	**42.4**	**48.7**	**39.3**	**24.8**	**65.6**	**71.7**	**60.3**	**53.0**
India	44.8	49.9	37.2	28.6	68.9	74.0	68.8	50.3
Pakistan/ Bangladesh	29.5	40.2	31.9	10.6	55.8	60.1	50.2	53.2
Afghanistan	27.7	—	—	—	45.3	—	—	—
Iran	55.9	59.7	—	—	76.7	82.6	—	—
Iraq	24.6	—	—	—	48.5	—	—	—
Israel/Palestine	66.0	63.8	—	—	78.9	80.9	—	—
Other West Asia	37.8	42.9	35.4	22.7	63.6	70.8	55.3	52.8
Africa	**49.3**	**55.0**	**45.7**	**30.4**	**72.6**	**75.3**	**77.0**	**56.4**
Africa, Blacks	51.4	57.4	49.2	32.0	72.6	76.1	76.5	53.5
Africa, Whites*	45.3	50.6	37.6	26.3	72.5	73.8	77.7	62.1
Europe/Canada	**44.8**	**50.8**	**40.3**	**21.5**	**67.2**	**73.0**	**62.5**	**45.0**
Former Soviet Union	38.9	56.7	35.2	16.2	59.2	73.9	53.5	45.4
Other Europe, Canada*	46.0	50.0	41.6	25.0	68.8	72.9	65.3	44.8
Other	**43.4**	**45.1**	**38.3**	**28.2**	**70.3**	**74.0**	**57.0**	**48.6**

REFERENCES

Bernstein, J., Brocht, C., & Spade-Aguilar, M. (2000). *How much is enough? Basic family budgets for working families.* Washington, DC: Economic Policy Institute.

Blake, J. (1985). Number of siblings and educational mobility. *American Sociological Review, 50,* 84–94.

Blake, J. (1989). *Family size and achievement.* Berkeley, CA: University of California Press.

Blau, P. M., & Duncan, O. D. (1967). *The American occupational structure.* New York: Wiley.

Boushey, H., Brocht, C., Gundersen, B., & Bernstein, Y. J. (2001). *Hardships in America: The real story of working families.* Washington, DC: Economic Policy Institute.

Cherlin, A. J. (1999). Going to extremes: Family structure, children's well-being, and social sciences. *Demography, 36,* 421–428.

Citro, D. F., & Michael, R. T. (1995). *Measuring poverty: A new approach.* Washington, DC: National Academy Press.

Duncan, G. J., & Brooks-Gunn, J. (Eds.). (1997). *Consequences of growing up poor.* New York: Russell Sage Foundation.

Featherman, D. L., & Hauser, R. (1978). Occupations and social mobility in the United States. *Sociological Microjournal, 12,* Fiche 62. Copenhagen: Sociological Institute.

Gormley, W. T., & Gayer, T. (2005). Promoting school readiness in Oklahoma: An evaluation of Tulsa's pre-K program. *Journal of Human Resources, 40*(3), 533–554.

Gormley, W. T., Gayer, T., Phillips, D., & Dawson, B. (2005). The effects of universal pre-K on cognitive development. *Developmental Psychology, 41,* 872–884.

Haskins, R., & Rouse, C. (2005, Spring). Closing achievement gaps. *The Future of Children* [Policy Brief]. Princeton, NJ: Princeton-Brookings.

Hernandez, D. J. (1986). Childhood in sociodemographic perspective. In R. H. Turner & J. F. Short Jr. (Eds.), *Annual Review of Sociology* (Vol. 12, pp. 159–180). Palo Alto, CA: Annual Reviews.

Hernandez, D. J., & Charney, E. (Eds.). (1998). *From generation to generation: The health and well-being of children in immigrant families.* Washington, DC: National Academy Press.

Hernandez, D. J., Denton, N. A., & Macartney, S. E. (2007). Child poverty in the U.S.: A new family budget approach with comparison to European countries. In H. Wintersberger, L. Alanen, T. Olk, & J. Qvortrup (Eds.), *Children's economic and social welfare* (pp. 176–201). Odense: University Press of Southern Denmark.

Hernandez, D. J., Denton, N. A., & Macartney, S. E. (in press). Early childhood education programs: Accounting for low enrollment in newcomer and native families. In M. Waters & R. Alba (Eds.), *The next generation: Immigrant youth and families in comparative perspective.* Ithaca, NY: Cornell University Press.

Hill-Scott, K. (2005). *Facilities technical report.* Los Angeles: First 5 LA.

Holloway, S. D., Fuller, B., Rambaud, M. F., & Eggers-Pierola, C. (1998). *Through my own eyes: Single mothers and the cultures of poverty.* Cambridge, MA: Harvard University Press.

Kao, G. (1999). Psychological well-being and educational achievement among immigrant youth. In D. J. Hernandez (Ed.), *Children of immigrants: Health, adjustment, and public assistance* (pp. 410–477). Washington, DC: National Academy Press.

Liang, X., Fuller, B., & Singer, J. D. (2000). Ethnic differences in child care selection: The influence of family structure, parental practices, and country-of-origin language. *Early Childhood Research Quarterly, 15,* 357–384.

Lynch, R. G. (2004). *Exceptional returns: Economic, fiscal and social benefits of investment in early childhood development.* Washington, DC: Economic Policy Institute.

Matthews, H., & Ewen, D. (2006). *Reaching all children? Understanding early care and education participation among immigrant families.* Washington, DC: Center for Law and Social Policy.

McLanahan, S., & Sandefur, G. (1994). *Growing up with a single parent: What hurts, what helps.* Cambridge, MA: Harvard University Press.

McLoyd, V. (1998). Socioeconomic disadvantage and child development. *American Psychologist, 53*(2), 185–204.

Mezey, J., Greenberg, M., & Schumacher, R. (2002). *The vast majority of federally-eligible children did not receive child care assistance in FY2000.* Washington, DC: Center for Law and Social Policy. Retrieved, March 16, 2005, from http://www.clasp.org/publications/1in7full.pdf

Organisation for Economic Co-operation and Development (OECD), Directorate of Education. (2006). *Early childhood education and care policy: Country note for Mexico.* Retrieved March 4, 2006, from www.oecd.org/dataoecd/11/39/34429196.pdf

Rumbaut, R. G. (1999). Passages to adulthood: The adaptation of children of immigrants in Southern California. In D. J. Hernandez (Ed.), *Children of immigrants: Health, adjustment, and public assistance* (pp. 478–545). Washington, DC: National Academy Press.

Sewell, W. H., & Hauser, R. M. (1975). *Education, occupation and earnings.* New York: Academic Press.

Sewell, W. H., Hauser, R. M., & Wolf, W. C. (1980). Sex, schooling and occupational status. *American Journal of Sociology, 86,* 551–583.

Shonkoff, J. P., & Phillips, D. A. (2000). *From neurons to neighborhoods: The science of early child development.* Washington, DC: National Academy Press.

Takanishi, R. (2004). Leveling the playing field: Supporting immigrant children from birth to eight. *The Future of Children, 14* [Special issue on Children of Immigrants], 61–79.

UNICEF. (2005). Child poverty in rich countries, 2005. *Innocenti Report Card No. 6.* Florence, Italy: UNICEF Innocenti Research Centre.

Utall, L. (1999). Using kin for child care: Embedment in the socioeconomic networks of extended families. *Journal of Marriage and the Family, 61,* 845–857.

Yoshikawa, H., McCartney, K., Myers, R., Bub, K., Lugo-Gil, J., Ramos, M., et al. (2006). Educacion preescolar en Mexico. In F. Reimers (Ed.), *Aprender mas y mejor: Politicas, programas y oportunidades de aprendizaje en educacion basica en Mexico* (pp. 121–139). Mexico City: Fonda Cultura y Economica.

CHAPTER 3

English Language Learners' Math and Reading Achievement Trajectories in the Elementary Grades

Claudia Galindo

In the United States, many English language learner (ELL) students lag behind native-English-speaking students in their educational achievement. Compared with English-speaking students, ELL students have lower math and reading test scores, academic grades, and educational and occupational aspirations (García & Frede, Chapter 1, this volume). This chapter focuses on language-minority students' achievement patterns and investigates the relationships between language skills at kindergarten entry, ethnicity, socioeconomic status, and achievement in elementary school. The early school years are crucial for children's later learning. As students acquire basic skills, they construct their identity as students (Farkas & Berton, 2004; Rouse, Brooks-Gunn, & McLanahan, 2005). Young students also learn to navigate the formal school setting, and teachers begin to sort students through ability groups, special education classes, and grade retention (Alexander, Entwisle, & Bedinger, 1994; Entwisle & Alexander, 1993). The early school years may be even more important for English language learners, given that these years coincide with the processes of English language acquisition and with their initial exposure to formal English.

The main aim of this chapter is to provide detailed *descriptive* analyses of the patterns of language-minority students' achievement, rather than to explain the primary causes of these patterns. This effort differs from and builds on previous research on language-minority students' education in several ways. First, instead of analyzing language-minority students as a homogenous group, my analyses disaggregate these students based on additional characteristics. Second, by analyzing longitudinal data, I go beyond a static measure of achievement to examine achievement trajectories over time. The results of these analyses can inform research on educational interventions for language-minority children prior to school entry.

A DESCRIPTION OF THE DATABASE USED IN THIS ANALYSIS

For my analysis of the achievement trajectory of linguistic-minority children, I used the database created by the Early Childhood Longitudinal Study-Kindergarten Cohort (ECLS-K), sponsored by the National Center for Education Statistics (National Center for Education Statistics, 2001). ECLS-K provides a nationally representative sample of approximately 21,000 kindergartners who were then followed over time. In this chapter, I present analyses of reading and math assessments from kindergarten through 5th grade (fall 1998, spring 1999, fall 1999, spring 2000, spring 2002, and spring 2004) in order to describe patterns in cognitive development among language-minority students.

The ECLS-K researchers based the math and reading assessment instruments on national and state standards to ensure that the assessments measured skills typically taught in the relevant grades. Trained data collectors individually administered these untimed, adaptive tests. Details of the assessments are provided in ECLS-K psychometric reports (Pollack, Narajian, Rock, Atkins-Burnett, & Hausken, 2005; Pollack, Rock, Weiss, Atkins-Burnett, Tourangeau, & West, 2005; Rock & Pollack, 2002).

Prior to conducting analyses, I converted the assessment scores to a common metric to allow for easy comparison across instruments and to analyze children's performance relative to their peers. An important advantage of using standardized scores is that they allow for interpretation and comparability with other research (Reardon & Galindo, 2009). In the analyses, I primarily focus on achievement "gaps," indicate the difference in scores between each group of interest and a reference group in standard deviation units. One standard deviation typically represents the achievement gap between children from low-income and middle-income families.

I classified a student as language minority if a language other than English is the primary language used at home. For most students, this information was available from their school records, or was gathered from teachers' reports. I used language-minority status classification at kindergarten to illuminate the relationship of skills at kindergarten entry to later school success. The ECLS-K data set also allowed me to control for race/ethnicity, socioeconomic status, and immigrant generational status (i.e., whether the grandparents, parents, or child were immigrants).

SAMPLE AND SAMPLE SELECTION

Results presented in this chapter are based on three different samples. The full ECLS-K sample is used to describe the language-minority student population in the kindergarten class of 98–99 (n = 21,260 students). Math learning achievement gap analyses are based on information from 11,792 students, and reading achievement gap analyses are based on 11,787 students. The numbers are different because, after each additional year of data collection, students' scores had to be re-estimated to include the most recent items so that test scores could be compared across waves. (See Galindo, 2009, for a full description of the samples and statistical methods used for each analysis.)

CHARACTERISTICS OF LANGUAGE-MINORITY
STUDENTS IN THE KINDERGARTEN CLASS OF 98–99

Using the full nationally representative sample in the ECLS-K data set (n = 21, 260), I identified some important characteristics of the language-minority population in kindergarten. (For a more detailed and specific report of the characteristics, see Galindo, 2009.) About 14% of students in the kindergarten class of 98–99 were identified by their teachers/schools as language minority and about half of these students (52.30%) were not proficient in oral English in the fall of kindergarten.

There are important differences between language-minority students and native-English-speaking students in this sample. On average, language-minority students are more likely to be in a racial/ethnic minority group, to have immigrant families, and to live in poverty. Only 7% of language-minority students are non-Hispanic Whites compared to 64% of native-English-speaking students. Also, 32% of language-minority students are in the lowest socioeconomic quintile, and only 6% belong to the highest quintile. The characteristics of this sample corroborate results from other studies showing that language-minority students not only have to overcome their language barriers, but they also face important economic and cultural barriers due to poverty and immigrant status (Gándara, Rumberger, Maxwell-Jolly, & Callahan, 2003; Maxwell-Jolly, Gándara, & Méndez Benavides, 2007; Schmid, 2001).

My analysis of the sample provides information about the two most predominant language-minority groups in the United States: Hispanics and Asians. Overall, at least half of Hispanic and Asian students are defined as language minority, which is not surprising given the large number of these students with foreign-born parents. A higher percentage of Asian students (60%) are classified as language minority compared with

Hispanic students (51%). However, Asian students are more likely than Hispanic children to be proficient in oral English at the beginning of kindergarten (62% vs. 41%).

There is important variability in socioeconomic status (SES) levels between Asian and Hispanic language-minority students. More than half of Hispanic language-minority students belong to the lowest SES quintile, but only 11% belong to the two highest SES quintiles. In contrast, 27% of Asian language-minority students belong to the highest SES quintiles, while 22% belong to the lowest SES quintile, suggesting two distinct populations of Asian language-minority students.

In terms of generational status, students from both racial/ethnic groups are equally likely to be second generation children (i.e., U.S.-born children with non-U.S.-born parents), but Asian students are more likely to be first generation (i.e., non-U.S.-born children with non-U.S.-born parents) than are Hispanic students. Thus, the economic and English proficiency differences observed between Asian and Hispanic language-minority students may have important consequences for these students' math and reading achievement trends over time.

ACHIEVEMENT GAP TRENDS FROM KINDERGARTEN TO 5TH GRADE

In an effort to better understand the patterns of achievement of young English language learners, I describe math and reading achievement gap trends from kindergarten to 5th grade disaggregating language-minority students by their oral English proficiency at kindergarten, socioeconomic status, and race/ethnicity. These achievement gap trends are depicted in Figures 3.1 to 3.6, all shown in the Appendix to this chapter.

Achievement Gap Trends by Oral English Proficiency

As Figure 3.1 indicates, compared to native-English-speaking students, language-minority students begin kindergarten with math scores that are about three-fourths of a standard deviation lower. By spring of 5th grade their scores remain about one-fourth of a standard deviation lower. The math achievement gap at the beginning of kindergarten is one standard deviation for students who are not proficient in English, but only one-third of a standard deviation for students who are proficient in oral English. By spring of 5th grade, the math achievement gap is reduced by more than half for the first group and is entirely eliminated for English proficient students, so that by 5th grade only non-English proficient language-minority students have lower math achievement than do native-English-speaking students. Nevertheless, as noted in Reardon and Galindo (2006), steeper gap decreases are observed for non-English proficient students than for English proficient students in math achievement over time.

Figure 3.2 in the Appendix shows that in reading, language-minority students' scores are roughly one-third of a standard deviation lower than those of native English speaking students at fall of kindergarten, and by spring of 5th grade the achievement gap remains about two-fifths of a standard deviation. Note that the achievement gap at the beginning of kindergarten denotes differences only between English proficient language minority and native-English-speaking students. This estimate likely underrepresents the "true" initial reading achievement gap given that it does not apply to language-minority students who are not proficient in English. Figure 3.2 also indicates that students who begin kindergarten proficient in oral English have better reading scores than students who are non-proficient. The reading achievement gap between native-English-speaking and English proficient language-minority students is eliminated by spring of 5th grade. For non-English proficient language-minority students, the reading gap slightly narrows between spring of 1st grade and spring of 5th grade, yet it remains large (about three-fourths of a standard deviation). By the spring of 5th grade, reading gaps are larger than math gaps. It appears that language-minority students who have limited English proficiency at kindergarten entry have much more difficulty making progress in reading than in math.

Given the concentration of economic disadvantages among language-minority students, it is also useful to examine trends in adjusted math and reading gaps after controlling for students' socioeconomic status. (For the specific results of these analyses, please see Galindo, 2009.) Overall, the trends are similar to those for the unadjusted gaps. However, math and reading achievement gaps are smaller by about half, at least in the first 2 years of schooling. Some, but not all, of the educational disadvantages of language-minority students are due to their economic circumstances and parental education and occupation.

Achievement Gap Trends by Socioeconomic Status

Figures 3.3 and 3.4 in the Appendix depict achievement differences between the average language-minority student in a given SES quintile and the average native-English-speaking student regardless of her or his socioeconomic status. Language-minority students' achievement gaps decrease as SES rises. Achievement gaps are large for language-minority students in the lowest SES quintiles, but students in the fourth quintile have relatively similar achievement levels, and students in the highest quintile have better achievement than the comparison group of native-English-speaking students. However, most language-minority students are in the lowest socioeconomic quintiles, so the cognitive advantages observed among the students in the highest socioeconomic quintile are experienced only by a small number of language-minority students.

Figure 3.3 reveals that language-minority students in the lowest SES quintile begin kindergarten with a math score about one standard deviation below native-English-speaking students. In contrast, language-minority students in the highest SES quintile begin kindergarten with a math score one-third of a standard deviation above their native-English-speaking counterparts. Math achievement gaps decrease by half between kindergarten and 5th grade for students in the lowest SES quintiles, falling from one standard deviation in the fall of kindergarten to roughly one half of a standard deviation in the spring of 5th grade. The math advantage of language-minority students in the highest SES quintile almost doubles by the end of 5th grade, rising to two-thirds of a standard deviation above native-English-speaking students.

Figure 3.4 shows similar patterns for initial gaps in reading achievement, but decreases in reading gaps over time are minimal. Language-minority students in the lowest SES quintile begin kindergarten with reading achievement scores two-fifths of a standard deviation below native-English-speaking students. In contrast, students in the highest SES quintile begin kindergarten with reading scores almost two-thirds of a standard deviation above their native-English counterparts. Between 1st and 5th grades, the reading achievement gaps of language-minority students remain relatively stable across the SES quintiles. For three of the quintiles, there is little or no progress toward closing the gap.

Achievement Patterns by Race/Ethnicity

From Figure 3.5, shown in the Appendix, it is clear that in math, language-minority Asian students significantly outperform language-minority Hispanic students and native-English-speaking Black students. Nevertheless, substantial math achievement gaps compared with White native English speakers are evident by 1st grade, if not earlier, for both language-minority groups. These gaps narrow over time. By the end of 5th grade, language-minority Asian students who were English proficient at kindergarten entry have surpassed White students by about one-third standard deviation, and language-minority Asian students generally have reached parity. For language-minority Hispanic children, the gap falls from more than one standard deviation to less than two-thirds of a standard deviation. Despite this gain, language-minority Hispanic children remain far behind White native English speakers in math and do not appear to be on a trajectory that would lead to much further closing of the gap. Black children fall behind through 5th grade and have a larger gap than language-minority Hispanic children by the end of 1st grade.

The trends for reading achievement are quite different, as can be seen in Figure 3.6 in the Appendix. There is little evidence that gaps close over time, particularly after 1st grade. If anything, language-minority Asian and Hispanic children fall somewhat further behind by the 3rd and the 5th grades, though the decline is not as steep as for Black children. By the end of 5th grade, language-minority Hispanic children are about at parity with Black children in reading achievement. Both are about three-quarters of a standard deviation behind White children. Language-minority Hispanic children who were proficient in English at kindergarten entry perform much better, but still lag by nearly half of a standard deviation. Asian language-minority children are just below one-quarter standard deviation behind White native English speakers; those who were proficient in English at kindergarten entry score slightly higher than White native English speakers.

ISOLATING THE EFFECTS OF ORAL
ENGLISH PROFICIENCY AT KINDERGARTEN ENTRY

A key question raised by the trends in achievement gaps is the extent to which English proficiency at school entry has an impact on language-minority students' achievement over time that is independent of other background characteristics such as gender, race/ethnicity, SES, immigrant status, and so on. I conducted a preliminary investigation and found that English proficiency at kindergarten entry was highly statistically significant, even when controlling for these other factors. (For a full report of the regression analysis, see Galindo, 2009.) These results support the hypothesis that oral language proficiency in English at kindergarten entry has an important independent effect on later achievement for language-minority children. They also suggest that the strength of this effect may increase over time for reading achievement.

CONCLUSION

In the past 30 years, there have been major advances in research on language development and literacy interventions for English language learners. Yet, discussions about how to help language-minority students successfully navigate the educational system are immersed in intense battles in political, public, and academic arenas. The manipulation of critical information and fragmented research affect and bias the debate about English language learners.

Many language-minority students are at risk of failing in school because of language barriers, family poverty, low parental education, and unfamiliarity with U.S. schools and society. Regardless of the substantial challenges that language-minority children pose to schools and society, these students also bring important cultural and linguistic assets. Language-minority children potentially can reach similar levels of competences in two different languages. Dual language skills are associated with cognitive and linguistic advantages, including greater cognitive flexibility, better classification and reasoning skills, and increased awareness and control over language (Cummins, 2000; Krashen, 1999; Winsler, Diaz, Espinosa, & Rodríguez, 1999). At the same time, language-minority students and their immigrant parents are reportedly more optimistic about the future and have higher educational expectations than children of native-born parents. They tend to cultivate cohesive ethnic communities that facilitate social control, affirm cultural values, and may provide exposure to positive role models (Hao & Bonstead-Bruns, 1998; Pong, Hao, & Gardner, 2005; Valenzuela & Dornbusch, 1994; Zhou & Bankston, 1994).

In this chapter, five important findings emerge. First, compared to native-English-speaking students, language-minority students, particularly students who lack oral English proficiency, have important educational disadvantages. At kindergarten entry, language-minority students have significantly lower scores than do native-English-speaking students and, although these differences are reduced over time, they remain significant through grade 5.

Second, there are important variations among language-minority student subgroups in their patterns of achievement. Larger achievement gaps are observed for three groups of students: (a) those who are not proficient in oral English at the fall of kindergarten, (b) Hispanic students, and (c) students in the lowest socioeconomic quintiles. In contrast, there are narrower achievement gaps for students who are proficient in oral English at entry to kindergarten, are Asian, or are from the highest socioeconomic quintiles.

Third, achievement gaps narrow over time, particularly in math, yet meaningful achievement gaps remain at the end of 5th grade. Language-minority Hispanic students score nearly two-thirds of a standard deviation lower than native-English-speaking White students in math and three-fourths of a standard deviation lower than native-English-speaking students in reading by the spring of 5th grade.

Fourth, oral English proficiency at kindergarten entry has a significant impact on students' math and reading achievement during the elementary school years. The effect of oral English proficiency remains strong over time, suggesting that improving language-minority students' English proficiency prior to kindergarten may be a critical mechanism to improve their later educational outcomes.

Fifth, different trends in achievement gaps are observed for reading and math across language-minority subgroups, suggesting that language background and oral English proficiency may have different consequences for children's content development. On average, math achievement gaps between language-minority groups and native-English-speaking students close steadily over time, yet reading achievement gaps remain stable between the spring of 3rd grade and 5th grade. By the spring of 5th grade, reading achievement gaps are much larger than math achievement gaps.

Given the rapid growth of the language-minority population, the United States will benefit from a thorough, comprehensive, and multifaceted approach to understanding these children's educational experiences and outcomes. This research shows that being a language minority is not a risk factor by itself for persistent poor achievement. Proficiency in oral English at kindergarten entry, the poverty levels commonly observed among these students, and other disadvantages most dramatically limit the students' long-term educational achievement.

The findings from this research have important implications for preschool education, given the dramatic math and reading achievement gaps already observed at the beginning of kindergarten and the strong association observed between oral English proficiency and math and reading achievement over time. It is important to point out that findings presented in this chapter should not be used as evidence to support English-only education given that I have not tested in my analyses different teaching strategies for non-English-speaking students nor have I incorporated issues about bilingualism and fluency in more than one language.

Effective preschool practices to support language-minority children and to increase their English ability may help neutralize their educational disadvantages. To redeem this promise, it will be necessary to identify specific teaching practices relating to language and other mechanisms through which English proficiency can be increased among young language-minority students. Future studies of language-minority students also will benefit from a longitudinal approach and from taking into account the diversity of the language-minority population and other key school-relevant variables (i.e., teacher quality, curricular richness, school characteristics, school segregation, student behavior, and family involvement) that affect students' educational experiences. Other studies find that school quality (Alexander et al. 1994; Downey, Von Hippel, & Broh, 2004; Entwisle & Alexander, 1993) and active parental involvement (Epstein, 2001) can help reduce the effects of social and economic disadvantages on students' educational outcomes. From a policy perspective, it is essential that research identify in detail key mechanisms that may contribute to the improvement of educational outcomes of the language-minority population in the United States. Policymakers should understand that interventions to improve language-minority students' educational paths should begin with preschool education. It is important to invest in the development of highly effective approaches and in those who can staff such programs.

The author thanks Steve Barnett, Ellen Frede, Eugene E. García, and Joyce Epstein—for useful comments and suggestions—and Sean Reardon and Joe Robinson for methodological and statistical guidance.

APPENDIX

FK = Fall Kindergarten, SK = Spring Kindergarten,
F1 = Fall 1st Grade, S1 = Spring 1st Grade,
S3= Spring 3rd Grade, S5= Spring 5th Grade,
LM = Language Minority, p = proficient, n = not proficient

FIGURE 3.1. Trends in Math Achievement Gaps for Language-Minority Students by Oral English Proficiency at Entry into Kindergarten

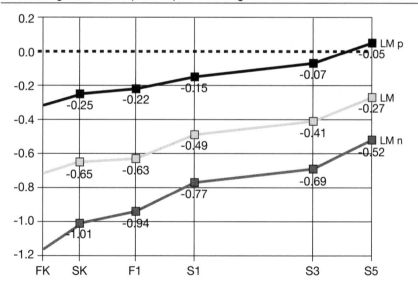

# of cases by group and time point

	FK	SK	F1	S1	S3	S5
LM: proficient at fall K	927	962	256	934	926	918
LM: not proficient at fall K	658	840	287	962	975	975

	FK	SK	F1	S1	S3	S5
LM	1,585	1,802	543	1,896	1,903	1,895

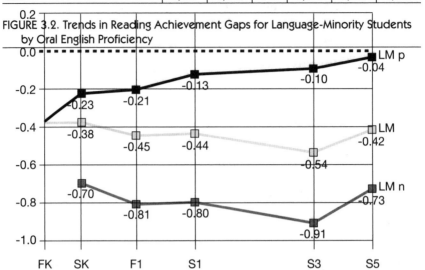

FIGURE 3.2. Trends in Reading Achievement Gaps for Language-Minority Students by Oral English Proficiency

# of cases by group and time point

	FK	SK	F1	S1	S3	S5
LM: proficient at fall K	924	958	256	932	923	917
LM: not proficient at fall K	0	368	156	734	970	973
LM	924	1,326	412	1,666	1,895	1,892

FIGURE 3.3. Trends in Math Achievement Gaps by Socioeconomic Status

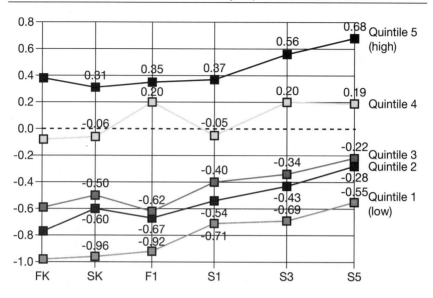

of cases by group and time point

	FK	SK	F1	S1	S3	S5
LM, quintile 1 (low)	710	787	243	823	820	822
LM, quintile 2	284	330	99	342	334	335
LM, quintile 3	187	214	63	231	232	237
LM, quintile 4	176	201	57	207	205	201
LM, quintile 5 (high)	179	202	66	204	208	204

FIGURE 3.4. Trends in Reading Achievement Gaps by Socioeconomic Status

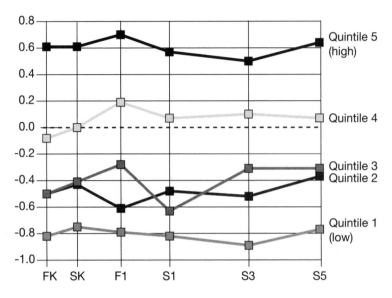

# of cases by group and time point

	FK	SK	F1	S1	S3	S5
LM, quintile 1 (low)	238	434	134	643	812	821
LM, quintile 2	182	261	82	310	335	335
LM, quintile 3	136	185	58	222	232	237
LM, quintile 4	159	194	57	205	205	201
LM, quintile 5 (high)	173	198	66	203	208	203

FIGURE 3.5. Trends in Math Achievement Gaps by Race/Ethnicity and Oral English
Proficiency

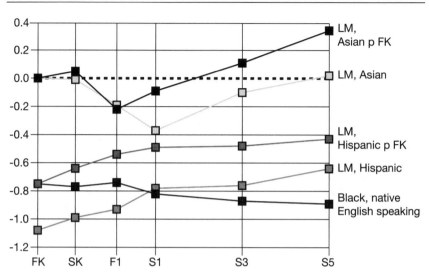

of cases by group and time point

	FK	SK	F1	S1	S3	S5
Black, native English speaking	1,157	1,267	420	1,249	1,221	1,241
LM, Asian	256	370	96	459	483	487
LM, Asian, proficient at FK	256	250	52	241	252	250
LM, Hispanic	516	776	258	1,014	1,215	1,216
LM, Hispanic, proficient at FK	516	507	142	497	482	480

FIGURE 3.6. Trends in Reading Achievement Gaps by Race/Ethnicity and Oral
English Proficiency

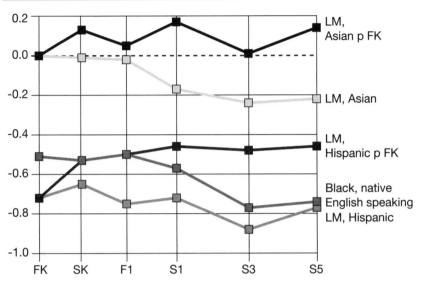

of cases by group and time point

	FK	SK	F1	S1	S3	S5
Black, native English speaking	1,157	1,267	420	1,249	1,221	1,241
LM, Asian	256	370	96	459	483	487
LM, Asian, proficient at FK	256	250	52	241	252	250
LM, Hispanic	516	776	258	1,014	1,215	1,216
LM, Hispanic, proficient at FK	516	507	142	497	482	480

Note for all Figures: Native-English-speaking White students are the reference group,
represented by the value of "0" on the "Y" axes.
Gaps are measured in pooled standard deviation units.

REFERENCES

Alexander, K. L., Entwisle, D. R., & Bedinger, S. D. (1994). When expectations work: Race and socioeconomic differences in school performance. *Social Psychology Quarterly, 57*(4), 283–299.

Cummins, J. (2000). *Language, power, and pedagogy: Bilingual children in the crossfire.* Buffalo, NY: Multilingual Matters.

Downey, D., Von Hippel, P., & Broh, B. A. (2004). Are schools the great equalizer? Cognitive inequality during the summer months and the school year. *American Sociological Review, 69*(5), 613–635.

Entwisle, D. R., & Alexander, K. L. (1993). Entry into school: The beginning school transition and educational stratification in the United States. *Annual Review of Sociology, 19*, 401–423.

Epstein, J. L. (2001). *School, family, and community partnerships: Preparing educators and improving schools.* Boulder, CO: Westview Press.

Farkas, G., & Berton, K. (2004). The detailed age trajectory of oral vocabulary knowledge: Differences by class and race. *Social Science Research, 33*(3), 464–497.

Galindo, C. (2009). *English language learners' math and reading achievement trajectories in the elementary grades: Full technical report* [NIEER Online Report]. New Brunswick, NJ: National Institute for Early Education Research. Retrieved January 31, 2010, from nieer.org/docs/index.php?DoeID=4.

Gándara, P., Rumberger, R., Maxwell-Jolly, J., & Callahan, R. (2003). English learners in California schools: Unequal resources, unequal outcomes. *Education Policy Analysis Archives, 11*(36). Retrieved February 18, 2008, from http://epaa.asu.edu

Hao, L., & Bonstead-Bruns, M. (1998). Parent-child differences in educational expectations and the academic achievement of immigrant and native students. *Sociology of Education, 51*, 175–198.

Krashen, S. D. (1999). *Condemned without a trial: Bogus arguments against bilingual education.* Portsmouth, NH: Heinemann.

Maxwell-Jolly, J., Gándara, P., & Méndez Benavides, L. (2007). *Promoting academic literacy among secondary English language learners: A synthesis of research and practice.* Davis: University of California–Davis, Linguistic Minority Research Institute. Retrieved February 15, 2009, from http://lmri.ucsb.edu

National Center for Education Statistics. (2001). *Early childhood longitudinal study–Kindergarten class of 1998–99 (ECLS-K), Base year public-use data file and user's manual* (NCES Report No. 2001-029). Washington, DC: U.S. Department of Education, Office of Educational Research and Improvement.

Pollack, J. M., Narajian, M., Rock, D. A., Atkins-Burnett, S., & Hausken, E. G. (2005). *Early childhood longitudinal study–Kindergarten class of 1998–99 (ECLS-K), Psychometric report for the fifth grade* (NCES Report No. 2006–036). Washington, DC: U.S. Department of Education, Office of Educational Research and Improvement.

Pollack, J. M., Rock, D. A., Weiss, M. J., Atkins-Burnett, S., Tourangeau, K., West, J., et al. (2005). *Early childhood longitudinal study–Kindergarten class of 1998–99 (ECLS-K), Psychometric report for the third grade* (NCES Report No. 2005–062). Washington, DC: U.S. Department of Education, Office of Educational Research and Improvement.

Pong, S.-L., Hao, L., & Gardner, E. (2005). The roles of parenting styles and social capital in the school performance of immigrant Asian and Hispanic adolescents. *Social Science Quarterly, 86*(4), 928–950.

Reardon, S. F., & Galindo, C. (2006). *Patterns of Hispanic students' math and English literacy test scores in the early elementary grades.* Tempe, AZ: National Task Force on Early Childhood Education for Hispanics. Retrieved February 11, 2009, from http://www.ecehispanic.org

Reardon, S., & Galindo, C. (2009). The Hispanic–White test score gap in the elementary years. *American Educational Research Journal, 46,* 853–891.

Rock, D., & Pollack, J. (2002). *Early childhood longitudinal study—Kindergarten Class 1998–99 (ECLS-K), Psychometric report for kindergarten through 1st grade* (NCES Report No. 2002–005). Washington, DC: U.S. Department of Education, National Center for Educational Statistics, Office of Educational Research and Improvement.

Rouse, C., Brooks-Gunn, J., & McLanahan, S. (2005). Introducing the issue in school readiness: Closing racial and ethnic gaps. *The Future of Children, 15,* 5–14.

Schmid, C. L. (2001). Educational achievement, language-minority students, and the new second generation. *Sociology of Education, 74*(Extra Issue: Current of Thought—Sociology of Education at the Dawn of the 21st Century), 71–87.

Valenzuela, A., & Dornbusch, S. (1994). Familism and social capital in the academic achievement of Mexican origin and Anglo adolescents. *Social Science Quarterly, 75*(1), 18–36.

Winsler, A., Diaz, R., Espinosa, L., & Rodríguez, J. (1999). When learning a second language does not mean losing the first: Bilingual language development in low-income, Spanish-speaking children attending bilingual preschool. *Child Development, 70*(2), 349–362.

Zhou, M., & Bankston, C. L. (1994). Social capital and the adaptation of the second generation: The case of Vietnamese youth in New Orleans. *International Migration Review, 28*(4), 821–845.

CHAPTER 4

Dual Language Development in Preschool Children

Fred Genesee

This chapter reviews research findings on dual language learning in preschool children. By dual language learning, I mean the acquisition of two, or more, languages during the preschool years, prior to age 5. Dual language learning in the preschool years can occur simultaneously, as, for example, when parents regularly use two languages with their child from birth; or it can occur successively, for example, when children are exposed to and speak only one language at home during the first 1 or 2 years of life and then attend day care or preschool programs where another language is used.

It is important to distinguish between these two forms of language learning, because there may be differences with respect to their patterns and rates of development and possibly even the ultimate level of proficiency in the second language. However, it is not always easy to distinguish between simultaneous and successive dual language learning, in part because we do not have an empirically determined age that can be used to distinguish between simultaneous versus successive dual language learning. As well, some children's exposure to and acquisition of two languages during the preschool years may not fit neatly into either of these categories, for example, a child who speaks only Spanish at home during the first 2 years of life and has periodic but limited and passive exposure to English through playmates or TV and, later, begins to attend a preschool program at age 2 or older in which he or she actively begins to need and use the language for interpersonal communication.

A scientifically based understanding of dual language learning in the preschool years is critical for a number of reasons. Many people, including parents, general educators, education specialists, professionals who work with young children (e.g., speech and language pathologists and doctors), and educational policymakers have misconceptions and apprehensions about young children acquiring more than one language (e.g.,

Beardsmore, 2003; Genesee, 2009). In the absence of a solid understanding of relevant scientific evidence, these individuals risk making the wrong or misguided decisions about young dual language learners. For example, the assumption that dual language learning during the preschool years is cognitively and linguistically burdensome for children could lead policymakers to disfavor dual language preschool programs when, in fact, the evidence does not support this assumption. Assessment and support services that are part and parcel of early childhood and primary school education also demand in-depth knowledge of dual language learning in its multiple forms. A lack of understanding of what can be expected of young dual language learners may lead evaluation or educational specialists to interpret a bilingual child's language performance as symptomatic of delay or even impairment when, in fact, it is typical of dual language learning.

The first part of this chapter reviews research on simultaneous dual language learning and the second part, successive dual language learning. This is followed by a consideration of major research questions that need attention.

SIMULTANEOUS DUAL LANGUAGE LEARNING: BASIC RESEARCH ISSUES

Underlying much of the research on simultaneous dual language learning, or what is often referred to in the scientific literature as bilingual first language acquisition (BFLA), is the question of whether a child's ability to learn language is challenged by the acquisition of two languages at the same time. There are three fundamental ways in which BFLA could differ from monolingual acquisition–rate and pattern of development and ultimate level of proficiency. Evidence that dual language learners take longer to attain critical milestones in language acquisition, such as babbling or first words, might be taken as evidence that dual language learning is burdensome and compromises development. Bilingual first language learners might also differ from monolingual learners with respect to their patterns of language development. One particularly strong version of this possibility is known as the unitary language system hypothesis (Genesee, 1989). Specifically, it has been hypothesized that infants with dual language exposure go through an initial stage when their languages are not differentiated but constitute a single underlying language system. Arguably, this occurs because learners treat input from the two languages as if it were part of a single language (see Genesee, 1989, for a historical review; Leopold, 1949; Volterra & Taeschner, 1978). This view can have particularly pernicious effects in families that speak minority languages because it may result in parents being counseled to discontinue use of the heritage language in favor of the societally dominant language on the assumption that the child will learn faster and better if they learn only one language.

Research on these issues has often compared the development of bilingual children to that of monolingual children acquiring the same languages. On the one hand, this comparison may be an inappropriate frame of reference because it uses monolingual acquisition as the gold standard and, thereby, risks attributing differences that bilingual children exhibit to deficits in children's capacity to acquire two languages at the same time. It has been argued that the linguistic competencies of bilingual children, like those of bilingual adults, should be examined and evaluated on their own merit (Cook, 2002; Grosjean, 1997). On the other hand, comparisons between bilingual and monolingual children are widespread in clinical and lay settings and can have important real-world implications. Scientific comparisons between bilingual and monolingual children can serve to reveal the extent to which BFLA actually differs from monolingual acquisition and, most importantly, what such differences mean (De Houwer, 1995).

The research findings reviewed in this chapter are primarily based on single case studies (except see Pearson, Fernández, & Oller, 1993, and other work by this team of researchers in Miami), and most often are based on children learning two languages in the home from their parents. Findings based on single case studies are valuable for identifying children's capacity for language acquisition—that is, what is possible or what children can do, other things being equal. However, findings from case studies cannot reveal typical patterns of language learning or variation in language development among dual language learners with all of the attendant variation that learning two languages entails, in other words, when learning conditions are not equal.

The research reviewed is international in scope; it includes studies of infants and children living in different national settings who were learning different combinations of languages from birth, for example, (a) children living in Quebec learning English and French; (b) children living in Germany learning German and French; or (c) children living in the United States or Britain learning Spanish and English. In most cases, the children under investigation were learning a societally dominant language (e.g., English in the United States or British studies) and a heritage or minority language (e.g., Spanish in these studies). In the case of most of the Canadian studies, the children were learning two official national languages—English and French. The children in all these studies were selected, although not always, because they were thought to have some minimum and extensive exposure to each language (e.g., 20%–30% of their waking day), thereby ensuring that they were likely to have adequate input in both languages to acquire them. This begs the question of what effects reduced or inconsistent exposure to either language would have on patterns, rates, and ultimate level of proficiency in dual language learners. Issues of socioeconomic and minority ethnolinguistic status have seldom been considered in these studies and, thus, their findings can be generalized to U.S. populations only with caution.

The following review of research on simultaneous bilingual development is organized around four questions:

1. Are the patterns and rates of language acquisition in simultaneous dual language learners altered in comparison to those of monolingual children and, if so, what do such differences mean?
2. Is bilingual code-mixing a sign of linguistic confusion or competence?
3. Can simultaneous dual language learners manage the additional demands of bilingual communication?
4. Are bilingual children with language impairment at greater risk for impaired language development than monolingual children with language impairment?

PATTERNS AND RATES OF
BILINGUAL FIRST LANGUAGE ACQUISITION

Morpho-Syntax

Most research on the morpho-syntactic (grammar and sentence structure) development of simultaneous dual language learners has examined oral production rather than oral comprehension. Findings from this research indicate that, contrary to the claims of the unitary language system hypothesis, these children acquire language-specific properties of the target languages early in development and these correspond, for the most part, to those exhibited by same-age monolingual children (see De Houwer, 1990, 1995; Deuchar & Quay, 2000; Genesee, 2001; Genesee & Nicoladis, 2007; Meisel, 2001, for more detailed reviews). Findings from research on BFLA also generally indicate that bilingual children exhibit the same rate of morpho-syntactic development as monolingual children, at least in their dominant language (see reviews in De Houwer, 1995; Nicoladis & Genesee, 1996; Paradis & Genesee, 1996). This is evident even in bilingual children who are identified as having a specific language impairment (Gutierrez-Clellen, Wagner, & Simón-Cereijido, 2008; Paradis, Crago, Genesee, & Rice, 2003).

There is also evidence of cross-linguistic transfer of specific morpho-syntactic features from one language into the other (Döpke, 2000; Hulk

& van der Linden, 1996; Müller, 1999; Nicoladis, 2002, 2003; Paradis & Navarro, 2003; Yip & Matthews, 2000). Döpke (2000), for example, found that Australian children learning English and German simultaneously used verb-object word order much more in all verbal clauses in their German than did native monolingual speakers of German. Evidence of cross-linguistic transfer tends to come from children who have incorporated morpho-syntactic structures from their dominant into their weaker language, rather than vice versa (Döpke, 1998; Petersen, 1988; Yip & Matthews, 2000). For example, Yip and Matthews (2000) found evidence of transfer from Cantonese to English in a Cantonese-English learning child during a period when he was dominant in Cantonese. Yip and Matthews (2000) have suggested that normal asynchronous development of specific features or structures in two languages might also explain instances of transfer of structures that are normally acquired earlier in one language (e.g., Chinese) to the language in which the corresponding structure is normally acquired later. Instances of cross-linguistic transfer that have been reported pertain to specific aspects of the child's developing grammar, and they appear to occur only under certain circumstances; in other words, they are not across-the-board effects.

Many, if not virtually all, simultaneous dual language learners acquire more proficiency in one language than in the other. This is often referred to as dominance. Researchers have noted that children's relative dominance in each language can change over time as a result of changes in the child's exposure to each language. There is surprisingly little empirical research on this topic (except see Pearson, Fernández, Lewedag, & Oller, 1997, in the next section). The limited available evidence suggests that reduced exposure of a dual language learner to any one language does not necessarily entail delayed morpho-syntactic development in comparison to monolinguals, but it may reduce dual language learners' use of certain syntactic forms (Paradis & Genesee, 1996; Paradis, Nicoladis, & Crago, 2007). Clearly, as Pearson et al. (1997) point out, exposure below some limit would surely be expected to impair the child's ability to acquire working knowledge of a language.

Vocabulary

In a particularly important set of studies on vocabulary/lexical development, Pearson, Fernández, Oller, and their colleagues studied Spanish-English bilinguals (8–30 months of age) living in Miami. They found that the children produced their first words at about the same age as monolingual children—at 12 to 13 months (see also Genesee, 2003; Patterson & Pearson, 2004; Petitto et al., 2001) and their rates of vocabulary growth generally fell within the range reported for same-age monolinguals, as long as both languages of bilinguals were considered together (Pearson & Fernández, 1994; Pearson et al., 1993). Nicoladis (2001) found that the distribution of lexical categories (e.g., noun, verb, etc.) in the early lexicons of bilingual children is similar to that observed in monolingual children.

Some studies report that the number of different words that preschool bilingual children know in each language is smaller than that of monolinguals learning the same languages (Ben-Zeev, 1977; Doyle, Champagne, & Segalowitz, 1978; Rosenblum & Pinker, 1983). However, Pearson et al. (1993) note that single language measures are inadequate because they fail to consider the child's total vocabulary. They found that the total conceptual vocabulary (i.e., the number of words they knew in either language for different concepts) of the bilingual children was, on average, equal to monolingual norms published for the MacArthur Communicative Development Inventory. They also found that the English vocabulary of English-dominant bilinguals was equal to that of the English norms and, likewise, the Spanish vocabulary of Spanish-dominant bilinguals was equal to that of the Spanish norms. Thus, it is clearly important to examine bilingual children's vocabulary in both languages or, at least, in their dominant language.

Finally, Pearson and her colleagues found a correlation of .68 between amount of exposure to Spanish and vocabulary size in Spanish (Pearson & Fernández, 1994; Pearson et al., 1997). Therefore, children exposed more to Spanish in their everyday environments were more likely to have higher vocabulary scores in Spanish. The relationship between exposure and vocabulary size was stronger in families that provided relatively consistent and balanced exposure to both languages compared to families with inconsistent and less balanced exposure. The link between exposure and size of vocabulary was more important for the minority language (Spanish) than for English. Similar findings have been reported for general measures of language proficiency among school-aged Spanish-English bilinguals in dual language programs (see Lindholm-Leary & Borsato, 2006, for a review).

BILINGUAL CODE-MIXING

Bilingual code-mixing (BCM) is the use of elements (phonological, lexical, morpho-syntactic) from two languages in the same utterance or stretch of conversation. It can occur within an utterance (intrautterance mixing—e.g., "see *cheval*" [horse]) or between utterances (interutterance mixing). When two languages are used in the same utterance, grammatical incompatibilities between the languages can arise (e.g., different word orders); these in turn can result in patterns of language use that are awkward or illicit. Research on intrautterance code-mixing in adult bilinguals has shown that it is grammatically constrained and serves a variety of metacommunicative purposes—for example, to mark ethnic identities or affiliations, to negotiate social roles and status, and to establish interpersonal intimacy or distance (Myers-Scotton, 1993; Poplack, 1980, 1987; Zentella, 1999).

Young bilingual children also code mix and do so from the earliest stages of language development. Rates of code-mixing in children have been found to vary depending on the form of mixing (intra- vs. interutterance), the nature of the mixed element (function vs. content words), the language of the conversation (the child's less proficient vs. the child's more proficient language), and the context (with interlocutors who are bilingual vs. those who are monolingual, for example) (see Genesee & Nicoladis, 2007, for a detailed review). Individual differences in both rates and style of mixing are widely reported, even within the same family (Vihman, 1998). Child BCM has often been interpreted as a sign of incompetence and even confusion (e.g., Volterra & Taeschner, 1978). Indeed, parents, educators, and other professionals often look unfavorably on BCM in children and often attempt to follow the one-parent-one-language role on the assumption that this will reduce the risk of linguistic confusion in children. Research on code-mixing in BFLA has examined both its grammatical and functional or communicative properties (see Genesee, 2002 and Genesee & Nicoladis, 2007 for reviews).

Grammatical Properties of Child Bilingual Code-Mixing

Researchers have examined grammatical constraints on intrautterance code-mixing by preschool dual language learners learning a variety of language pairs, for example, French and German (Meisel, 1994), French and English (Paradis, Nicoladis, & Genesee, 2000; Sauve & Genesee, 2000), English and Norwegian (Lanza, 1997a), English and Estonian (Vihman, 1998), and Inuktitut and English (Allen, Genesee, Fish, & Crago, 2002). There is consistent evidence that child BCM is grammatically constrained (see Allen, Genesee, Fish, & Crago, 2008). Most researchers also report that the constraints that operate on child BCM are essentially the same as those that have been reported in adults (except see Meisel, 1994). There does not appear to be a stage in BFLA when grammatical constraints do not operate, albeit the nature of the constraints may change as bilingual children's grammars change. These findings reinforce results reviewed earlier indicating that, for the most part, bilingual children acquire language-specific morpho-syntactic properties of each language early in development and, moreover, they can access these constraints simultaneously during production.

Functional Properties of Child Bilingual Code-Mixing

Research reviewed in the preceding sections indicates that BCM is not due to fusion of the child's underlying representations of their two languages. The question arises: Why then do they code mix? There are at least three functional explanations of why young bilingual children code-mix: gap filling, context-sensitivity, and pragmatic or symbolic reasons. In support of the gap-filling hypothesis, it has been found that young bilingual children mix more when they use their less proficient than when they use their more proficient language (Genesee, Nicoladis, & Paradis, 1995; Lanvers, 2001). While mixing to fill lexical gaps because of incomplete mastery of their languages is one explanation of child code-mixing, it can also be true for otherwise fully proficient, older bilinguals because lexical knowledge in both languages of the bilingual is seldom equivalent. Evidence for grammatical gap-filling comes from Petersen (1988) and Lanza (1997b) who report that bilingual children often mix function words and inflectional morphemes from their more proficient language with content words from their less proficient language, but seldom the reverse, and from Gawlitzek-Maiwald and Tracy (1996) who argue that young bilingual children use syntactic patterns from their stronger language to bootstrap the grammar of their less proficient language. Both lexical and morpho-syntactic mixing of these types attest to the young bilingual child's ability to access and use the lexical and morpho-syntactic resources of both languages creatively online during language production.

There is considerable evidence that bilingual children's code-mixing is sensitive to contextual variables, including those related to the language of the person to whom the child is directing her/his speech (Deuchar & Quay, 2000; Genesee, Boivin, & Nicoladis, 1996; Genesee et al., 1995; Lanza, 1997b; Meisel, 1990; Vihman, 1998, among others), the topic (Lanvers, 2001), and the purpose of the interaction (Vihman, 1998). Bilingual children usually use their languages appropriately with different individuals so that, for example, children who are raised in bilingual homes where parents tend to use only their native/dominant language with the child generally use more of each parent's language with that parent than with the other parent (e.g., De Houwer, 1990; Deuchar & Quay, 2000; Genesee et al., 1995; Lanza, 1997b; Vihman, 1998). There is also evidence that their use of code-mixing is sensitive to the nature of the situation; both Sprott and Kemper (1987) and Vihman (1998) found that bilingual children as young as 3 years of age were less likely to code mix with authority figures (unfamiliar experimenter or parent) than with peers.

Child BCM has also been associated with a variety of pragmatic functions, even in quite young bilingual children. Lanvers (2001) reports that her two German-English children (1 year, 6 months, to 2 years, 11 months) used language to emphasize (see also Goodz, 1989), to appeal, to quote a parent, and for topic shift (see also Vihman, 1998).Vihman (1998) also presents evidence that the unmarked language choice for her bilingual children when playing together was a mixture of English and Estonian, which she argued was a reflection of their dual identity with the Estonian and English speakers in their lives (see also Pan, 1995, for evidence concerning the use of BCM to mark identity in 4- to 6-year-old Mandarin-English bilingual children).

COMMUNICATIVE COMPETENCE
IN SIMULTANEOUS DUAL LANGUAGE LEARNERS

Simultaneous dual language learners face the same communication challenges as monolingual children, but, at the same time, the ability to communicate appropriately and effectively in two languages entails an understanding of interpersonal communication that exceeds that required for monolingual communication, including, among other things, an understanding of when it is appropriate to use code-mixing and that breakdowns in communication may be due to language choice. In question is how bilingual children accommodate the specific demands of bilingual communication and when, in the development, they can do so.

Fundamental to bilingual communicative competence is the ability to make appropriate language choices with interlocutors who speak different languages and/or engage differentially in code-mixing. Numerous researchers have found that even bilingual children in the one-word and early two-word stages of development are able to use their languages differentially and appropriately with others–for example, with parents who habitually speak different languages with them (Nicoladis & Genesee, 1996) and with strangers with whom they have had no prior experience (Genesee et al., 1996). It has also been found that they can adjust their rates of code-mixing to match those of unfamiliar interlocutors who change rates of mixing from one occasion to another (Comeau, Genesee, & Lapaquette, 2003; see Petitto et al., 2001, for similar evidence from children learning oral and sign languages simultaneously). Additional evidence of young bilingual children's capacity to manage the use of their two languages effectively comes from Comeau, Genesee, and Mendelson (2007), who found that 2-year, 6-month-old French-English bilingual children were able to modify their choice of language (switched from French to English, or vice versa) when their interlocutor expressed lack of comprehension and requested clarification when the child used the language the interlocutor did not prefer. In short, the additional challenges of bilingual communication are well within the competence of typically developing children.

Lanza (1997b, 2001) has argued that parental discourse strategies with respect to language use in the home serve to socialize their children to adopt specific bilingual practices. Bilingual parents who engage in code-mixing themselves model mixing and, thereby, condone and possibly even encourage their children to code mix; in contrast, parents who disapprove of code-mixing and avoid it discourage their children from mixing. In a related vein, Döpke (1992) found that bilingual families in Australia that actively used explicit strategies to favor the use of the minority language (German) over the majority language (English) were more successful at getting their children to use the minority language in the face of social pressures that favored English.

CHILDREN WITH LANGUAGE LEARNING IMPAIRMENT

Children with language learning difficulties are often thought to be poor candidates for dual language learning on the assumption that the challenges they face learning language will be exacerbated by learning two languages during the formative years. Children with specific language impairment (SLI), estimated to be between 5% and 10% of children (Leonard, 1998), exhibit language that is delayed and below that of age-matched peers, but they are typical in other aspects of their development; in other words, they have no known perceptuo-motor, neurocognitive, or socioemotional problems that could account for their language learning difficulty. Children with SLI can exhibit difficulties with lexical, morpho-syntactic, and pragmatic aspects of language (see Leonard, 1998, for a review of research on monolingual children, and Goldstein, 2004, for research on Spanish-English children); but, difficulty learning specific morpho-syntactic features of language is an especially robust indicator of SLI and one that has received the lion's share of research attention.

The extant, albeit limited, evidence concerning dual language learners with language impairment indicates that such learners exhibit the same language-specific morpho-syntactic difficulties in each of their two languages as monolinguals and, as well, that their language impairment is of the same magnitude as that exhibited by monolingual learners of the same languages (Gutierrez-Clellen et al., 2008; Paradis et al., 2003). At the same time, these children can acquire bilingual competence within the limits of their learning ability. Gutierrez-Clellen and her colleagues examined Spanish-English bilingual children (4 years, 5 months, to 6 years, 5 months of age) in the United States, and Paradis and her colleagues, French-English bilingual children (mean age of 6 years, 11 months) in Canada. While the young subjects of Paradis et al. were clearly simultaneous bilinguals, it appears that Gutierrez-Clellen's Spanish-English sample included some simultaneous and some very young successive bilinguals. Nevertheless, both studies found that the bilingual children with SLI did not differ from monolingual English-speaking children with SLI of the same age (see Goldstein, 2004, for more research on Spanish-speaking children with SLI).

An additional issue concerning bilingual children with language impairment is intervention and, in particular, whether intervention should be provided in only one language (and, if so, which one) or both. Intervention studies with bilingual children with language impairment (both simultaneous and sequential bilinguals) have demonstrated that outcomes following bilingual treatment are just as positive or even more positive than monolingual treatment (Gutierrez-Clellen, 1999; Perozzi & Sanchez, 1992; Thordardottir, Weismer, & Smith, 1997). Reviewing a variety of relevant research on bilingual acquisition, Kohnert and Derr (2004) argue that "the overall goal in language intervention is to affect positive change in both languages used by a bilingual child with language impairment in an effort to maximize his or her potential to communicate effectively" with important people, such as family members, schoolmates, and teachers. Kohnert and Derr recommend, therefore, that interventions for bilingual children with language impairment use both languages. They go on to point out that this does not mean that both languages should be used at all times in all intervention sessions but, rather, that a bilingual or cross-linguistic approach be used depending on whether the focus of intervention is on underlying cognitive processes or linguistic features that are common to both languages or on features and processes that are unique to each language (see Kohnert & Derr, 2004, pp. 324–333).

SECOND LANGUAGE ACQUISITION

This section reviews research on children under 5 years of age who begin to learn a second language (L2) after first language learning has begun and is established. This review is limited to L2 learners who are less than 5 years of age for purely practical reasons—namely, that this is the customary age for identifying preschool from school-age children. It is also based on the assumption that evidence concerning L2 learners' language development during the preschool years (and not subsequently) is critical for developing policy and professional practice for this group.

There are important policy-related and practical reasons for examining preschool L2 learners independently of simultaneous bilinguals, on the one hand, and "school-age" L2 learners, on the other hand. There is growing scientific evidence that critical foundations for academic language and literacy development are established during the preschool years (see Genesee, Lindholm-Leary, Saunders, & Christian, 2006). It is commonly believed among parents, educators, and researchers that second language acquisition during the preschool years is unproblematic, occurs quickly and easily, and can be as successful as first language learning with respect to ultimate competence in the second language. In fact, however, our understanding of preschool L2 learning is far from precise. A major reason for this state of affairs is that there is relatively little research on child second language learners of any age. Moreover, data from studies on preschool second language learners have been aggregated with data on simultaneous bilinguals (see, for example, work by Guttierrez-Clellen et al., 2008) or with data from children who are 4 or 5 years of age or older upon first exposure to the second language and/or at the time of data collection. In a notable exception, Tabors (2008) used ethnographic techniques to study the acquisition of English as a second language by 15 preschoolers who ranged in age from 2 years, 9 months, to 5 years, 0 months of age. The children spoke a variety of first languages and came from a variety of countries and home backgrounds. Tabors did not include objective measures of specific aspects of language development; rather, her focus was on the children's strategies for acquiring and using English as a second language and not on their actual developing linguistic competence or their acquisition milestones. She noted that the children passed through general stages of language development (except for the first stage) that are very similar to those seen in monolingual children, even though they come to the task of learning English later than monolinguals. The stages are (a) home language use, (b) nonverbal period, (c) telegraphic and formulaic use, and (d) productive language use. Tabor's report provides rich descriptions of the communication strategies of young English language learners (ELLs) and can be useful in similar settings to monitor other ELL learners' progress.

A comprehensive review by Unsworth (2005) of studies on child-L2 acquisition that were published since approximately 1995 illustrates how data on preschool L2 learners has often been aggregated with school-age learner data. Unsworth defined child-L2 learners as those who begin L2 acquisition after 4 years of age and before 8 years of age on the assumption that most grammatical principles of language are established in first language learners by the age of 4. Even though some of the children included in the studies she reviewed were first exposed to a second language before 5 years of age, their language development was not actually examined until after 5 years of age. While Unsworth's cut-off age of 4 has some conceptual merit, it is arbitrary, as she recognizes (Unsworth, personal communication, May 2009), and it begs the question of whether child-L2 acquisition under 5 years of age is like L1-acquisition and, if not, in what ways it is different. Unsworth concluded her review:

The evidence regarding the question of whether L2 children pass through the same developmental stages as L1 children is rather inconclusive. Although it is clear that as a result of L1 transfer, these two groups differ from each other and as such their developmental sequences will differ, the question of whether certain developmental stages found in child L1 development also characterize child L2 development remains largely unanswered. As yet, the child L2 data are rather limited in terms both of the linguistic phenomena which have been systematically investigated and the language combinations of the L2 children who have been studied. (Unsworth, 2005, p. 54).

Understanding the language development of preschool second language learners is complicated by the fact that they can begin learning a second language at different ages, and this might influence their patterns and rates of development. The question of when simultaneous bilingual acquisition ends and child-L2 acquisition begins remains to be answered. Some researchers have argued that the cut-off occurs as early as 1 year of age or younger (De Houwer, 1995); others have suggested that it occurs at 3 (McLaughlin, 1978) or 4 years of age (Unsworth, 2005). Whether there is a critical age during the preschool or early childhood period that demarcates the ability to acquire a second language like a first language in all respects—and if there is, what is it—are open questions at this time.

SECOND LANGUAGE LEARNERS
WITH LANGUAGE LEARNING IMPAIRMENT

There are significant challenges in identifying child L2 learners with language learning impairment above and beyond the challenges associated with identifying monolingual children with language learning impairment because there are no clinical markers that are unique to an endogenous impairment in learning language versus common difficulties that even typical L2 learners face. Take tense-marking, for example—while monolingual English-speaking children with specific language impairment exhibit delays in many aspects of language development, including vocabulary, they exhibit particularly protracted delays in acquiring tense-marking morphology. Verb tense is also produced variably and, initially, with low accuracy by typically developing L2 learners of English. In other words, typically developing ELLs exhibit the same difficulty acquiring tense marking as monolingual children with SLI. As a result, typically developing ELLs could be diagnosed inappropriately as having SLI if their status as L2 learners were not considered appropriately. Paradis (2008) has reported preliminary results from two preschool children with SLI who were learning English as a second language in Edmonton,

Canada, indicating that they had difficulties acquiring tense marking in English that exceeded the difficulties exhibited by typically developing L2 learners. Given the small sample size and variation (not reported here) between the two learners in this study, these results must be viewed with some caution, but they are important in suggesting that it may be possible to distinguish difficulties learning English as a second language that are a result of an underlying language learning impairment from difficulties learning English as a second language that are typical of L2 learners using standard test instruments.

SUMMARY AND FUTURE DIRECTIONS FOR RESEARCH

Research on simultaneous bilingual acquisition in children from diverse language communities around the world is broad in scope and in the linguistic and family backgrounds of the children who have been studied. However, there has been little systematic investigation of the role of family background factors in their development. Taken together, findings from this body of research indicate that, other things being equal, language acquisition in simultaneous bilingual children is as natural as learning one language—it is systematic and exhibits the same critical milestones, at approximately the same ages, as that documented in monolingual children acquiring the same languages. Simultaneous bilingual acquisition is not a burden on infants' and toddlers' capacity to acquire language and does not compromise their competence in comparison to monolingual children, provided they receive adequate exposure to each language. In short, the human neurocognitive capacity for learning language is as adept learning two languages simultaneously as one. At the same time, simultaneous bilingual children are different from monolingual children, often in ways that appear to be due to input and exposure. For example, they may have smaller vocabularies in each language than monolinguals, although not always (Nicoladis & Paradis, 2008). When such differences occur, they are probably due to the distributed nature of their exposure to vocabulary in each language and their reduced input in each language in comparison to monolinguals. In other words, vocabulary differences exhibited by bilingual children do not reflect limitations in children's ability to acquire two languages. Simultaneous bilinguals also differ from monolinguals in that they code mix their two languages. Extensive research on this topic indicates that their code-mixing is a reflection of dual language competence and serves useful communicative functions.

Our understanding of preschool child L2 learning is incomplete at present because data on such learners has often been aggregated with that of either simultaneous dual language learners or school-age L2 learners (see Paradis, 2008, for a review of second language acquisition in childhood, including school-age children). As a result, there is a substantial lack of longitudinal developmental data on preschool L2 learners and, thus, a lack of understanding of dual language learning in children who begin learning a second language after first language acquisition has begun and before the age of school entry (taken to be age 5). Research on school-age minority language students in dual language programs in the United States (Lindholm-Leary & Borsato, 2006) indicates that such students can acquire competence in English that exceeds that of similar language-minority students in all-English programs and, moreover, is equal to, and in some cases superior to, that of native English-speaking children. In addition, both the National Literacy Panel and the Center for Research on Education, Diversity and Excellence reports on literacy development in ELLs concluded that there is considerable positive transfer of home language skills to the development of literacy in English as a second language, resulting in facilitation in the acquisition of literacy skills in English as a second language (August & Shanahan, 2006; Genesee et al., 2006). Taken together, these findings indicate that contrary to the time-on-task notion, support for the development of ELLs' home languages in school actually facilitates their acquisition of English as a second language. These findings, in turn, support conclusions from research on simultaneous bilingual acquisition that dual language learning does not compromise minority language students' acquisition of language; to the contrary, it enhances it (see Barnett, Yarosz, Thomas, Jung, & Blanco, 2007, for similar evidence from a dual language preschool program).

Extant findings on early dual language learners are based on studies of children who were selected because researchers deemed their learning environments to be sufficient to allow them to become bilingual. In other words, these learners were in additive bilingual learning environments. This is not always the case. Research in the United States has shown that dual language acquisition by minority language children in all-English school programs often leads to a shift in dominance from the home language to English and to a loss of the home language as English becomes stronger (Anderson, 2004; Jia & Aaronson, 2003; Kohnert, 2004; Kohnert & Bates, 2002; Pease-Alvarez, Hakuta, & Bayley, 1996). Both lexical and morpho-syntactic skills in the home language can undergo shift and loss as they become more proficient in English. A number of factors have been proposed to explain such shifts, including early exposure to English (Wong Fillmore, 1991; except see Winsler, Diaz, Espinosa, & Rodríguez, 1999), level of community support for the minority language (Winsler et al., 1999), attitudes toward English and the home language (Jia & Aaronson, 2003), and depth of immigration to the United States along with personal commitment to the home language (e.g., Pease-Alvarez et al., 1996). While researchers have shed some light on the nature and extent of language shift and loss in minority dual language learners, more research is needed in order to further elucidate the exact nature of these shifts and of factors in the home, community, and school that precipitate them.

In addition, research on the following topics with respect to preschool dual language learning in children from minority language backgrounds in the United States would extend our understanding of these children and, thereby, benefit the early childhood education community:

1. the prevalence of simultaneous and successive dual language learning in minority language children in the United States;
2. the nature of the preschool language learning environments in which minority language children acquire English along with the home language (e.g., sources of input for each language, nature, and extent of exposure to each language, continuity in exposure, community variables, etc.);
3. social and linguistic factors in the home, community, and school that serve to maintain minority language children's competence in the home language as their competence in English increases;
4. family-related factors that shape minority language children's language learning environments during the preschool years (e.g., parents' language backgrounds, education, job status, and attitudes to the home language and English) and the specific ways in which these factors shape the child's learning environment;
5. the morpho-syntactic development of simultaneous and successive preschool dual language learners from major minority language groups in the United States (Kindler, 2002);
6. the acquisition of discourse/conversational skills of preschool dual language learners from major minority language groups and, in particular, the learner's ability to use language to perform cognitively demanding tasks that are age appropriate, as well as their ability to use language for routine social interactions;
7. the acquisition of skills that are thought to be precursors to later literacy and academic language development (see August & Shanahan, 2006; Genesee et al., 2006)—for example, advanced vocabulary skills, phonological awareness, letter-sound knowledge, print-related knowledge, use of anaphor and connectives in discourse, etc;
8. normative studies on rates and patterns of development of preschool dual language learners for clinical purposes;

9. the influence of amount of exposure to the home language and English on maintenance of the home language; and

10. the validity of standard test instruments in English for identifying child L2 learners with language impairment.

REFERENCES

Allen, S. E. M., Genesee, F. H., Fish, S. A., & Crago, M. B. (2002). Patterns of code mixing in English—Inuktitut bilinguals. In M. Andronis, C. Ball, H. Elston, & S. Neuvel (Eds.), *Proceedings of the 37th annual meeting of the Chicago Linguistic Society* (Vol. 2, pp. 171–188). Chicago, IL: Chicago Linguistic Society.

Allen, S. E. M., Genesee, F. H., Fish, S. A., & Crago, M. B. (2008). Typological constraints on code mixing in Inuktitut-English bilingual adults. In N. Tersis & M. A. Mahieu (Eds.), *Variations on polysynthesis: The Eskaleut languages* (pp. 273–306). Amsterdam: Benjamins.

Anderson, R. (2004). First language loss in Spanish-speaking children: Patterns of loss and implications for clinical practice. In B. Goldstein (Ed.), *Bilingual language development and disorders in Spanish-English speakers* (pp. 187–212). Baltimore: Brookes.

August, D., & Shanahan, T. (Eds.). (2006). *Developing literacy in second-language learners.* Mahwah, NJ: Erlbaum.

Barnett, W. S., Yarosz, D. J., Thomas, J., Jung, K., & Blanco, D. (2007). Two-way and monolingual English immersion in preschool education: An experimental comparison. *Early Childhood Research Quarterly, 22*(3), 277–293.

Beardsmore, H. B. (2003). Who is afraid of bilingualism? In J. M. Dewaele, A. Housen, & L. Wei (Eds.), *Bilingualism: Beyond basic principles* (pp. 10–27). Clevedon, UK: Multilingual Matters.

Ben-Zeev, S. (1977). The influence of bilingualism on cognitive strategy and cognitive development. *Child Development, 48*(3), 1009–1018.

Comeau, L., Genesee, F., & Lapaquette, L. (2003). The modeling hypothesis and child bilingual code-mixing. *International Journal of Bilingualism, 7*(2), 113–126.

Comeau, L., Genesee, F., & Mendelson, M. (2007). Bilingual children's repairs of breakdowns in communication. *Journal of Child Language. 34*(1), 159–174.

Cook, V. (2002). Background to the L2 user. In V. Cook (Ed.), *Portraits of the L2 user* (pp. 1–28). Clevedon, UK: Multilingual Matters.

De Houwer, A. (1990). *The acquisition of two languages from birth: A case study.* Cambridge, UK: Cambridge University Press.

De Houwer, A. (1995). Bilingual language acquisition. In P. Fletcher & B. MacWhinney (Eds.), *The handbook of child language* (pp. 219–250). Oxford, UK: Blackwell.

Deuchar, M., & Quay, S. (2000). *Bilingual acquisition: Theoretical implications of a case study.* Oxford, UK: Oxford University Press.

Döpke, S. (1992). *One parent one language: An interactional approach.* Amsterdam: John Benjamins.

Döpke, S. (1998). Competing language structures: The acquisition of verb place-ment by bilingual German-English children. *Journal of Child Language, 25*(2), 555–584.

Döpke, S. (2000). Generation of and retraction from cross-linguistically motivated structures in bilingual first language acquisition. *Bilingualism: Language and Cognition, 3*(3), 209–226.

Doyle, A., Champagne, M., & Segalowitz, N. (1978). Some issues in the assessment of linguistic consequences of early bilingualism. In M. Paradis (Ed.), *Aspects of bilingualism* (pp. 13–21). Columbia, SC: Hornbeam Press.

Gawlitzek-Maiwald, I., & Tracy, R. (1996). Bilingual bootstrapping. *Linguistics, 34*(5), 901–926.

Genesee, F. (1989). Early bilingual development: One language or two? *Journal of Child Language, 16*(1), 161–179.

Genesee, F. (2001). Bilingual first language acquisition: Exploring the limits of the language faculty. In M. McGroarty (Ed.), *21st annual review of applied linguistics* (pp. 153–168). Cambridge, UK: Cambridge University Press.

Genesee, F. (2002). Portrait of the bilingual child. In V. Cook (Ed.), *Portraits of the second language user* (pp. 170–196). Clevedon, UK: Multilingual Matters.

Genesee, F. (2003). Rethinking bilingual acquisition. In J. M. deWaele (Ed.), *Bilingualism: Challenges and directions for future research* (pp. 158–182). Clevedon, UK: Multilingual Matters.

Genesee, F. (2009). Early childhood bilingualism: Perils and possibilities. *Journal of Applied Research on Learning, 2*. Retrieved March 10, 2007, from http://search. ccl-cca.ca/CCL/Reports/Journal/JARLApr09_Vol2_SpecialIssue1_Art2

Genesee, F., Boivin, I., & Nicoladis, E. (1996). Talking with strangers: A study of bilingual children's communicative competence. *Applied Psycholinguistics, 17*(4), 427–442.

Genesee, F., Lindholm-Leary, K., Saunders, W., & Christian, D. (2006). *Educating English language learners.* Cambridge, UK: Cambridge University Press.

Genesee, F., & Nicoladis, E. (2007). Bilingual acquisition. In E. Hoff & M. Shatz (Eds.), *Handbook of Language Development* (pp. 324–342). Oxford, UK: Blackwell.

Genesee, F., Nicoladis, E., & Paradis, J. (1995). Language differentiation in early bilingual development. *Journal of Child Language, 22*(3), 611–631.

Goldstein, B. A. (2004). *Bilingual language development and disorders in Spanish-English speakers.* Baltimore, MD: Brookes.

Goodz, N. S. (1989). Parental language mixing in bilingual families. *Journal of Infant Mental Health, 10*(1), 25–44.

Grosjean, F. (1997). The bilingual individual. *Interpreting, 2*(1/2), 163–187.

Gutierrez-Clellen, V. F. (1999). Language choice in intervention with bilingual chil-dren. *American Journal of Speech-Language Pathology, 8*(4), 291–302.

Gutierrez-Clellen, V. F., Wagner, C., & Simón-Cereijido, G. (2008). Bilingual chil-dren with language impairment. *Applied Psycholinguistics, 29*(1), 3–19.

Hulk, A. C. J., & van der Linden, E. (1996). Language mixing in a French-Dutch bilingual child. In E. Kellerman, B. Weltens, & T. Bongaerts (Eds.), *Eurosla 6: A selection of papers* (pp. 89–103). Amsterdam: John Benjamins.

Jia, G., & Aaronson, D. (2003). A longitudinal study of Chinese children and adolescents learning English in the United States. *Applied Psycholinguistics, 24*(1), 131–161.

Kindler, A. L. (2002). *Survey of the states' limited English proficient students and available educational programs and services: 2000–2001 summary report.* Washington, DC: National Clearinghouse for English Language Acquisition and Language Instruction Education Programs.

Kohnert, K. (2004). Processing skills in early sequential bilinguals. In B. Goldstein (Ed.), *Bilingual language development and disorders in Spanish-English speakers* (pp. 53–76). Baltimore: Brookes.

Kohnert, K., & Bates, E. (2002). Balancing bilinguals II: Lexical comprehension and cognitive processing in children learning Spanish and English. *Journal of Speech, Language and Hearing Research, 45*(2), 347–359.

Kohnert, K., & Derr, A. (2004). Language intervention with bilingual children. In B. Goldstein (Ed.), *Bilingual language development and disorders in Spanish-English speakers* (pp. 311–338). Baltimore: Brookes.

Lanvers, U. (2001). Language alternation in infant bilinguals: A developmental approach to codeswitching. *International Journal of Bilingualism, 5*(4), 437–464.

Lanza, E. (1997a). Language contact in bilingual two-year-olds and code-switching: Language encounters of a different kind? *International Journal of Bilingualism, 1*(2), 135–162.

Lanza, E. (1997b). *Language mixing in infant bilingualism: A sociolinguistic perspective.* Oxford, UK: Clarendon Press.

Lanza, E. (2001). Bilingual first language acquisition: A discourse perspective on language contact in parent-child interaction. In J. Cenoz & F. Genesee (Eds.), *Trends in bilingual acquisition* (pp. 201–230). Amsterdam: John Benjamins.

Leonard, L. (1998). *Children with specific language impairment.* Cambridge, MA: MIT Press.

Leopold, W. (1949). *Speech development of a bilingual child* (Vol. 4). Evanston, IL: Northwestern University Press.

Lindholm-Leary, K., & Borsato, G. (2006). Academic achievement. In F. Genesee, K. Lindholm-Leary, W. Saunders, & D. Christian (Eds.), *Educating English language learners* (pp. 176–223). Cambridge, UK: Cambridge University Press.

McLaughlin, B. (1978). *Second language acquisition in childhood.* Hillsdale, NJ: Lawrence Erlbaum.

Meisel, J. M. (1990). *Two first languages: Early grammatical development in bilingual children.* Dordrecht, Netherlands: Foris.

Meisel, J. M. (1994). Code-switching in young bilingual children: The acquisition of grammatical constraints. *Studies in Second Language Acquisition, 16*, 413–441.

Meisel, J. M. (2001). The simultaneous acquisition of two first languages: Early differentiation and subsequent development of grammars. In J. Cenoz & F. Genesee (Eds.), *Trends in bilingual acquisition* (pp. 11–42). Amsterdam: John Benjamins.

Müller, N. (1999). Transfer in bilingual first language acquisition. *Bilingualism: Language and Cognition, 1*(3), 151–171.

Myers-Scotton, C. (1993). *Social motivation for codeswitching: Evidence from Africa.* Oxford, UK: Oxford University Press.

Nicoladis, E. (2001). Finding first words in the input. In J. Cenoz & F. Genesee (Eds.), *Trends in bilingual acquisition* (pp. 131–147). Amsterdam: John Benjamins.

Nicoladis, E. (2002). What's the difference between "toilet paper" and "paper toilet"? French-English bilingual children's crosslinguistic transfer in compound nouns. *Journal of Child Language, 29*(4), 843–863.

Nicoladis, E. (2003). Cross-linguistic transfer in deverbal compounds of preschool bilingual children. *Bilingualism: Language and Cognition, 6*(1), 17–31.

Nicoladis, E., & Genesee, F. (1996). A longitudinal study of pragmatic differentiation in young bilingual children. *Language Learning, 46*(3), 439–464.

Nicoladis, E., & Paradis, J. (2008, October). *Are all bilingual children delayed in vocabulary development? How Canadian French-English bilingual children are different.* Paper presented at the International Conference on Models of Interaction in Bilinguals. ESRC Center for Research on Bilingualism in Theory and Practice. Bangor, Wales, UK.

Pan, B. A. (1995). Code negotiation in bilingual families: "My body starts speaking English." *Journal of Multilingual and Multicultural Development, 16*(4), 315–327.

Paradis, J. (2008). Tense as a clinical marker in English L2 acquisition with language delay/impairment. In E. Gavruseva & B. Haznedar (Eds.), *Current trends in child second language acquisition: A generative perspective* (pp. 337–356). Amsterdam: John Benjamins.

Paradis, J., Crago, M., Genesee, F., & Rice, M. (2003). Bilingual children with specific language impairment: How do they compare with their monolingual peers? *Journal of Speech, Language and Hearing Research, 46*(1), 113–127.

Paradis, J., & Genesee, F. (1996). Syntactic acquisition in bilingual children: Autonomous or interdependent? *Studies in Second Language Acquisition, 18*(1), 1–25.

Paradis, J., & Navarro, S. (2003). Subject realization and cross linguistic interference in the bilingual acquisition of Spanish and English: What is the role of the input? *Journal of Child Language, 30*(2), 371–393.

Paradis, J., Nicoladis, E., & Crago, M. (2007). French-English bilingual children's acquisition of past tense. In H. Caunt-Nulton, S. Kulatilake & I-H Woo (Eds.), *BUCLD 31 Proceedings* (pp. 497–507). Somerville, MA: Cascadilla Press.

Paradis, J., Nicoladis, E., & Genesee, F. (2000). Early emergence of structural constraints on code-mixing: Evidence from French-English bilingual children. *Bilingualism: Language and Cognition, 3*(3), 245–261.

Patterson, J. L., & Pearson, B. Z. (2004). Bilingual lexical development: Influences, contexts, and processes. In B. A. Goldstein (Ed.), *Bilingual language development and disorders in Spanish-English speakers* (pp. 77–104). Baltimore: Paul H. Brookes.

Pearson, B. Z., & Fernández, S. C. (1994). Patterns of interaction in the lexical growth in two languages of bilingual infants and toddlers. *Language Learning, 44*(4), 617–654.

Pearson, B. Z., Fernández, S. C., Lewedag, V., & Oller, D. K. (1997). The relation of input factors to lexical learning by bilingual infants (ages 10 to 30 months). *Applied Psycholinguistics, 18*(1), 41–58.

Pearson, B. Z., Fernández, S. C., & Oller, D. K. (1993). Lexical development in bilingual infants and toddlers: Comparison to monolingual norms. *Language Learning, 43*(1), 93–120.

Pease-Alvarez, L., Hakuta, K., & Bayley, R. (1996). Spanish proficiency and language use in a California Mexicano community. *Southwest Journal of Linguistics, 15*(1/2), 137–151.

Perozzi, J. A., & Sanchez, M. L. C. (1992). The effect of instruction in L1 on receptive acquisition of L2 for bilingual children with language delay. *Language, Speech, and Hearing Services in Schools, 23*(4), 348–352.

Petersen, J. (1988). Word-internal code-switching constraints in a bilingual child's grammar. *Linguistics, 26*(1), 479–493.

Petitto, L. A., Katerelos, M., Levy, B. G., Gauna, K., Tetreault, K., & Ferraro, V. (2001). Bilingual signed and spoken language acquisition from birth: Implications for the mechanism underlying early bilingual language acquisition. *Journal of Child Language, 28*(2), 453–496.

Poplack, S. (1980). "Sometimes I start a sentence in English y termino en Espanol": Toward a typology of code-switching. *Linguistics, 18*, 581–618.

Poplack, S. (1987). Contrasting patterns of code-switching in two communities. In E. Wande, J. Anward, B. Nordberg, L. Steensland, & M. Thelander (Eds.), *Aspects of multilingualism* (pp. 51–77). Uppsala, Sweden: Borgströms, Motala.

Rosenblum, T., & Pinker, S. A. (1983). Word magic revisited: Monolingual and bilingual children's understanding of the word-object relationship. *Child Development, 54*(3), 587–599.

Sauve, D., & Genesee, F. (2000, March). *Grammatical constraints on child bilingual code-mixing.* Paper presented at the annual meeting of the American Association for Applied Linguistics, Vancouver, Canada.

Sprott, R. A., & Kemper, S. (1987). The development of children's code-switching: A study of six bilingual children across two situations. *Working Papers on Language Development, 2*, 116–134.

Tabors, P. (2008). *One child, two languages.* Baltimore: Brookes.

Thordardottir, E. T., Weismer, S. E., & Smith, M. E. (1997). Vocabulary learning in bilingual and monolingual clinical intervention. *Child Language Teaching and Therapy, 13*(3), 215–227.

Unsworth, S. (2005). *Child L2, adult L2, child L1: Differences and similarities.* Utrecht, Netherlands: LOT.

Vihman, M. (1998). A developmental perspective on codeswitching: Conversations between a pair of bilingual siblings. *International Journal of Bilingualism, 2*(1), 45–84.

Volterra, V., & Taeschner, T. (1978). The acquisition and development of language by bilingual children. *Journal of Child Language, 5*(2), 311–326.

Winsler, A., Díaz, R., Espinosa, L. & Rodríguez, J. (1999). When learning a second language does not mean losing the first: Bilingual language development in low-income, Spanish-speaking children attending bilingual preschool. *Child Development, 70*(2), 349–362.

Wong Fillmore, L. (1991). When learning a second language means losing the first. *Early Childhood Research Quarterly, 6*, 323–346.

Yip, V., & Matthews, S. (2000). Syntactic transfer in a Cantonese-English bilingual child. *Bilingualism: Language and Cognition, 3*(3), 193–208.

Zentella, A. C. (1999). *Growing up bilingual.* Malden, MA: Blackwell.

CHAPTER 5

Bilingualism and Cognitive Processing in Young Children

José E. Náñez Sr.

This chapter provides a review of some of the most relevant literature exploring the bilingualism-cognition relationship. The chapter is divided into several sections, each stemming from the broader topic concerning whether bilingualism is associated with brain plasticity (malleability in linguistic neural network function or structure). This topic is the springboard for considering a number of more focused questions regarding bilingualism and cognition: What is known about the interaction between bilingualism and cognition in early childhood? What does brain research reveal about bilingualism and cognition? What are some potential areas of cognitive benefits for bilingual children that should be explored in future research?

PERCEPTUAL AND COGNITIVE NEUROPLASTICITY

Neuroplasticity, defined as a change in neuronal structure or function, in response to repeated environmental experience has been demonstrated on a variety of nonlinguistic tasks. For example, expert London taxicab drivers, compared with frequent but non-taxicab drivers in the same city, showed a significantly larger posterior part of the hippocampus. Further, there was a positive correlation between time spent driving and posterior hippocampus growth between the cab drivers. "These data are in accordance with the idea that the posterior hippocampus stores a spatial representation of the environment and can expand regionally to accommodate elaboration of this representation in people with a dependence on navigational skills. It seems that there is a capacity for local plastic change in the structure of a healthy adult human brain in response to environmental demands" (Maguire et al., 2000, p. 4398). Another study (Johansson, 2006) reported that musicians showed plasticity in the brain area corresponding to the little finger of the left hand in right-handed players of string instruments, while conductors exhibited increased spatial tuning ability relative to nonmusicians or piano players. Like Maguire et al. (2000), Johansson (2006) found a correlation between plasticity and age at training initiation. Draganski et al. (2004) reported that novice jugglers exhibited structural brain plasticity "in brain areas that are associated with the processing and storage of complex visual motions" (p. 311). Together, these studies demonstrate that the brain responds with functional and structural plasticity to new motor and visual environmental experiences. The question remains concerning how these findings relate to plasticity in more cognitively demanding tasks, such as acquiring a second language.

Is There Plasticity Associated with Acquisition of a Second Language (Bilingualism)?

Numerous studies regarding the relationship between bilingualism and cognitive abilities reveal growing research evidence indicating that the experience of acquiring a second language leads to plasticity in language processing neural networks. Specifically, positive cognitive outcomes in brain plasticity also accrue to emergent bilinguals. For example, Kim, Relkin, Lee, and Hirsch (1997) and Mechelli et al. (2004) found functional (changes in what neurons do) and structural (increased gray brain matter) plasticity respectively in proficient bilinguals. (See section titled "How Do Age at the Time of Bilingual Acquisition and Bilingual Proficiency Correlate with Bilingualism-Induced Plasticity" for detailed discussion of the Kim et al. and the Mechelli findings.) A contrasting view is that bilingual acquisition disrupts cognitive processes through information overload or by confusing second language learners. This idea stems from the early *balance effect theory* that storage for a first and second language occurs separately in the brain (Macnamara, 1966), as if each language was a "balloon" with limited inflation capacity as the bilingual's lexicons increase, less storage space is available for either language. This would then lead to lower proficiency in both of the bilingual's languages relative to monolinguals, whose language ability is expected to be higher given that their balloon is wholly dedicated to one language. Second, as one of the bilingual's balloons inflates, the other deflates (i.e., increased experience and proficiency in one language comes at the "cost" of decreased proficiency in the other). The balance effect theory would specify that "promoting skills in one of a bilingual's two languages would inevitably lead to a decrease in proficiency in the other" (Cummins, 1981, p. 27).

Cummins disagreed with this view. Instead he proposed the *think tank model* that makes three assumptions concerning bilingual acquisition:

First, talking usually reflects thinking, and the thinking that underlies talk in L1 is essentially the same as the thinking that underlies talk in L2. In other words, there is only one Think Tank. . . .

Second, although the same basic ability underlies the processing of meanings in L1 and L2, these meanings are not always directly translatable across languages. Thus, some information or operations . . . may be much easier to express in one of the bilingual's two languages. . . . However, the important point is that all the information is stored in the same Think Tank, and the individual potentially has access to (can inspect) all the information so stored.

. . . third[,] an individual's experience with language is extremely important for the operation and development of the Think Tank. Thus, understanding, speaking, reading, and writing in *either language* contributes to the development of the *total* Think Tank. However, if an individual's proficiency in one of the languages is low, then the amount and quality of both input and output flowing between the Think Tank and the environment through that channel will be reduced. (Cummins, 1981, pp. 29–30).

For almost half a century, the bulk of the research evidence has not supported the cognitive disruption or limited processing capacity theories. In fact, the most current research indicates that there is a strong positive correlation between bilingualism and functional (Kim et al., 1997) and structural (Mechelli et al., 2004) plasticity in language processing neural networks.

WHAT IS KNOWN ABOUT THE INTERACTION
BETWEEN BILINGUALISM AND COGNITION IN EARLY CHILDHOOD

This section considers evidence regarding the possible cognitive benefits or costs of learning a second language. Historically, research has identified three possible interactions between bilingualism and cognition: negative, neutral, and positive.

Evidence for a Negative Correlation Between Bilingualism and Cognition

Research through the early 1960s tended to report that bilinguals suffer an intellectual "handicap" relative to monolinguals, attributable to manifested mental confusion, decreased intelligence, impoverished cognitive processing, or limited language processing capacity (e.g., Darcy, 1946; Goodenough, 1926). This negative consideration of bilingualism was based on results of studies conducted during the first half of the 20th century with minority-English language groups in the United States and other countries.

Peal and Lambert (1962) conducted a thorough review of early studies that explored the relationship between bilingualism and "intelligence," which was defined mostly as IQ test scores and, occasionally, as academic achievement scores. The studies reviewed by Peal and Lambert routinely revealed a strong tendency for monolinguals to outscore bilinguals on verbal scales of standardized IQ tests. Based on this finding, some prominent researchers of the time (e.g., Brown, 1922; Goodenough, 1926; Thompson, 1952) held a negative view of nonnative English speakers. The following quote was typical: "Use of a foreign language in the home is one of the chief factors in producing mental retardation as measured by intelligence tests. A more probable explanation is that those nationality-groups whose average intellectual ability is inferior do not readily learn the new language" (Goodenough 1926, pp. 392–393).

Peal and Lambert (1962) reported that as a whole, the studies that showed a negative relationship between bilingualism and IQ tended to suffer from a variety of methodological flaws or failure to control for possible confounding factors. Most prominent among these confounds was a failure to adequately control for socioeconomic status (SES) differences between the families of the subjects (e.g., Pintner, 1932; Saer, 1923). Jones conducted a series of studies correlating bilingualism with IQ (e.g., Jones & Stewart, 1951) and concluded that observed differences between monolinguals and bilinguals on nonverbal IQ tests, common to all his studies, were likely due to SES differences between the two language groups.

Some early studies failed to provide adequate matching for age (e.g., Graham, 1925; Mead, 1927; Rigg, 1928; Wang, 1926). Still others compared subjects who were quite young and who might easily overcome any deficit with time and experience (Darcy, 1946). Indeed, the correlation between IQ and age decreases over time (Brody, 1992; Honzik, MacFarlane, & Allen, 1948; McCall, Appelbaum, & Hogarty, 1973). Lilienfeld, Lynn, Namy, & Woolf (2009) sum up the issue by stating that with the exception of very low IQ (under 50) that predicts adult retardation, IQ scores for infants and very young children do not correlate well with adult outcomes.

Other early studies did not control for bilingual proficiency or failed to provide adequate measures of bilingualism. This represented a problem especially if the bilinguals were native speakers of languages other than English, but were tested with IQ tests that were not standardized on their native-speaking population (Altus, 1953; Darcy, 1946; Jones & Stuart, 1951; Pintner, 1932; Pintner & Keller, 1922; Saer, 1923). For example, Pintner (1932) classified children as bilinguals based on their last names. Pintner and Keller (1922) and Altus (1953) make no mention of using a bilingualism measure. Darcy (1946) adequately controlled for age, sex, and SES differences among her subjects but relied on maternal reports for linguistic group classification and, also, failed to mention the language in which the

Stanford-Binet test was administered. From the description of the methodology, the most parsimonious conclusion is that both groups of children were tested with the English version of the test. It is very likely that at this young stage of development, Darcy's bilingual subjects were not as proficient in English (L2) as in Italian (L1). Thus, if the standardized English version of the test was used, then the reported verbal IQ "handicap" could be due to the "bilingual" subjects' lower English proficiency.

Several subsequent reviews of the early literature (e.g., Cummins, 1976; Diaz 1985; Hakuta & Diaz, 1985) found the same flaws identified by Peal and Lambert as common among the studies. For example, Cummins (1976) pointed out that the problem of inadequate assessment of bilingual proficiency was common in early studies that tended to utilize bilingual subjects with declining L1 proficiency. Cummins identifies a "balance effect" where the bilinguals "pay for" L2 competence gains with L1 competence decrease or loss (p. 2). Cummins concludes that the studies failed to compare proficient bilinguals with monolinguals. Like Peal and Lambert (1962), Hakuta and Diaz's (1985) review of the early literature also found lax socioeconomic status control and lack of adequate definitions of bilingualism. According to Hakuta and Diaz, bilingualism was "mostly assumed by foreignness of their parents" and, further, that "it is difficult to ascertain whether the bilingual subjects of many of the early studies were indeed bilingual or just monolingual of a minority language" (p. 321).

Some more recent studies have also found negative cognitive outcomes for bilinguals. Bilingual infants' word-based knowledge (memory) in either language is said to lag behind that of their monolingual counterparts. Bee and Boyd (2004) cite several studies in which the authors conclude that the deficits persist through the early school years and into adulthood (Gollan & Silverberg, 2001; McElree, Jia, & Litvak, 2000). Patterson (1998) reported that while the overall receptive and expressive vocabularies of monolingual and bilingual infants are similar, the bilinguals' vocabulary is smaller. Another suggested problem is that many preschool and school-age children are not balanced in both of their languages, which may lead them to think and react slower to cognitive stimuli in their language of schooling.

Evidence for a Lack of Correlation Between Bilingualism and Cognition

A number of the early studies reviewed by Peal and Lambert reported finding no evidence of a correlation between bilingualism and intelligence. These studies, however, suffer from some of the same confounds as those described above. Darsie (1926), for example, reported that differences in general mental capacity on IQ tests between Japanese and American children were not significant. However, Peal and Lambert (1962) noted that due to differences in social class and a lack of bilingual proficiency measures, Darsie's findings were not easily interpretable.

Even the best designed studies of the time (e.g., Hill, 1936) contained methodological inadequacies. Among other important demographic factors, Hill documented bilingual proficiency but failed to find a significant difference in IQ between monolingual and bilingual Italian American children. Peal and Lambert (1962) pointed out that by matching mental age, in effect, Hill had controlled for possible language group differences in intelligence test scores. Spoerl (1944) also conducted a well-controlled study and found that group IQs did not differ significantly. However, as a whole, the bilingual subjects performed better academically than the monolinguals.

More recently, Bialystok and colleagues reported several studies that did not find definitive differences on most of their measures. The one exception was on a phoneme separation task on which monolingual children outperformed bilinguals (Bialystok, Majumder, & Martin, 2003).

Evidence for a Positive Correlation Between Bilingualism and Cognition

Overall Intelligence. Based on the results of their literature review, Peal and Lambert (1962) relayed that "a large proportion of investigators have concluded [that] . . . bilingualism has a detrimental effect on intellectual functioning. The bilingual child is described as being hampered in his [or her] performance on intelligence tests in comparison to the monolingual child" (p. 1). Given the propensity for negative or neutral findings reported by other researchers, Peal and Lambert did not expect to find differences in nonverbal IQ between bilingual and monolingual children in their study. In fact, their bilingual subjects not only outperformed the monolinguals on this task, but they exhibited an advantage in verbal IQ as well.

Numerous studies in the 1970s and 1980s supported Peal and Lambert's findings. Such studies (e.g., Ben-Zeev, 1977; Cummins, 1976; Ianco-Worrall, 1972) reported that bilinguals outperformed monolinguals on a variety of cognitive measures, including improved metalinguistic awareness (see comprehensive reviews by Cummins 1976; Diaz 1985; Hakuta, Ferdman, & Diaz, 1987 of other studies conducted during the 1970s and 1980s).

More recent studies have reported similar results. Martin and Bialystok (2003) found that 4-year-old bilinguals exhibited significantly faster reaction time than their monolingual counterparts on both congruent and incongruent trials on the Simon cognitive interference task (Simon & Wolf, 1963). A number of other studies cited by Bialystok et al. (2005) reported bilingual advantages on a variety of other interference tasks, including language (Bialystok, 1988; Cromdal, 1999; Galambos & Goldin-Meadow,

1990), quantity (Bialystok & Codd, 1997; Saxe, 1988), spatial concepts (Bialystok & Majumder, 1998), and problem solving (Kessler & Quinn, 1987; Secada, 1991). Bialystok, Shenfield, and Codd (2000) documented bilingual advantages in writing ability that may translate to improved reading ability later in childhood. Greater attention focus on language tasks, which benefits bilinguals in grasping the connection between sounds and symbols in the early stages of learning to read, has also been reported (e.g., Bialystok, 1997; Bialystok & Majumder, 1998; Oller, Eilers, Neal, & Cobo-Lewis, 1998). Further benefits have been attributed to bilinguals, including linguistic and cognitive creativity (Kessler & Quinn, 1987), improved cognitive abilities (e.g., creative thinking, word order correction, and word reading; Ricciardelli, 1992), and metalinguistic skills (Cromdal, 1999).

Overall Language Development. Berk (2008) identified a group of studies whose findings provide further evidence for the benefits of bilingualism. Infants who learn two or more languages from the beginning show signs from earliest development of separating the sounds, gaining mastery of equivalent words inherent in each language, and reaching language development milestones at appropriate times (Bosch & Sebastian-Galles, 2001; Conboy & Thal, 2006; Holowka, Brosseau-Lapré, & Petitto, 2002). Genesee (2001) found that preschoolers maintain native language proficiency in L1 and acquire good-to-native proficiency in L2 with sufficient exposure to both languages.

It appears that some metalinguistic factors may represent cases in which bilingualism does not offer a clear, overall cognitive advantage; but neither does it constitute a cognitive disadvantage or handicap. For example, Bialystok (2001) reviewed the data comparing bilinguals and monolinguals on three metalinguistic tasks: word awareness (children's understanding of word function as symbols), phonological awareness ("understanding of sound units that make up words" [p. 175]), and syntactic awareness ("need to make a judgment about the grammatical acceptability of a sentences" [p. 173]). The results of a multitude of studies in these and other metalinguistic and metacognitive tasks clearly conclude that bilinguals possess enhanced perceptual and cognitive abilities relative to monolinguals on a range of cognitive interference tasks, such as grammatical judgment tasks. For example, several studies compared bilingual and monolingual subjects on a grammatical judgment task that requires children to judge whether a statement such as "Apples grow on noses" (p. 174) is grammatically correct.

> This sentence is grammatically correct, but the semantic anomaly is highly distracting and children would like to say that the sentence is wrong. In repeated

studies, it has been shown that bilingual children are better than monolinguals at ignoring this irrelevant information and identifying the sentences as correct (Bialystok, 1988; Bialystok & Majumder, 1998; Cromdal, 1999). Again, there is a bilingual advantage on a specific metalinguistic task but not a global advantage over the paradigm. (Bialystok, 2001, p. 174).

Bialystok et al. (2005) suggest a reason for the increase in cognitive control exhibited by bilinguals on tasks such as grammatical judgment and the Simon and Stroop: "The same control processes are used both to solve these misleading problems and to manage two active language systems. Bilingual children therefore have had more opportunity than monolinguals to exercise a crucial cognitive skill and this practice may then accelerate the development of that skill" (p. 40). Bialystok et al. (2005) make the point that the cognitive control processes required for regulation and inhibition of such cues develop in late childhood: This "delay has been attributed to late development of the frontal lobes that mediate these skills (Diamond, 2002). Therefore, bilingualism may have the salutary effect of boosting control processes in nonverbal domains because those same general processes are required to manage two-language systems" (p. 40). Being "bilingual in specific languages may be (an advantage) . . . children who speak a second language with similar phonological structure and alphabetic orthographic system (e.g., Spanish) may have some advantage when learning to read in English, whereas those children who speak a second language (e.g., Chinese) that is phonologically and orthographically different may require additional help in understanding these concepts (in English)" (Bialystok et al., 2003, p. 42).

Executive Functions. Current research in favor of the positive effects theory continues to be steadily compiled. Bilinguals demonstrate advantages over monolinguals on a variety of metalinguistic tasks (e.g., word, syntactic, and phonological awareness) (see Bialystok, 2001; Bialystok et al., 2003). Carlson and Meltzoff (2008) looked at numerous personal and behavioral child factors (e.g., self-control and verbal ability) and parental factors (demographic, SES, and household rules), as well as nine measures of executive function (e.g., visually cued recall and delay of gratification), in kindergartners. Subjects in the bilingual group learned Spanish and English simultaneously from birth; the immersion group received education in multiple subjects in English for half of the day and in either Spanish or Japanese for the remaining half; the control group consisted of monolinguals from English-speaking homes who were enrolled in all-day monolingual English kindergarten instruction. For the purpose of this chapter, Carlson and Meltzoff's executive function results are most relevant. The raw data did not reveal differences on executive function between the language groups. However, when the likely confounding effects of age, SES, and expressive vocabulary were statistically controlled, the simultaneous bilinguals exhibited a significant advantage over the other two language groups on a composite factor consisting of the nine executive function measures. The authors conclude that the observed bilingual executive function advantage "strongly suggests that there are genuine cognitive differences in the ability to resolve conflicting attention demands in bilingual versus monolingual speakers, which do not simply boil down to sociocultural parental attitudes, but may be due specifically to the cognitive 'exercise' of thinking in two languages: holding in mind the relevant language and inhibiting activation of the nonrelevant language" (Carlson & Meltzoff, 2008, p. 295).

In sum, there is significant evidence that bilingual children outperform their monolingual counterparts on tasks requiring high cognitive control, including the ability to focus on relevant information while disregarding distracting events or cues, which represents an obvious advantage for academic success in the busy classroom setting. Further, as with other cognitive effects, there does not appear to be a "cost" in representational processes for bilingual children (i.e., there are no negative cognitive effects associated with bilingualism).

SUMMARY OF THE RESEARCH

Researchers in the United States, Canada, and other countries with large bilingual populations have undertaken extensive examination of the relationship between bilingualism and cognition, especially during the early part of the developmental process, in a concerted effort to identify best practices for informing and implementing high-quality bilingual education. Beginning with Peal and Lambert and continuing for nearly half a century since their article, research has consistently revealed compelling evidence for the existence of a strong positive correlation between bilingualism and a variety of cognitive-intellectual tasks.

WHAT DOES BRAIN RESEARCH REVEAL
ABOUT BILINGUALISM AND COGNITION?

Methodological approaches for studying bilingual cognitive processes have ranged from behavioral research and psychophysics to employing the most recent neuroimaging technology and sophisticated statistical computational techniques.

Behavioral Psychophysics Research

Information gained regarding brain processes through this meth-odology is valuable for understanding *what* the brain does. Behavioral psychophysics studies have also provided some general cues regarding *where* within the brain such information (e.g., perceptual, behavioral, and cognitive responses to environmental stimuli) is processed. It has been known for some time that two left hemisphere areas of the human brain are involved in language processing. Specifically, Broca's area, located for-ward of the inferior frontal gyrus in the left hemisphere, has historically been identified as essential for controlling motor mechanisms that govern speech and sign language production, while Wernicke's area, located in the posterior part of the temporal lobe of the left hemisphere, functions in language comprehension. While knowledge of the broad functions of the brain areas involved in language processing is important, behavioral psychophysics methodology has failed to reveal specific brain structures or their function in language processing either in general or specific to bilingual processing.

Neurological Research

Neurological methodology shows significant promise for gaining in-creased understanding concerning *where* (brain areas), *what* (specific neu-rons or neural networks are involved), and *how* (functional and structural changes) bilingual processing occurs. The most relevant of the neurologi-cal techniques and methods used to conduct bilingualism research include those used for recording brain waves and mapping brain activity.

Recording Brain Waves. The two prevalent methods for recording brain waves are electroencephalography (EEG), which records brain activity via strategically placed scalp electrodes, and magnetoencephalography (MEG), which measures the magnetic component resulting from electrical activity produced by the brain. EEG results in an inability to disambiguate brain noise (i.e., brain activity that is irrelevant to the task) from relevant neural activity that is of importance for the task at hand and, thus, has led some researchers to consider it to be too unreliable to adequately investigate the bilingualism-cognition interaction. An advantage of using MEG (magnetic fields) over EEG (electrical fields) is that the former is not as susceptible to interference by incidental noise from neurons in other brain areas. It "is impossible to determine the generator of an effect since the same effect is compatible with an infinite number of different neural generators ('the inverse problem,' see Kutas, Federmeier, & Sereno, 2000, for recent innova-tions aimed at addressing this problem)" (Green, 2001, p. 101).

Mapping Brain Activity. Of the methods used for mapping brain activity, magnetic resonance imaging (MRI) and functional magnetic resonance imaging (fMRI) are most appropriate for research on bilingualism. Other methods pose risks to the subject through the use of x rays and are less precise. MRI techniques produce images of body tissues using magnetic and radio waves. Powerful radio waves are sent through the body, forcing the hydrogen nuclei (i.e., protons) temporarily out of alignment. As the nuclei resettle into alignment, they emit their own radio waves that are picked up by the scanner and transformed into a computerized picture (NetDoctor.com, 2008). The fMRI technique is among the most recently developed and widely used magnetic neuroimaging techniques. Most research with this technology uses blood-oxygen-level dependent (BOLD-fMRI) activity which indicates what areas of the brain are most active within a 1 to 5 second delay from cell activation.

Computational Methods. Near infrared spectroscopy (NIRS) measures brain responses within the near infrared region (from about 800 nm to 2500 nm). This technology is used to detect changes in blood hemoglobin concentrations resulting from neural activity. In medical research, this method can be used in conjunction with other MRI technology to produce tissue or structure image slices. Voxel-based morphometry (VBM) combines neuroimaging with statistical modeling. The brains of the subjects in a study are scanned, registered into a template, and smoothed into an average. Like near infrared spectroscopy, this methodology can be combined with MRI procedures.

WHAT CONTRIBUTIONS CAN NEUROIMAGING MAKE TO INCREASED UNDERSTANDING OF THE BILINGUALISM-COGNITION RELATIONSHIP?

Neuroimaging methodology and statistical data smoothing techniques have been used to address a number of general questions related to language processing. The studies discussed in the section below are among those that have utilized neuroimaging to investigate the bilingualism-cognition interaction at a deeper level of the brain than is possible through behavioral and psychophysical methodology alone.

While still in its infancy of investigating bilingual brain function and structure, neuroimaging is generating increased understanding of bilingual development and cognitive processes and shows promising potential to benefit bilingual and second language learners in applied learning settings. For example, neuroimaging may reveal differences in brain structure or function between bilingual readers who are poor, average, and good readers. Pictorial (neural image) differences can potentially assist researchers in the quest for identifying neural correlates of reading problems. This knowledge could in turn lead to development of specific perceptual and cognitive exercises designed to improve reading ability (plasticity in reading areas of the brain) in normal (nonclinical) slow readers and clinical (dyslexic) bilingual and monolingual individuals. Such programs could be administered to the child in the applied classroom setting. Changes in reading ability scores coupled with changes in neural structure and/or function would serve as corroborative evidence for the effect of a perceptual, behavioral, or cognitive intervention for improved reading ability.

WHAT ARE SOME POTENTIAL AREAS OF COGNITIVE BENEFIT FOR BILINGUAL CHILDREN THAT SHOULD BE EXPLORED IN FUTURE RESEARCH?

Neuroimaging is being used effectively to gain greater clarification regarding long-standing questions that cannot be fully addressed through behavioral and psychophysical research alone. These questions include the following: Are the bilingual's two languages processed in the same language areas as in monolinguals or is bilingual processing modular? How do age at the time of bilingual acquisition and bilingual proficiency correlate with bilingualism-induced plasticity? Neural mapping is also allowing researchers to address, for the first time, the intriguing question: Are there structural-functional differences in bilinguals' neuronal processing? The impact of this knowledge would be that any observed structural-functional differences in brain areas, such as those involved in reading, could potentially be used to develop interventions that enhance plasticity and, therefore, performance.

Do Bilinguals and Monolinguals Process Language in the Same Areas of the Brain or Is Bilingual Processing Modular?

There is evidence in the literature both that bilingual's two languages are processed in the same language areas as the monolingual's language is processed and that bilingual processing is modular. DeBleser et al. (2003) used positron emission tomography (PET) neuroimaging, in which a tracer dye is injected into the subject and tracked (scanned) while the subject performs a mental task. Movement of the dye indicates the brain location(s) involved in processing the task. In their study, DeBleser et al. (2003) examined cortical activity during covert naming of pictures representing cognates and noncognates between Belgian Flemish/Dutch L1 and French L2 speakers. They concluded that there is much overlap in the cortical area activated during cognate and noncognate naming in L1 and L2. This result is in line with the hypothesis that language processing occurs in the same general brain vicinity (see also, Bialystok et al., 2005; Grady, 2002). However, in a study using magnetoencephalography neuroimaging, Bialystok et al. (2005) observed that bilinguals exhibited faster reaction time (RT) on the Simon task (see Bialystok et al., 2005, p. 43 for a detailed description of the Simon task) "and greater activity in superior and middle temporal, cingulate, and superior and inferior frontal regions, largely in the left hemisphere. The monolinguals demonstrated faster reaction times with activation in middle frontal regions. The interpretation is that the management of two language systems led to systematic changes in frontal executive functions" (p. 40). The positive relationship between faster RT and greater involvement of higher brain areas implies that the bilingual brain "enjoys" a cognitive advantage in faster neural RT and cognitive processing on tasks that require focusing on central (task relevant) and controlling noncentral (task-irrelevant) information. In short, bilinguals are more efficient processors on tasks that require focus and cognitive control.

Chee, Soon, Lee, and Pallier (2004) used fMRI to map brain activity on a phonological word memory reaction time and target-identification task. Their subjects were equal (high English-Chinese linguistic proficiency) and unequal (English proficient, non-Chinese proficient) Chinese-English speakers with some 10 years of bilingual experience. Differences were observed in the brain areas that were activated and deactivated. "Taken together, these observations support the overall construct that unequal bilinguals . . . show differences in neural activations that may belie a less efficient processing strategy that correlates with poorer second-language attainment. The extent to which such processing differences are the cause or consequence of impaired second-language attainment remains to be explored" (p. 15270). How can such differences in working memory be explained? Perani (2005) suggests that if certain brain anatomy "foster(s) the development of extra-ordinary abilities" (p. 212), then, specific anatomical structures would be required for acquisition of advanced cognitive skills such as L2 acquisition and proficiency. Those possessing the structures would enjoy an advantage in acquiring such abilities.

However, there is strong counterevidence indicating that changes in brain anatomical structure in highly proficient bilinguals may result from long-term L1-L2 linguistic experience (Chen, Vaid, & Bortfeld, 2008). Additionally, Chen et al. showed that differences in language-processing ability may also depend on the properties of the specific languages involved. Responding to Chinese- or English-involved activation of the same overall left hemisphere areas, however, there were differences in the most utilized areas. The researchers attribute their findings to the fact that the two languages differ in how they are represented by their writing systems.

Given the observed differences, Chen et al. (2008) posit that the activation of the left middle frontal gyrus among English readers was due to the fact that the words selected for the study were simple and high frequency (commonly used), as opposed to words that appear with lower frequency. Neuroimaging results such as those described in Chen et al. indicate that linguistic neural processing is not uniform within and across languages. In general, orthographic-based languages, such as Chinese, that utilize symbols activate different brain areas than phonemic-based languages such as English. However, interestingly, processing simple, high frequency English words involved activation of the same area (left middle frontal gyrus) as processing Chinese. The important point here is that neuroimaging revealed some of the intricacies involved in linguistic processing within and between languages that linguistic researchers should be aware of. Such fine-grained brain processes would not be detected through behavioral-psychophysical research methodology. Possible implications of such findings for bilingual children in the classroom or other applied learning settings remain to be determined by future research.

The hypothesis of Chen et al. (2008) is in line with earlier research (Seidenberg, 1985) that reports that in Chinese and English writing systems a large number of higher frequency words were visually recognized in the absence of phonological mediation. Coltheart, Rastle, Perry, Langdon, & Zeigler (2001) attribute such findings to a computational dual route model, with one route for recognizing words visually and another for reading aloud. Perfetti et al. (2007) offer the explanation that the left middle frontal gyrus is involved in memory for orthographic information while a subject is involved in phonological processing, that is, orthographic processing has greater significance for reading Chinese. Another possible explanation for the observed modularity in late bilinguals versus overlapping language processing areas in early bilinguals is offered by Kim et al. (1997). "Human infants, initially capable of discriminating all phonetically 'relevant' differences (Kuhl, 2004; Kuhl, Tsao, & Liu, 2003; Miyawaki et al., 1975), may eventually modify the perceptual acoustic space, based on early and repeated exposure to their native languages. It is possible that representations of languages in Broca's area that are developed by exposure early in life are not subsequently modified. This could necessitate the utilization of adjacent cortical areas for the second language learned as an adult" (Kim et al., 1997, p. 173).

How Do Age at the Time of Bilingual Acquisition and Bilingual Proficiency Correlate with Bilingualism-Induced Plasticity?

Kim et al. (1997) examined processing in Broca's and Wernicke's areas in six proficient "early" bilinguals (simultaneous L1-L2 acquisition from infancy) and six "late" bilinguals (mean age at L2 exposure = 11.2 years; mean age of L2 conversational proficiency attainment = 19.2 years). All subjects were tested as young adults (mean age at testing = 29.3 years). In Broca's area, the "typical" late bilingual individual showed that separate, distinct neuronal areas function in L1 and L2 processing of a "silent, internally expressive linguistic task" (Kim et al., 1997, p. 171). The same results were observed for the late bilinguals as a group. The study also showed that in Wernicke's area, basically the same neurons were involved during L1 and L2 processing of the task. Alternatively, the early bilinguals showed no difference in neuronal processing at either neural area. Kim et al. interpret their findings of functional differences as suggesting "that age of language acquisition may be a significant factor in determining the functional organization of this (Broca's) area in the human brain" (Kim et al., 1997, p. 173). The findings provide clear pictorial biophysical evidence for the hypothesis that Broca's and Wernicke's areas play distinct roles in language processes. The importance of the observed differences in language comprehension (Broca's area) is the indication that to achieve maximal benefit of learning two or more languages, it is best to provide learners with bilingual or multiple language exposure from birth or shortly thereafter.

Tan and colleagues (2003) used functional MRI to compare reading ability between adult Chinese-English bilinguals who learned to speak English after 12 years of age and monolingual native-English speakers. Their results present convincing evidence that previous experience learning a second language well early in development serves a strategic function of tuning the cortex. Further evidence for the increased benefits of early (simultaneous) versus later (sequential) L2 acquisition is provided by Mechelli et al. (2004), who found that to gain maximum cognitive benefit (increased gray matter density leading to improved linguistic processing) it is best to experience simultaneous L2 acquisition from early in development (birth to 5 years). Fortunately, gray matter was also generated (albeit to a lesser degree than for early bilinguals) in later acquisition bilinguals who acquired L2 between 10 and 15 years.

Are There Structural-Functional Differences in Bilingual Neural Processing?

Convincing evidence for functional differences in neural structures and increased gray matter within the language production areas of proficient bilinguals' brains has been found (Kim et al., 1997; Mechelli et al., 2004). Neuroimaging studies by Kim et al. and Mechelli et al. provide indisputable neurological evidence that the brain responds with structural and functional plasticity to multiple language exposure and learning.

It should be noted that although evidence for modularity-generalized function (whether two languages involve separate [modularity] or the same [generalized] brain function or structures), *age/proficiency-related* differences, and *structural-functional* neural change is discussed separately above, this is only for the sake of readability. In reality, the three processes are intricately intertwined in a complex symbiotic fashion. For example, Kim et al. showed evidence supporting the *functional change hypothesis*. Mechelli et al. showed a significant increase in gray matter in the inferior parietal cortex (which has been documented to function in L2 learning) of the bilinguals (also supporting the *structural change hypothesis*) relative to the monolinguals (supporting the *bilingual proficiency hypothesis*). The greatest increase occurred in the left hemisphere, although a trend toward gray matter increase was also observed in the right hemisphere of the bilinguals (supporting the *modularity hypothesis*). While increased gray matter was observed in both bilingual groups, the increase in the early bilinguals was significantly greater in the inferior parietal cortex of both hemispheres relative to the late bilinguals (supporting the *age of bilingual acquisition hypothesis*). Neuroimaging technology is assisting researchers to reduce investigation of the bilingualism-cognition interaction to the level of the neuron. Collectively, the resulting research findings indicate that neural plasticity is a general adaptive brain response to environmental experiences.

CONCLUSION

Research amassed over the 8 decades covered in this chapter strongly favors the theory that bilingualism is significantly correlated with cognitive benefits and with differences in the brain for proficient bilinguals. It is time for cognitive neuroscientists and education scholars to change the focus of their independent and collective research efforts to identifying ways to use what has been learned through behavioral, psychophysical, and neuroimaging research to benefit children in applied learning settings.

With continued sophistication and technological advances, neuroimaging shows promise for supplementing behavioral and psychophysical research to further uncover the secrets underlying bilingual processes that may lead to a fuller understanding of the bilingual child's cognitive operations in real time. A next logical step would be to apply this knowledge to help bilingual and monolingual children excel in the ecological systems in which they interact daily, such as the classroom and other applied-learning settings, peer interactions within and outside of the academic setting, or social group interactions in their communities.

Thanks to Tina Drury for her help in compiling the literature used by the author to write this chapter. Thanks also to Professor Darryl Hattenhauer for his helpful editing comments on an earlier version of the chapter.

REFERENCES

Altus, G. T. (1953). WISC patterns of a selective sample of bilingual school children. *Journal of Genetic Psychology, 83,* 241–248.

Bee, H., & Boyd, D. (2004). *The developing child* (10th ed.). Boston: Pearson.

Ben-Zeev, S. (1977). The influence of bilingualism on cognitive strategy and cognitive development. *Child Development, 48*(3), 1009–1018.

Berk, L. (2008), *Infants & children* (6th ed.). Boston: Pearson.

Bialystok, E. (1988). Levels of bilingualism and levels of linguistic awareness. *Developmental Psychology, 24*(4), 560–567.

Bialystok, E. (1997). Effects of bilingualism and biliteracy on children's emerging concepts of print. *Developmental Psychology, 33*(3), 429–440.

Bialystok, E. (2001). Metalinguistic aspects of bilingual processing. *Annual Review of Applied Linguistics, 21,* 169–181.

Bialystok, E., & Codd, J. (1997). Cardinal limits: Evidence from language awareness and bilingualism for developing concepts of number. *Cognitive Development, 12*(1), 85–106.

Bialystok, E., Craik, F. I. M., Grady, C., Chau, W., Ishii, R., Gunji, A., et al. (2005). Effect of bilingualism on cognitive control in the Simon task: Evidence from MEG. *NeuroImage, 24*(1), 40–49.

Bialystok, E., & Majumder, S. (1998). The relationship between bilingualism and the development of cognitive processes in problem solving. *Applied Psycholinguistics, 19*(1), 69–85.

Bialystok, E., Majumder, S., & Martin, M. M., (2003). Developing phonological awareness: Is there a bilingual advantage? *Applied Psycholinguistics, 24*(1), 27–44.

Bialystok, E., Shenfield, T., & Codd, J. (2000). Languages, scripts, and the environment: Factors in developing concepts of print. *Developmental Psychology, 36*(1), 66–76.

Bosch, L., & Sebastion-Galles, N. (2001). Early language differentiation in bilingual infants. In J. Cenoz & F. Genesee (Eds.), *Trends in bilingual acquisition* (pp. 71–94). Amsterdam: Johns Benjamin.

Brody, N. (1992). *Intelligence* (2nd ed.). San Diego: Academic Press.

Brown, G. L. (1922). Intelligence as related to nationality. *Journal of Educational Research, 5*(4), 324.

Carlson, S. M., & Meltzoff, A. N. (2008). Bilingual experience and executive functioning in young children. *Developmental Science, 11*(2), 282–298.

Chee, M. W., Soon, C. S., Lee, H. L., & Pallier, C. (2004). Left insula activation: A marker for language attainment in bilinguals. *Proceedings of the National Academy of Sciences, U.S.A., 101,* 15265–15270.

Chen, H., Vaid, J., & Bortfeld, H. (2008). Optical imaging of phonological processing in two distinct orthographies. *Experimental Brain Research, 184,* 427–433.

Coltheart, M., Rastle, K., Perry, C., Langdon, R., & Zeigler, J. (2001). DRC: A dual route cascaded model of visual word recognition and reading aloud. *Psychological Review, 108,* 204–256.

Conboy, B. T., & Thal, D. J. (2006). Ties between the lexicon and grammar: Cross-sectional and longitudinal studies of bilingual toddlers. *Child Development, 77*(3), 712–735.

Cromdal, J., (1999). Childhood bilingualism and metalinguistic skills: Analysis and control in young Swedish-English bilinguals. *Applied Psycholinguistics, 20,* 1–20.

Cummins, J. (1976). The influence of bilingualism on cognitive growth: A synthesis of research findings and explanatory hypothesis. *Working Papers on Bilingualism, 9,* 1–43.

Cummins, J. (1981). *Bilingualism and minority-language children.* Ontario, Canada: Ontario Institute for Studies in Education Press.

Darcy, N. T. (1946). The effect of bilingualism upon the measurement of the intelligence of children of preschool age. *Journal of Educational Psychology, 37,* 21–44.

Darsie, M. L. (1926). The mental capacity of American-born Japanese children. *Comparative Psychological Monographs, 3*(5), 89.

DeBleser, R., Dupont, P., Postler, J., Bormans, G., Speelman, D., Mortelmans, L., et al. (2003). The organization of the bilingual lexicon: A PET study. *Journal of Neurolinguistics, 16,* 439–456.

Diamond, A. (2002). Normal development of prefrontal cortex from birth to young adulthood: Cognitive functions, anatomy, and biochemistry. In D. T. Studd & R. T. Knight (Eds.), *Principles of frontal lobe function* (pp. 466–503). New York: Oxford University Press.

Diaz, R. M. (1985). Bilingual cognitive development: Addressing three gaps in current research. *Child Development, 56,* 1376–1388.

Draganski, B., Gaser, C., Busch, V., Schuierer, G, Bogdahn, U., & May, A. (2004). Changes in grey matter induced by training: Newly honed juggling skills show up as a transient feature on a brain-imaging scan. *Nature, 427,* 311–312.

Galambos, S. J., & Goldin-Meadow, S. (1990). The effects of learning two languages on levels of metalinguistic awareness. *Cognition, 34,* 1–56.

Gennesee, F. (2001). Bilingual first language acquisition: Exploring the limits of the language faculty. In M. McGroarty (Ed.), *21st Annual Review of Applied Linguistics* (pp. 153–168). Cambridge, UK: Cambridge University Press.

Gollan, T. H., & Silverberg, N. B. (2001). Tip-of-the-tongue states in Hebrew-English bilinguals. *Bilingualism, Language and Cognition, 4*(1), 63–83.

Goodenough, F. L. (1926). Racial differences in the intelligence of school children. *Journal of Experimental Psychology, 9,* 388–397.

Grady, C. L. (2002). Age-related differences in face processing: A meta-analysis of three functional neuroimaging components. *Canada Journal of Experimental Psychology, 56,* 208–220.

Graham, V. T. (1925). The intelligence of Italian and Jewish children. *Journal of Abnormal Psychology, 20,* 371–376.

Green, D. W. (2001). Introduction. *Bilingualism: Language and Cognition, 4*(2), 101–103.

Hakuta, K., & Diaz, R. M. (1985). The relationship between degree of bilingualism and cognitive ability: A critical discussion and some new longitudinal data. *Children's Language, 5,* 319–344.

Hakuta, K., Ferdman, B. M., & Diaz, R. M. (1987). Bilingualism and cognitive development: Three perspectives. In S. E. Rosenberg (Ed.), *Advances in Applied Psycholinguistics* (Vol. 2, pp. 284–319). New York: Cambridge University Press.

Hill, H. S. (1936). The effects of bilingualism on the measured intelligence of elementary school children of Italian parentage. *Journal of Experimental Education, 5*(1), 75–79.

Holowka, S., Brosseau-Lapré, F., & Petitto, L. A. (2002). Semantic and conceptual knowledge underlying bilingual babies' first signs and words. *Language Learning, 52*(2), 205–262.

Honzik, M. P., MacFarlane, J. W., & Allen, L. (1948). The stability of mental test performance between two and eighteen years. *Journal of Experimental Education, 17*(2), 309–324.

Ianco-Worrall, A. (1972). Bilingualism and cognitive development. *Child Development, 43,* 1390–1400.

Johansson, B. B. (2006). Music and brain plasticity. *European Review, 14,* 49–64.

Jones, W. R., & Stewart, W. A. (1951). Bilingualism and verbal intelligence. *British Journal of Psychology, 4,* 3–8.

Kessler, C., & Quinn, M. E. (1987). Language minority children's linguistic and cognitive creativity. *Journal of Multilingual and Multicultural Development, 8*(1/2), 173–186.

Kim, K. H. S., Relkin, N. R., Lee, K. M., & Hirsch, J. (1997). Distinct cortical areas associated with native and second languages. *Nature, 388,* 171–174.

Kuhl, P. K. (2004). Early language acquisition: Cracking the speech code. *Nature Reviews: Neuroscience, 5*(11), 831–843.

Kuhl, P. K., Tsao, F. M., & Liu, H. M. (2003). Foreign-language experience in infancy: Effects of short-term exposure and social interaction on phonetic learning. *PNAS, 100*(15), 9096–9101.

Kutas, M., Federmeier, K. D., & Sereno, M. I. (2000). Current approaches to mapping language in electromagnetic space. In C. Brown & P. Hagoort (Eds.), *The Neurocognition of Language* (pp. 359–392). Oxford, UK: Oxford University Press.

Lilienfeld, S. O., Lynn, S. J., Namy, L. L., & Woolf, N. J. (2009). *Psychology: From inquiry to understanding.* Boston: Pearson Education.

Macnamara, J. (1966). *Bilingualism and primary education: A study of Irish experience.* Edinburgh, UK: Edinburgh University Press.

Maguire, E. A., Gadian, D. G., Johnsrude, I. S., Good, C. D., Ashburner, J., Frachowiak, R. S. J., et al. (2000). Navigational-related structural change in the hippocampi of taxi drivers. *PNAS, 97*(8), 4398–4403.

Martin, M. M., & Bialystok, E., (2003, October). *The development of two kinds of inhibition in monolingual and bilingual children: Simon vs. Stroop.* Poster presented at the annual meeting of the Cognitive Development Society, Park City, Utah.

McCall, R. B., Appelbaum, M. I., & Hogarty, P. S. (1973). Developmental changes in mental performance. *Monographs of the Society for Research in Child Development, 38*(3), 1–84.

McElree, B., Jia, G., & Litvak, A. (2000). The time course of conceptual processing in three bilingual populations. *Journal of Memory and Language, 42,* 229–254.

Mead, M. (1927). Group intelligence and linguistic disability among Italian children. *School Sociology, 25,* 456–468.

Mechelli, A., Crinion, J. T., Noppeney, U., O'Doherty, J., Ashburner, J., Frackowiak, R. S., et al. (2004). Structural plasticity in the bilingual brain: Proficiency in a second language and age at acquisition affect grey-matter density. *Nature, 431*(7010), 757–756.

Miyawaki, K., Strange, W., Verbrugge, R., Liberman, A. M., Jenkins, J. J., & Fujimura, O. (1975). An effect of linguistic experience: The discrimination of [r] and [l] by native speakers of Japanese. *Perception and Psychophysics, 18*, 331–340.

NetDoctor.com. (2008). *MRI scan*. Retrieved May 19, 2008, from http://www.Net-Doctor.co.uk/health_advice/examinations/mriscan.htm

Oller, D. K., Eilers, R. E., Neal, A. R., & Cobo-Lewis, A. B. (1998). Late onset canonical babbling: A possible early marker of abnormal development. *American Association on Mental Retardation, 103*(3), 249–263.

Patterson, J. L. (1998). Expressive vocabulary development and word combinations of Spanish-English bilingual toddlers. *American Journal of Speech-Language Pathology, 7*(4), 46–56.

Peal, E., & Lambert, W. E. (1962). The relation of bilingualism to intelligence. *Psychological Monographs: General and Applied, 76*(27), Whole No. 546.

Perani, D. (2005). The neural basis of language talent in bilinguals. *TRENDS in Cognitive Sciences, 9*(5), 211–213.

Perfetti, C. A., Liu, Y., Fiez, J., Nelson, J., Bolger, D. J., & Tan, L. H., (2007). Reading in two writing systems: Accommodation and assimilation of the brain's reading network. *Bilingualism, Language and Cognition, 10,* 131–146.

Pintner, R., (1932). The influence of language background on intelligence tests. *Journal of Social Psychology, 3*, 325–240.

Pintner, R., & Keller, R., (1922). Intelligence tests of foreign children. *Journal of Educational Psychology, 13*, 214–222.

Ricciardelli, L. A. (1992). Bilingualism and cognitive development in relation to threshold theory. *Journal of Psycholinguistic Research, 21*(4), 301–316.

Rigg, M. (1928). Some further data on the language handicap. *Journal of Educational Psychology, 19*, 252–257.

Saer, D. J. (1923). The effects of bilingualism on intelligence. *British Journal of Psychology, 14*, 25–38.

Saxe, G. B. (1988). Linking language problems with mathematics achievement: Problems and prospects. In R. R. Cocking & J. P. Mestre (Ed.), *Linguistic and cultural influences on learning mathematics* (pp. 47–62). Hillsdale, NJ: Erlbaum.

Secada, W. G. (1991). Degree of bilingualism and arithmetic problem solving in Hispanic 1st graders. *The Elementary School Journal, 92*(2), 213–231.

Seidenberg, M. S. (1985). The time course of phonological code activation in two writing systems. *Cognition, 19*, 1–30.

Simon, J. R., & Wolf, J. D. (1963). Choice reaction time as a function of angular stimulus-response correspondence and age. *Ergonomics, 6*(1), 99–105.

Spoerl, D. T. (1944). The academic and verbal adjustment of college age bilingual students. *The Journal of Genetic Psychology, 64*, 139–157.

Tan, L. H., Spinks, J. A., Feng, C.-M., Siok, W. T., Perfettic, C. A., Xiong, J., et al. (2003). Neural systems of second language reading are shaped by native language. *Human Brain Mapping, 18*, 158–166.

Thompson, G. G. (1952). *Child psychology*. Boston: Houghton Mifflin.

Wang, S. L. A. (1926). A demonstration of the language difficulty involved in comparing racial groups by means of verbal intelligence tests. *Journal of Applied Psychology, 10*, 102–106.

CHAPTER 6

A Research Perspective on the Involvement of Linguistic-Minority Families on Their Children's Learning

Flora V. Rodríguez-Brown

As their children's first and most important teachers, parents play an important role in their children's early learning. When children enter school, teachers can take advantage of this fact if they view parents as potential resources and can facilitate parents' understanding of their continuing role as teachers. This understanding is especially critical for new immigrant parents and for parents who are culturally and/or linguistically different from the mainstream.

Children of immigrants comprise one out of five K–12 students in the United States (Capps, Fix, Murray, Ost, & Herwantoro, 2005; U.S. Census Bureau, 2004). Getting these parents actively and effectively involved in their children's learning at home has great potential. However, linguistic-minority families must cope with the values and expectations of at least two different cultures as they participate in the process of educating their children in U.S. schools. The way educational institutions support these children's learning at home and at school can have an impact, not only on their families, but also on the whole country's economy and well-being. By responding to the learning needs of preschool children, schools and families can make education more relevant for them and prepare them to succeed in school.

This chapter reports on research findings from studies of home learning environments and family practices that support early learning and school readiness for preschool children from low socioeconomic status (SES) backgrounds and for whom English is not the language used at home. Although the chapter focuses on Latinos, it also discusses barriers that linguistic-minority families, especially new immigrants, have to overcome in order to be successful in supporting their preschool children's learning at home and in helping them to make the transition from home to school. Also discussed are successful practices that support linguistic-minority families as they learn the expectations of U.S. schools and become involved in their children's education.

A RESEARCH PERSPECTIVE
ON LEARNING AT HOME FOR PRESCHOOL CHILDREN

It is widely recognized that young children acquire basic cognitive and linguistic skills within the context of the family and that all children benefit from home environments that foster cognitive, language, and literacy development (Heath, 1983). Research has shown that a positive home environment has an impact on children's success in school (Blevins-Knabe & Musun-Miller, 1996; Heath, 1983; Morrow, 1995; Peters, 1998; Taylor & Dorsey-Gaines, 1988). Such an environment could include activities such as rhyming and counting games, songs, telling stories, read alouds, playing store, and answering questions.

Traditional Studies

In the majority of studies, however, the home literacy environment is conceptualized as parent-child joint book-reading and its influence on children's language and literacy acquisition (Burgess, 1997; Senechal, LeFevre, Thomas, & Daley, 1998) and the child's motivation to learn (Baker & Scher, 2002). For example, Teale and Sulzby (1986) described the role of parent-child interactions with books and how these interactions affected children's emergent literate behaviors and literacy learning.

Other studies have focused on the development of mathematical concepts through a variety of related activities in the home (Anderson, 1997; Blevins-Knabe & Musun-Miller, 1996; Peters, 1998). Anderson (1997) described how parents used a variety of materials at home to teach, explicitly or through games, mathematical concepts during the early years. Peters (1998) found that when parents were trained to teach math through games in school settings, they used the game strategies to teach rote counting, enumeration, and sequencing to their preschool children at home.

Research on both emergent literacy and math learning at home has examined the effects of parents' efforts and found that even parents from low SES backgrounds and low educational levels contributed to their preschool-age children's early learning (Blevins-Knabe & Musun-Miller, 1996; Taylor & Dorsey-Gaines, 1988).

An area of interest in home learning environments is the parents' role in motivating their preschool children to read. One of the few studies on motivation compared parental attitudes toward early reading and children's interest in reading (Baker & Scher, 2002). Authors found that parents who identified the reason for reading as pleasure predicted a higher motivation with respect to their children's enjoyment and value of literacy than parents who associated book reading interactions with learning (which produced a negative impact on their children's interest in literacy).

Data from the National Head Start Research and Evaluation Project, which includes data on 3,001 children, their caregivers/mothers, and 785 fathers has generated a number of studies over the years that relate home literacy environments to the language, literacy, and cognitive development of low-income and minority infants and toddlers. The findings from the studies also have important implications for the development of interventions. In general, findings show a consistent predictive relationship between home literacy environment and children's language development. Bradley, Corwyn, McAdoo, and Coll (2001) found that low-income families were less likely to read (at least several times a week) with their young children than middle-class families. Raikes et al. (2004), using a subset of the Head Start data, studied maternal and children's characteristics that affect the frequency of reading and book availability, and what the reciprocal effects of book reading and children's language skills are over time. Mothers reported that they read more to girls than to boys. Mothers who were high school graduates and White, African American, or English-speaking Latino read more to their toddlers than non-high school graduates and non-English-speaking Latino mothers. Availability of books in the home paralleled the frequency of book reading.

At each age level for which data were collected, shared reading was significantly related to child language skills at that age and predicted reading achievement at subsequent ages. A study by Nord, Lennon, Liu, & Chandler (1999) showed that Latino mothers shared fewer storytelling activities in either Spanish or English with their preschool-age children compared with non-Latino mothers. Machida, Taylor, and Kim (2002) found that parents' beliefs and self-efficacy serve as mediators in determining home learning activities with preschool children. Stress was a debilitating factor in the self-efficacy demonstrated by Mexican American mothers in the study.

Language-Based Research

Research studies on learning at home involving linguistic-minority families often overlook the English proficiency and native language proficiency of both children and parents. Research findings could vary if subjects' bilingual capabilities were considered. These concerns are raised by Snow (2004), who questioned the findings of some of the studies, especially those involving second language homes in the sample, since a large percentage of Head Start participants are Latino. Issues raised include whether there is equivalency in the vocabulary outcomes for children tested in Spanish and in English; how research studies account for different environments and access to materials in the native language available for bilingual children at home and in school; and whether researchers consider the language input and experiences of bilingual children when collecting data. These are questions that cannot be overlooked in future research on the effects of the home literacy environment in linguistic-minority children's cognitive development and knowledge acquisition.

Most of the studies that explore the contributions of linguistic-minority families to the cognitive development of their preschool children involve Latino families. These studies examine the role of the family in early literacy and math learning. Looking at emergent literacy, Quiróz (2004) studied the influence of narratives on knowledge, memory, and language acquisition with 50 bilingual (Spanish/English) families. She investigated the relationship between the interaction styles of bilingual parents during book reading and homework and their children's language skills. Results showed that bilingual mothers tended to use slightly more narrative than descriptive styles while interacting with their children. Narrative style, mostly joint book reading, was positively associated with typical indicators of home literacy environment (e.g., number of books at home, income). Descriptive language styles, which involved interaction between parents and children, were positively associated with discourse markers, such as questions and answers observed in parent-child interactions.

The most significant finding from the Quiróz study was that narrative style in Spanish was a significant and strong predictor of children's language development in English. The quality of the interaction was what counted, rather than the language that was used. This study also showed the value of parents using the language they know better (Spanish or English) in order to enhance interaction with their children, such as questioning, extending of stories, and other discourse markers that contribute to the cognitive, linguistic, and literacy development of young children. This finding demonstrates the need to make parents aware that when they share literacy with their young children, they are acting as models. It is better for them to use their native language, rather than a second language they are just learning, to play games, sing songs, extend the content of the stories, ask questions, or develop new stories.

Research on English Language Learners

Other research has identified home literacy practices that are beneficial for preschoolers who are English language learners (ELL). Snow and Paez (2004) found that language experiences and early exposure to literacy for bilingual preschool-age children were precursors to language development and acquisition, in particular vocabulary, concepts of print, and phonological awareness. Baker and Scher (2002) found similar results using data from the Early Childhood Study of Language and Literacy Development of Spanish-Speaking Children. They provide a deeper understanding of how cultural practices combine with other factors to shape the parents' behaviors in supporting their children's learning in the early years. Delgado and Ford (1998) found that parents' perceptions of child development are influenced by a complex interaction of cultural, social, and economic factors. This might explain how parents from different ethnicities foster the development of different skills in their preschool children. In interviews with parents, they found that for Mexican parents the development of social attributes was as important as cognitive development or motor skills. The researchers see a need for teachers to know about these differences when suggesting interventions based on expectations of mainstream groups.

More recently, López, Barrueco, Feinauer, and Miles (2007) examined parents' behaviors and children's developmental outcomes. Results indicated that, although few differences exist in parenting behaviors across ethnic groups, Latino families are less likely to read books and share stories with their children than parents from other ethnic backgrounds. The findings could benefit linguistic-minority families, as they learn to engage more effectively and influence the cognitive, social, language, and literacy development of their young children.

Recommendations from the Research

Research indicates that book reading and storytelling are two important behaviors related to children's learning outcomes (Flores, Tomany-Korman, & Olson, 2005). Based on their findings, López et al. (2007) suggest that Latino families increase the frequency of book reading, storytelling, and other language activities beginning in their children's first year of life in order to support the development of their children's skills to the level found in mainstream children. They call for support for linguistic-minority families in understanding their role in and expectations for their children's bilingual language development. In order to enhance the nature and quality of interactions, they also suggest the need for parent training that models effective practices in shared readings and the importance of using the language parents know better when sharing knowledge with their children.

In the area of math, studies show that preschool-age children learn math concepts at home through a variety of activities (counting, singing number songs, matching games). Blevins-Knabe and Musun-Miller (1996) found a relationship between the number of math activities reported at home and children's performance on the Test of Early Math Ability (TEMA-2). The number of activities was consistent across ethnicities, but the predictive performance of children varied for ethnic groups. Peters (1998) reported on the effect of an intervention based on the belief that games are more effective in enhancing math learning at home when a sensitive adult is available to support and extend children's learning. Parents learned about ways to share math with their preschoolers at home by serving as aides to teachers in school classrooms. Greater gains in math activities at home occurred in tasks that involved counting, enumeration, and recognition of number patterns.

Cross-cultural research on math learning at home has compared practices among Chinese, Chinese Americans, and Euro-American families with preschool children (Huntsinger, Jose, Liaw, & Ching, 1997). Chinese and Chinese American parents taught math more formally and in a direct manner in comparison with the Euro-American group. They also structured their children's activities and encouraged more math at home. Euro-American parents used more incidental, informal methods related to conceptual knowledge embedded in context rather than basic skills. On the TEMA-2, the Chinese and Chinese American children performed better than the Euro-American children. Analysis showed that ethnicity, parents' beliefs about their children's learning, and parents' work-oriented practices predicted the math-related outcomes.

Although these studies showed a positive relationship between home literacy environments, literacy practices, interaction styles, and language and literacy acquisition, the designs of the studies were based on what is expected from nonminority, White, middle-class populations. The measures used and the observations made might not be relevant in culturally and linguistically different settings. The following section discusses research conducted from a different perspective.

RESEARCH ON LEARNING AT HOME FROM A SOCIOCULTURAL PERSPECTIVE

Studies conducted from a sociocultural perspective show discontinuities between cultural ways of learning at home and at school for Latinos as well as for other ethnic minorities (Foster, 1995; Gallimore, Boggs, & Jordan, 1974; Laureau, 1989; Moll, 1994; Purcell-Gates, 1995; Reese & Gallimore, 2000; Trueba, Jacobs, & Kirton, 1990; Valdes, 1996). Linguistic-minority parents engage in culturally relevant talk and play activities with their preschool children in ways that might contrast with mainstream activities (Riojas-Cortes, Flores, Smith, & Clark, 2003). In addition, Cazden (1986) and Tharp (1989) have documented existing discontinuities for some cultural groups between home and school in such areas as linguistic codes, narrative patterns, motivation, participant structures, teaching strategies, and learning styles. Issues of discontinuity become problematic when differences are viewed as deficits by educators.

Some researchers (e.g., Gutierrez & Rogoff, 2003; Weisner, 1997) believe that there is a problem with studying issues of discontinuity between home and school under the assumptions that culture is static and categorical, and that differences also can be defined as traits. They call for an approach to the study of home-school discontinuities for linguistic minorities that takes into account the histories and valued practices of cultural groups.

Studies with linguistic-minority subjects have indicated that variability among people within cultural groups and the ways they adapt to change and to new circumstances can affect the literacy acquisition of their children (Chandler, Argyris, Barnes, Goodman, & Snow, 1985; Weisner, Gallimore, & Jordan, 1988). Using a cultural model approach specifically related to early literacy development, Reese and Gallimore (2000) studied changes in beliefs and home literacy practices among Mexican immigrant families. These changes in the Mexican parents' cultural models were not seen as threats to their traditional values. For example, once parents learned that reading to children at home supported literacy learning at school, they complied with teachers' requests. Because of the flexible nature of the parents' cultural model, Reese and Gallimore found that continuities and discontinuities coexist in home-school literacy interactions. This finding contrasts with previous research that describes discontinuities and no commonalities between learning at home and school (Goldenberg & Gallimore, 1995).

Results of research on successful home learning practices for preschool children emphasize the need to develop programs and/or activities from which parents learn about the importance of providing their children with opportunities for learning at home, for parents to become models of learning as a way to support their children's learning, and for parents to learn and add new methods of interaction with their children as they share books, play math games, tell stories, and talk to their children (Gutierrez & Rogoff, 2003).

Cultural Differences and Parental Involvement

Since the majority of the ELL population served by preschool programs is Latino, the focus of research on cultural differences has been with Latino populations. Delgado and Ford (1998) discussed parents' perceptions of child development and explained how those perceptions were influenced by an interaction of cultural, social, and economic factors. One perception was about life in the United States. The participants wanted their children to understand from an early age the need to learn English, to retain their

Spanish and home culture (including beliefs and values), and to learn to face discrimination.

Research on parental involvement suggests that cultural and socioeconomic status determine how parents define their role in their children's education (Laureau, 1989). Several concepts are central to understanding how Latino parents define their role. If not understood by the educational system, these concepts can act as barriers to parental involvement. The first is the concept of *familia* (family), which includes not only parents and children, but also extended families and networks. According to Abi-Nader (1991), this concept is central to life for Latinos. It provides individuals with a sense of belonging and interdependence; it implies, even requires, loyalty and obligation. The concept includes responsibilities to other members of the group, depending on one's status in the family (elder, parent, child). Usually the familia takes responsibility for the education of the children, so it is not only the parents that support them in becoming good people and doing well in school. It is important for schools to understand that the extended family supports young children as they learn and develop (De La Vega, 2007). Latino children usually have more resources available to support their learning than might be evident if one were to consider only the education and skills of the parents.

Another Latino concept involves the distinction between the terms *to educate* and *to teach*. Several researchers (e.g., Goldenberg, 1989; Goldenberg & Gallimore, 1995; Reese, Gallimore, Goldenberg, & Garnier, 1999; Rodríguez-Brown, 2001; Valdes, 1996) have described how these two concepts define Latino parents' role in their young children's education. Parents, especially new immigrants, distinguish between *educar* (to educate) and *enseñar* (to teach) when they talk about their role in their children's lives. Their role is to educate, or to instill morals and values in their children and help them become good people. Children are taught to be respectful, obedient, and reserved. When asked how they support their children's learning at home, Latino parents explain that they teach their children to be *bien educados* (well-educated). When asked directly whether they teach their preschool children about literacy or math at home, they react with surprise. They believe that it is the role of the school to teach (enseñar) such subjects as reading, writing, and math. Similar beliefs and values were discussed by Rodríguez and Olswang (2003), who described Mexican American parents as more authoritarian, traditional, and conforming in educational and childrearing practices. However, Rodríguez and Olswang recognize that there is variability in beliefs and values within ethnic groups as a result of different degrees of acculturation or identification with native and mainstream cultures.

The third concept is that Latino parents believe it is disrespectful to interfere with the teacher's role of educating their children. Latinos show great *respeto* (respect) for teachers and schools (Valdes, 1996). According to Saracho and Hancock (1986), Latino culture includes respect toward elders or those in power and positions of authority, such as teachers, within the home, school, state, and church. Since teachers have more schooling, they are more knowledgeable; therefore, Latino parents view schools and teachers with respeto and believe parents should not interfere with the way their children are educated (Flores, Cousin, & Diaz, 1991). However, these parents are often open to learning better ways to support their preschool children's cognitive and language development.

Delgado-Gaitán (1992) and Shannon (1996), among others, argue that teachers and schools do not have accurate perceptions about new immigrant families' attitudes about learning at home and school. Often teachers expect parents to serve as an extension of the school in support of their children's learning, but Latino parents believe it is the responsibility of the school to teach their children and support their academic development (Carrasquillo & London, 1993). These differing expectations of teachers and parents can produce misunderstandings that interfere with the development of relationships between new immigrant families and the schools and with successful parental involvement.

Barriers for Linguistic-Minority Parents' Involvement

Many Latino parents find it surprising that teachers expect them to work with their children at home to support their literacy development, and the parents explain that they do not have the education to teach their children school-related subjects (Rodríguez-Brown, 2004, 2009; Valdes, 1996). In general, linguistic-minority parents believe that their lack of English proficiency precludes them from supporting their preschool children's learning at home. These parents do want to support their children and they feel proud and validated when anyone clarifies to them that not all knowledge comes from schooling and that they have a lot of knowledge that they could share with their children to support their learning at school.

Another barrier to family involvement among linguistic-minority families is lack of knowledge about schooling in the United States (Delgado-Gaitán & Trueba, 1991; Valdes, 1996). Moll (1992) and Valdes (1996) have found that Latino parents lack familiarity with the educational system and what happens in U.S. schools and classrooms. As a result, parents tend to participate in their children's education based on things that they can do at home or based on their prior school experiences in their native countries, which are often different from school expectations here. New immigrant families need support from the school and the community to learn about the U.S. school system and ways they can support their children's learning.

In preschool and school settings, linguistically different parents, particularly those who are new immigrants and English language learners, need to feel welcome and wanted by the schools and the teachers in order to actively participate (Bright, 1996). Often these parents report feeling unwelcome at school and are discouraged from getting involved (Scribner, Young, & Pedroza, 1999). Schools can encourage more linguistic-minority parental involvement through teacher training and the enhancement of the school environment to make it more appealing to diverse families.

School or program personnel often lack understanding of parents' cultural and linguistic differences and can hold negative stereotypes about minority populations. Lack of communication between families and teachers can result in teachers' low expectations for performance from children who are culturally and linguistically different, which in turn affects children's achievement (Alexsaht-Snider, 1991).

Delgado-Gaitán (2001) found that 98% of the teachers in a predominately Latino community considered parental involvement to be very important to school success, but they reported that Latino parents did not provide enough support for their children's learning at home. Research indicates that teachers perceive linguistic-minority parents to be disinterested in their children's education because they don't participate in school activities such as PTA meetings, when, in fact, many times the activities are directed toward mainstream populations (Floyd, 1998; Moles, 1994; Vasquez, Pease-Alvarez, & Shannon, 1994). According to Inger (1992), "many school administrators and teachers misread the reserve, the non-confrontational manners, and the non-involvement of Hispanic parents to mean that they are uncaring about their children's education" (p. 1).

In contrast, research that examines linguistic-minority parents' perceptions of their role in their children's education shows that these parents care very much about their children's education regardless of cultural background (Delgado & Ford, 1998; Rodríguez & Olswang, 2003; Trumbull, Rothstein-Fish, Greenfield, & Quiróz, 2001). Latino parents, in particular, have high aspirations for their children and want to be involved in their young children's education (López, 2001; Shannon, 1996).

The discrepancy between the perception of teachers and administrators and linguistic-minority parents about parental involvement can be explained by each group's definition of involvement (Delgado & Ford, 1998). Scribner et al. (1999) found that while teachers defined parental involvement as participation in formal activities, such as school events and meetings, linguistic-minority parents defined involvement in terms of informal activities such as checking homework or reading to their young children. In addition, teachers connected parental involvement to improvement in school achievement, whereas linguistic-minority parents viewed their involvement as a way to support their children's overall well-being. The perceptions of linguistic-minority parents about parental involvement in schools result from their views about the distinct specific roles of families and schools in educating children. Bermúdez and Padrón (1989) see a need for teacher training programs and for school districts to provide formal training on parental involvement in diverse settings.

Creating Successful Home-School Connections

School programs and activities that support linguistic-minority, particularly Latino, parents' involvement in their young children's learning need to be based on principles of respeto (respect) and *confianza* (mutual trust within a defined community network that leads to support and understanding beyond expectations). According to De La Vega (2007), confianza is central to working with the Latino community and developing relationships with Latino parents. When confianza is established, the teacher or school becomes more effective in conveying their expectations regarding parents' involvement in their children's learning and in making parents feel welcome in the school. This will enhance the parents' self-efficacy in supporting their preschool-age children's learning at home (Izzo, Weiss, Shanahan, & Rodríguez-Brown, 2000; Machida et al., 2002).

It is through confianza that the community and the school are able to work together to create programs for linguistic-minority families that are relevant to different types of parents and that lead to self-efficacy for parents. When parents feel confident, they are able to support their children's learning through new techniques validated by the school, while using their cultural ways of sharing knowledge with their children at home. They become active participants in their children's education in ways that are congruent with the schools' expectations and their own families' culture and values (Izzo et al., 2000). Then, linguistic-minority parents become partners with the school in creating continuity in learning at home and school, thus supporting their children's school success.

In order to attain this goal, it is important that the schools and teachers learn about cultural ways and discourses used by the linguistic-minority families at home in order to create some continuity between learning at home and learning at school. Successful connections between "educators and Latino families must be based on mutual respect for our cultural differences, without exaggerating them to the point that they obscure our shared humanity and dreams" (Zentella, 2005, p. 29).

It is important to pay attention to what linguistic-minority parents do at home as well as how they use personal resources and knowledge to support their children's learning. Saracho (2007) shows that Hispanic fathers have a role in motivating and helping their children to develop, acquire, and use literacy at home. They participate in their children's literacy learning, especially when they know that the teachers use the children's home-based learning to enrich school practices. The role of the Hispanic fathers indicates that they are a positive influence on their children's early reading achievement. They are also resources to literacy learning at home, and their responses to their children's questions related to text have shown an effect on their young children's knowledge of literacy. Issues of congruency between home and school learning are critical in creating home-school connections that will support English language learners in school settings (De La Vega, 2007; Moll, 1992; Valdes, 1996). Educators need to learn how parents define their role as teachers at home. This could raise the teachers' awareness about the cultural learning models used at home by culturally and linguistically different families in support of their children's learning (Rodríguez-Brown, 2004, 2009).

According to Delgado-Gaitán and Trueba (1991), the success or failure of a school intervention or program for Latino parents depends on whether there is collaboration with the parents and/or the community in the development of the program. Delgado-Gaitán (1992) found that when systematic linkages between teachers and Latino parents existed, the interventions or programs were co-constructed in a mutual and respectful manner. Programs created according to what the school thinks the parents need to know to support their children are not very successful. Programs which take into account and respect parents' knowledge, cultural ways, and discourse differences are more relevant to minority parents and often more successful (Rodríguez-Brown, 2004, 2009). Delgado-Gaitán (1996) found that Mexican parents who participated in the creation of a family literacy program were very committed and interested in the activities taught due to their involvement in the planning of the program activities. Similarly, Vasquez et al. (1994) found that parents were interested in supporting their children's learning through a community-based program when the activities planned were relevant to them.

Linguistic-minority parents need to know that personal experiences are valuable resources when used to support their preschool-age children's learning at home, and they should be incorporated into children's learning activities. Most linguistic-minority parents, and particularly Latino parents, prefer to be told explicitly how they best can support their children's learning, and how they can use their own cultural ways and native language as they learn new ways to work with their young children at home. Programs directed toward linguistic-minority families should recognize the cultural capital that these families bring to the learning situation and design activities that use that knowledge as a starting point for program activities.

CONCLUSION

Some of the research related to home literacy environments that enhance preschool children's learning at home and preparedness for school describes concepts that are central to linguistic-minority families' lives and help shape their beliefs and values. These beliefs and values are sometimes in conflict with the expectations of mainstream society and, more specifically, with the expectations of U.S. schools. Many linguistic-minority parents perceive their lack of formal education and English proficiency as barriers that hinder communication with the schools and their expectations for their children's school readiness and development. They also feel that they are not welcomed and wanted by schools and that what their children learn at home is not valued at school. As discussed before, most of the current research about barriers to parents' involvement has been done with Latino families, but Li (2002) has described similar barriers for Chinese families, particularly those in which the parents are recent immigrants and lack education.

Research on early learning experiences at home show how shared book reading, counting, singing number songs, storytelling, and language interactions support school preparedness. These studies show that parents who are not English proficient do not participate in these activities at home as often as mainstream parents (Baker & Scher, 2002). Although linguistic-minority parents want their children to learn English, they also expect them to keep their native language, values, and beliefs (Delgado & Ford, 1998; Rodríguez & Olswang, 2003).

Many linguistic-minority parents, particularly Latinos, see their role in education as one of helping their children become good people. Therefore, they emphasize the learning of values and morals over the learning of language, math, and literacy. Research shows that new immigrant parents are very curious about their children's schooling in the United States. They want to support their children's learning, but they do not understand the expectations of the schools. They do not know how to teach their children at home in ways that are relevant to schools, but they are very willing to work with schools to support their children's learning, provided that this learning is not in conflict with their cultural beliefs and values (Rodríguez-Brown, 2009). Some research shows that linguistic-minority parents prefer explicit instruction from schools and teachers on how to best teach their children at home. This approach enhances the parents' self-efficacy in supporting their young children's learning (Izzo et al., 2000; Reese & Gallimore, 2000).

Research studies also describe ways to work with parents through programs that facilitate their understanding of their role as the first and most important teachers for their children. This research shows that programs directed toward linguistic-minority families need to explicitly explain to participants the role of language used in their interactions with their children. Even if the language used at home is not English, parents' sharing of knowledge with their children benefits their language and literacy development once they enter school.

Research also shows that parents prefer to participate in programs in which they can be partners in the planning of program activities. They are more open to programs that respect and recognize their cultural ways and linguistic differences as stepping stones to learning about different ways in which they can support their children's learning. It is through these types of programs that parents create congruency between learning at home and at school, facilitate their children's transition to formal education in the United States, and improve student learning and educational success (Delgado-Gaitán, 1996, Rodríguez-Brown, 2009).

FUTURE RESEARCH NEEDS

Much research is needed on the contributions of linguistic minority families to their children's learning at home, particularly with Asian and other immigrant groups other than Hispanics. Research on literacy and math learning at home with specific language-minority groups should explain the variability of learning outcomes within the specific population studied. Also needed are studies on the effect of different home learning environments on preschool children's learning, using variables other than SES and ethnicity. With linguistic minorities, new variables should account for cultural differences in ways of learning and different discourses used at home. Research on the effects of interventions with linguistic-minority groups is needed to compare the effects of "functional" (top-down) versus "critical" (enrichment) models (Rodríguez-Brown, 2009) of family training.

Lastly, the use of mixed methods is a must in studies about learning at home with diverse groups. The use of qualitative methods in the development of these studies seems relevant to descriptions of the context where learning at home takes place. Qualitative data collected from linguistic-minority families could contribute to the development of new hypotheses that then could be studied quantitatively with larger populations. This type of data also could contribute to the development of new variables (related to such constructs as cultural ways, discourse factors, etc.), which could be defined in a quantifiable manner for use in future studies. The use of qualitative methods would also contribute to the validation of findings and facilitate possible explanations of findings from large-scale studies.

REFERENCES

Abi-Nader, J. (1991, April). *Family values and the motivation of Hispanic youth.* Paper presented at the annual meeting of the American Educational Research Association, Chicago.

Alexsaht-Snider, M. (1991). *When school goes home and families come to school* [Unpublished dissertation]. Santa Barbara: University of California, Santa Barbara.

Anderson, A. (1997). Families and mathematics: A study of parent-child interactions. *Journal of Research in Mathematics Education, 28*(4), 484–511.

Baker, L., & Scher, D. (2002). Beginning readers' motivation for reading in relation to parental beliefs and home reading experiences. *Reading Psychology 23*(3), 239–269.

Bermúdez, A., & Padrón, Y. N. (1989). Improving language skills for Hispanic students through home-school partnerships. *The Journal of Educational Issues of Language Minority Students, 6,* 33–43.

Blevins-Knabe, B., & Musun-Miller, L. (1996). Number use at home by children and their parents and its relationship to early mathematical performance. *Early Development and Parenting, 5*(1), 35–45.

Bradley, R., Corwyn, R., McAdoo, H. P., & Coll, C. G. (2001). The home environments of children in the United States Part I: Variations by age, ethnicity and poverty status. *Child Development, 72*(6), 1844–1867.

Bright, J. A. (1996). Partners: An urban Black community perspective on the school and home working together. *New Schools, New Communities, 12*(3), 32–37.

Burgess, S. (1997). The role of shared reading in the development of phonological awareness: A longitudinal study of middle to upper middle class children. *Early Child Development and Care, 70,* 37–43.

Capps, R., Fix, M., Murray, J., Ost, J., & Herwantoro, S. (2005). *The new demography of America's schools: Immigration and No Child Left Behind Act.* Washington, DC: Urban Institute.

Carrasquillo, A. L., & London, C. B. G. (1993). *Parents and schools: A source book.* New York: Garland.

Cazden, C. (1986). Classroom discourse. In M. C. Wittrock (Ed.), *Handbook of research on teaching* (3rd ed., pp. 432–463). New York: Macmillan.

Chandler, J., Argyris, D., Barnes, W., Goodman, I., & Snow, C. (1985). Parents as teachers: Observations of low-income parents and children in a homework-like task. In B. Schieffelin & P. Gilmore (Eds.), *The acquisition of literacy: Ethnographic perspectives* (pp. 171–187). Norwood, NJ: Ablex.

De La Vega, E. (2007, April). *Culture, confianza, and caring: A key to connections between Mexicana/Latina mothers and schools.* Paper presented at the annual meeting of the American Educational Research Association, Chicago.

Delgado, B. M., & Ford, L. (1998). Parental perceptions of child development among low-income Mexican American families. *Journal of Child and Family Studies, 7*(4), 469–481.

Delgado-Gaitán, C. (1992). School matters in the Mexican-American home: Socializing children to education. *American Educational Research Journal, 29*(3), 495–513.

Delgado-Gaitán, C. (1996). *Protean literacy: Extending the discourse on empowerment.*

Washington, DC: Farmer Press.

Delgado-Gaitán, C. (2001). *The power of community: Mobilizing for family and schooling.* Lanham, MD: Rowman and Littlefield.

Delgado-Gaitán, C., & Trueba, H. (1991). *Crossing cultural borders.* London: Farmer.

Flores, B., Cousin, P. T., & Diaz, E. (1991). Transforming the deficit myths about learning, language, and culture. *Language Arts, 68,* 369–379.

Flores, G., Tomany-Korman, S. C., & Olson, L. (2005). Does disadvantage start at home? Racial and ethnic disparities in health-related early childhood home routines and safety practices. *Archives of Pediatric and Adolescent Medicine, 159*(2), 158–165.

Floyd, L. (1998). Joining hands: A parental involvement program. *Urban Education, 33*(1), 123–135.

Foster, M. (1995). African American teachers and culturally relevant pedagogy. In J. A. Banks & C. A. M. Banks (Eds.), *Handbook of research in multicultural education* (pp. 570–581). New York: Macmillan.

Gallimore, R., Boggs, J. W., & Jordan, C. (1974). *Culture, behavior and education: A study of Hawaiian-Americans.* Beverly Hills, CA: Sage.

Goldenberg, C. N. (1989). Parents' effects on academic grouping for reading: Three case studies. *American Educational Research Journal, 26*(3), 329–352.

Goldenberg, C. N., & Gallimore, R. (1995). Immigrant Latino parents' values and beliefs about their children's education: Continuities and discontinuities across cultures and generations. In P. Pintrich & M. Maehr (Eds.), *Advances in motivation and achievement* (Vol. 9, pp. 183–228). Greenwich, CT: Ablex.

Gutierrez, K. D., & Rogoff, B. (2003). Cultural ways of learning: Individual traits or repertoires of practice. *Educational Researcher, 32*(5), 15–25.

Heath, S. B. (1983). *Ways with words: Language, life and work in community and classrooms.* Cambridge, UK: Cambridge University Press.

Huntsinger, C. S., Jose, P. E., Liaw, F. R., & Ching, W. D. (1997). Cultural differences in early mathematics learning: A comparison of Euro-American, Chinese-American and Taiwan-Chinese families. *International Journal of Behavioral Development, 21*(2), 371–388.

Inger, M. (1992). *Increasing the school involvement of Hispanic parents.* (ERIC Document Reproduction Service No. EDO-UD-92-3).

Izzo, C., Weiss, L., Shanahan, T., & Rodríguez-Brown, F. V. (2000). Parental self-efficacy and social support as predictors of parenting practices and children's socioemotional adjustment in Mexican immigrant families. *Journal of Prevention and Intervention in the Community, 20*(1/2), 197–213.

Laureau, A. (1989). *Home advantage: Social class and parental intervention.* New York: Farmer Press.

Li, G. (2002). *"East is east, west is west?" Home literacy, culture, and schooling.* New York: Peter Lang.

López, G. R. (2001). The value of hard work: Lessons on parent involvement from an (im)migrant household. *Harvard Education Review, 71*(3), 416–437.

López, M. L., Barrueco, S., Feinauer, E., & Miles, J. C. (2007, June). Young Latino infants and families: Parental involvement implications from a recent national study. *Research Digest.* Cambridge, MA: Fine Network, Harvard Family Research Project.

Machida, S., Taylor, A., & Kim, J. (2002). The role of maternal beliefs in predicting home language activities in Head Start families. *Family Relations, 51*(2), 176–184.

Moles, O. (1994). Who wants parent involvement? *Education and Urban Society, 19*(2), 137–145.

Moll, L. C. (1992). Bilingual classroom studies and community analysis: Some recent trends. *Educational Researcher, 21*(3), 20–24.

Moll, L. C. (1994). Literacy research in community and classrooms: A sociocultural approach. In R. B. Ruddell, M. R. Ruddell & H. Singer (Eds.), *Theoretical models and processes of reading* (pp. 179–207). Newark, DE: International Reading Association.

Morrow, L. M. (Ed.). (1995). *Family literacy: Connections in schools and communities*. Newark, DE: International Reading Association.

Nord, C. W., Lennon, J., Liu, B., & Chandler, K. (1999). Home literacy activities and signs of children emerging literacy, 1993–1999. *Statistics in brief* (NCES Publication No. 2000–026 Rev). Washington, DC: U.S. Department of Education, National Center for Education Statistics.

Peters, S. (1998). Playing games and learning mathematics: The results of two intervention studies. *International Journal of Early Years Education, 6*(1), 49–58.

Purcell-Gates, V. (1995). *Other people's words: The cycle of illiteracy*. Cambridge, MA: Harvard University Press.

Quiróz, B. (2004, June). *Mothers' narratives and children's literacy skills in Spanish-speaking families*. Paper presented at Head Start's 7th National Research Conference, Washington, DC.

Raikes, H. H., Pan, B. A., Luze, G., Tamis-LeMonda, C. S., Brooks-Gunn, J., Constantine, J., et al. (2004, June). *Predictors of mother-toddler book reading in low-income families and child language and cognitive outcomes at 14, 24 and 36 months*. Paper presented at Head Start's 7th National Research Conference, Washington, DC.

Reese, L., & Gallimore, R. (2000). Immigrant Latinos' cultural models of literacy development: An alternative perspective on home-school discontinuities. *American Journal of Education, 108*(2), 103–134.

Reese, L., Gallimore, R., Goldenberg, C. N., & Garnier, H. (1999). Job-required literacy, home literacy environments, and school reading: Early literacy experiences of immigrant Latino children. In J. G. Lipson & L. A. McSpadden (Eds.), *Negotiating power and place at the margins: Selected papers on refugees and immigrants* (Vol. 7, pp. 232–269). Washington, DC: American Anthropological Association.

Riojas-Cortés, M., Flores, B. B., Smith, H. L., & Clark, E. R. (2003) Cuéntame un cuento (Tell me a story): Bridging family literacy traditions with school literacy. *Language Arts, 81*(1), 62–71.

Rodríguez, B. L., & Olswang, L. B. (2003). Mexican-American and Anglo-American mothers' beliefs and values about child rearing, education and language impairment. *American Journal of Speech-Language Pathology, 12*, 452–462.

Rodríguez-Brown, F. V. (2001). Home-school collaboration: Successful models in the Hispanic community. In P. Mosenthal & P. Schmitt (Eds.), *Reconceptualizing literacy in the new age of pluralism and multiculturalism, Advances in reading & language research* (pp. 273–288). Greenwich, CT: Information Age Publishing.

Rodríguez-Brown, F. V. (2004). Project FLAME: A parent support family literacy model. In B. Wasik (Ed.), *Handbook of family literacy* (pp. 213–229). Mahwah, NJ: Erlbaum.

Rodríguez-Brown, F. V. (2009). *Home-school connection: Lessons learned in a culturally and linguistically diverse community.* New York: Taylor and Francis.

Saracho, O. N. (2007). Hispanic father-child sociocultural literacy practices. *Journal of Hispanic Higher Education, 6*(3), 272–283.

Saracho, O. N., & Hancock, F. M. (1986). Mexican-American culture. In O. N. Saracho & B. Spodek (Eds.), *Understanding the multicultural experience in early childhood education* (3rd ed., pp. 3–15). Washington, DC: National Association for the Education of Young Children.

Scribner, J. D., Young, M. D., & Pedroza, A. (1999). Building collaborative relationships with parents. In P. Reyes, J. D. Scribner, & A. P. Scribner (Eds.), *Lessons from high-performing Hispanic schools: Creating learning communities* (pp. 36–60). New York: Teachers College Press.

Senechal, M., LeFevre, J., Thomas, E., & Daley, K. (1998). Differential effects of home literacy experiences on the development of oral and written language. *Reading Research Quarterly, 33*(1), 96–116.

Shannon, S. M. (1996). Minority parent involvement: A Mexican mother's experience and a teacher's interpretation. *Education and Urban Society, 29*(1), 71–84.

Snow, C. E. (2004, June). *Language and literacy environments of toddlers in low-income families: Relations to cognitive and language development.* Discussant at Head Start's 7th National Research Conference, Washington, DC.

Snow, C. E., & Paez, M. M. (2004). The Head Start classroom as an oral language environment: What should the performance standards be? In E. Ziegler & S. Styfco (Eds.), *The Head Start debates: Are we failing the most at risk?* (pp. 113–128). Baltimore, MD: Brookes Publishing.

Taylor, D., & Dorsey-Gaines, C. (1988). *Growing up literate: Learning from inner-city families.* Portsmouth, NH: Heinemann.

Teale, W. H., & Sulzby, E. (Eds.). (1986). *Emergent literacy: Writing and reading.* Norwood, NJ: Ablex.

Tharp, R. G. (1989). Culturally compatible education: A formula for designing effective classrooms. In H. T. Trueba, G. Spindler, & L. Spindler (Eds.), *What do anthropologists have to say about dropouts?* (pp. 51–66). New York: Farmer Press.

Trueba, H., Jacobs, L., & Kirton, E. (1990). *Cultural conflict and adaptation: The case of Hmong children in American society.* New York: Farmer Press.

Trumbull, E., Rothstein-Fish, C., Greenfield, P. M., & Quiróz, B. (2001). *Bridging cultures between home and schools: A guide for teachers.* Mahwah, NJ: Erlbaum.

U.S. Census Bureau. (2004). Table 4: Annual estimates of the population by sex and age for the United States: April 1, 2000, to July 1, 2003 (NC-EST2003-04-3, 5, 7, 12, & 13).

Valdes, G. (1996). *Con respeto: Bridging the differences between culturally diverse families and schools.* New York: Teachers College Press.

Vasquez, O. A., Pease-Alvarez, L., & Shannon, S. M. (1994). *Pushing boundaries: Language and culture in a Mexicano community.* New York: Cambridge University Press.

Weisner, T. (1997). The ecocultural project of human development: Why ethnography and its findings matter. *Ethos, 25*(2), 1977–1990.

Weisner, T., Gallimore, R., & Jordan, C. (1988). Unpackaging cultural effects on classroom learning: Native Hawaiian peer assistance and child-generated activity. *Anthropology and Education Quarterly, 19*(4), 327–353.

Zentella, A. C. (Ed.). (2005). *Building on strength: Language and literacy in Latino families and communities.* New York: Teachers College Press.

CHAPTER 7

Assessment of Young English Language Learners

Linda M. Espinosa

All early childhood programs, whether they are informal, family-based child care or more structured, school-based pre-K programs, have important goals for young children's development. These goals are often stated in terms of learning expectations, preschool foundations, child outcome frameworks, desired results, or early childhood learning standards. The goals most often cover the learning domains of language, literacy, cognitive development, social-emotional development, mathematics, social sciences and, less frequently, arts, health, and physical development (Scott-Little, Kagan, & Frelow, 2005). Increasingly, programs are asked to document that all children, including English language learners (ELLs), are making sufficient progress toward the stated goals and outcomes. Individual child assessments that include linguistically, culturally, and developmentally appropriate tools and procedures and that are aligned with the curriculum goals (National Association for the Education of Young Children [NAEYC]/National Association of Early Childhood Specialists in State Departments of Education [NAECS/SDE], 2003) will provide the information necessary to measure how children are progressing and what educational decisions need to be made (NAEYC & NAECS/SDE, 2003; Niemeyer & Scott-Little, 2001).

In this chapter, I describe the challenges presented in designing appropriate assessment systems for ELLs, summarize issues of assessment for ELL populations that are common across multiple assessment measures, detail by developmental domain the limitations of a few of the most widely used existing assessment instruments, present some of the promising new developments in ELL assessment, and, finally, present recommendations for assessing young ELLs and for future research.

While assessing the progress of young ELLs toward meeting learning objectives sounds straightforward and logical, the process becomes more complex when the children we are assessing are not yet 6 years of age and come from diverse backgrounds, when the purposes for the assessment are multiple and not well defined, when the consequences may be enormous for the children and programs, and when the assessors are not adequately trained (Ray, Bowman, & Robbins, 2006). Fortunately, there have been advances in the last decade in approaches to early childhood assessment including conceptual clarification (Maxwell & Clifford, 2004), understanding of important curriculum goals (National Early Literacy Panel, 2007), improved technical quality of instruments and procedures (Farver, Nakamoto, & Lonigan, 2007), and national guidelines for the collection and use of assessment data (American Educational Research Association, 1999; American Psychological Association, 1990; NAEYC & NAECS/SDE, 2003).

The central challenge in the accurate assessment of young ELL children is to determine what each child knows in each language, how much of the curriculum was learned, and how the learning environment should be adapted to maximize future learning. This requires individual child assessments that address all the important domains that are responsive to the linguistic, cultural, social, and developmental attributes of each child.

ISSUES IN ASSESSMENT THAT ARE SPECIFIC TO ELL CHILDREN

Young ELL children present all of the challenges inherent in accurate assessment of young children (Mesiels, 2007) in addition to their lack of English fluency (Neill, 2005). If a young child is asked to "put the block *on top of* the table" and responds by staring at the examiner or picking up the block and holding it in his hand, it is almost impossible to know if he does not understand the concept *on top of* or does not understand the English vocabulary sufficiently to respond correctly. If the assessors have no familiarity with the child's home language, it is difficult to determine the child's linguistic proficiency and conceptual knowledge in his or her first language (L1). There may also be cultural influences that make the task confusing for the child, even when he or she understands the directions. To determine the child's developmental progress, it is necessary to assess the child's abilities in his or her home language in addition to the child's level and stage of English development, early language-learning environment, and conceptual knowledge in each language. Given the reality that there may be a dozen different languages/cultures represented in a single program, it is highly unlikely that there are sufficient staff with the training or background to assess in all the languages represented in many programs. In addition, our current language measures include, at best, Spanish and English, which makes accurate assessment for ELL children a formidable challenge.

Furthermore, determining who is an ELL and who is not is an inconsistent process without standard definitions or criteria for inclusion. For some national data sets, a short screening tool to measure English fluency is administered with a predetermined cutoff score (see, for example, National Center for Education Statistics, 2001). Children who fall below that cutoff score are considered ELL and assessments are administered in their home language, typically Spanish, when possible. However, none of these large-scale studies requires that all children who fail the screener and are judged to be not fluent enough in English to continue with the assessment in English will then be assessed in their home language. Instead many ELL children who are neither English- nor Spanish-speaking are omitted from large national studies of children's development, resulting in fewer data being collected on this population.

In addition, almost all the instruments and procedures currently in use to assess language proficiency and early academic achievement were designed, normed, and validated on monolingual children (Espinosa & López, 2007). The samples used to develop the tests most frequently consisted of native English speakers and, occasionally, monolingual Spanish speakers, but rarely of dual language or bilingual children.

Diversity Within the ELL Population

Analysis of the Early Childhood Longitudinal Study-Kindergarten Cohort (ECLS-K) (National Center for Educational Statistics, 2001) data set reveals that young Latino English language learners at kindergarten entry are more likely to live in low-income homes (Espinosa, Laffey, & Whittaker, 2006) with both parents and a mother who is less likely to work outside the home than their White or African American peers (Crosnoe, 2005). Low-income Hispanic children in the ECLS-K sample also scored more than half a standard deviation below the national average in math and reading achievement at kindergarten entry (Lee & Burkam, 2002). In addition, children who are not native English speakers continue to have substantially lower levels of educational achievement, including lower high school completion and lower college enrollment rates than their peers from English-only backgrounds (Gandara, Rumberger, Maxwell-Jolly, & Callahan, 2003; Rumberger & Anguiano, 2004). However, these findings should be interpreted cautiously, as some researchers have suggested that poverty may account for a greater proportion of the achievement gap than minority or ELL status, given the disproportionately higher representation of such population subgroups who are living in poverty (Brooks-Gunn & Markman, 2005; Duncan & Magnuson, 2005).

To further illustrate the variability across ELL subgroups, when the ECLS-K data are disaggregated according to which language is spoken in the home (English, European–non-Spanish, Asian, or Spanish), and the socioeconomic status (SES) of the home, the discrepancies in the initial achievement scores as well as the amount of growth over time are greatly reduced, and not all language groups show depressed development and achievement (Espinosa et. al., 2006). In addition, this analysis of the ECLS-K data revealed that when comparing groups, all groups of ELL children scored below their native English-speaking peers on math and reading assessments, but when compared to other ELL groups by language type, the findings were more nuanced.

> In general, . . . children from European and Asian speaking homes do as well or better than their English speaking counterparts. Children from Spanish speaking homes are behind all other language groups. The difference is pronounced when the achievement scores of the Spanish speaking children who score lower than the cutoff are compared to the English speaking children or to the Spanish speaking children who score above the cutoff score. (Espinosa et al., 2006, p. 52)

The Spanish-speaking children who had basic English fluency (passed the language screener) and were not in the lowest SES quintiles achieved at rates that were comparable to their monolingual English-speaking peers.

Clearly, the economic and educational resources of the family influence the child's academic knowledge at kindergarten entry. Based on other research on the language learning opportunities and overall language development of children living in poverty (Hart & Risley, 1995), it is quite possible that these Spanish-speaking children are also behind in their native language abilities. There is other research showing that low-income, Spanish-speaking children growing up in the United States score below their monolingual English and Spanish-speaking peers in both Spanish and English, respectively, on standardized tests of language ability (Pearson, 1988; Tabors, Paez, & López, 2004). Thus, it is important to remember that there is great diversity within the ELL population; ELLs vary in the home language they speak, the age at which they were first exposed to English, their fluency in both their first language and English, and in the level of family and community resources available to them. These variations have implications for assessment policy and practices.

Assessment Implications from the Changing Population Demographics

The demographic data presented in this volume emphasize the clear and dramatic increase in the number and percentage of culturally and linguistically diverse children across the country. Similarly, the data regarding the characteristics of children between birth and age 5 also reflect the increasingly diverse population as a whole, both nationally and, to an even higher degree, within certain states and localities. These recent demographic changes and the inherent complexities and variability of bilingual language development, not only have implications for the nature and timing of instructional practices within classrooms, but also for the types of ELL assessment strategies implemented for individual child assessment.

It is important to take into consideration the fact that poverty has been shown to be one of the characteristics most strongly associated with lower performance on many common assessment measures (Duncan & Magnuson, 2005). Given the disproportionately higher representation of culturally and linguistically diverse (predominately Spanish-speaking) ELL children within the overall population of children living in poverty, it is not clear whether the frequently discussed "racial disparities" found in children's academic performance or assessment scores in English are more attributable to poverty, the children's cultural and linguistic traits, or some combination of the two. Thus, it is important to distinguish between issues associated with children growing up in poverty and those uniquely associated with the experience of being bilingual.

Within the context of the ELL population, it is important to understand and take into consideration some of the key dimensions associated with the variability in ELL children's language and literacy development, as they do not represent a single, homogeneous group. The above data highlight the fact that *within* the population of ELL children and families there is considerable variability across a number of important factors and characteristics that have been shown to predict important differences in children's rate and level of development. Thus, the child assessment approaches must be responsive to such *within* group language variability, as well as to differences between monolingual and dual language children.

STRENGTHS AND LIMITATIONS OF CURRENT ELL ASSESSMENT MEASURES AND ASSESSMENT STRATEGIES: RELIABILITY, VALIDITY, AND UTILITY

In order for ELL children's outcomes to be fairly and appropriately assessed, it is important to understand some of the major limitations to many of the currently available measures for young children. A more detailed review of the technical characteristics of common ELL assessment measures (e.g., how the measure was developed, nature of normative sample, intended use of measure, validity, reliability, predictive ability, relationship to other more in-depth assessments, prior use with similar populations, etc.) can be found in a recently compiled compendium of ELL assessment measures (Barrueco, López, Ong, & Lozano, 2007). Similarly, it is critical that users pay particular attention to the background information on standardization procedures contained in the respective assessment manuals for each measure. This is important both to guide the initial selection of the most appropriate assessment measure or measures, and to better understand any key concerns or limitations related to the interpretation of the results derived from individual assessments.

Not intended to be an exhaustive summary of considerations or limitations, the following discussion highlights some of the issues and general limitations across assessment measures and procedures for ELLs:

1. Despite the tremendous recent growth in the population of young ELL children, the corresponding development of a range of different types of appropriate measures for ELL children has lagged far behind. The limitations relate both to the overall number of available measures, and to the domains of skills and abilities covered by such measures.

2. Many of the currently available measures for ELL children have been developed essentially as basic translations or adaptations of existing English language versions of measures, with varying levels of attention to ensuring comparability in the conceptual, linguistic or semantic content and/or level of difficulty of the translated items across languages. As such, the content validity and construct validity may not be the same for the Spanish as for the English version of the same measure.

3. Unless a test were specifically normed with a sample of similar ELL children, the tests are still less accurate and valid for dual language learners who have been judged sufficiently fluent in English to be assessed in English. Often, the reliability coefficients for many standardized tests are lower for ELL children, even if they have been designated as fully proficient in English (Abedi, Leon, & Mirocha, 2001) meaning that the score for an individual child may not be an accurate measure of that specific child's abilities. The concurrent validity scores for some assessments have also been shown to be substantially lower for ELL students, again making the accuracy less dependable.

4. The actual developmental construct that is being assessed by a measure may vary from one language to the next. On several common measures assessing different aspects of phonemic awareness, a child may be asked either to add to or take away parts of words to form new words. On English versions of such tasks, compound words are often used. For example, a child may be asked to say a word such as *mailbox* and then say it without *mail* (*box*), or blend the words *mail* and *box* together to form a new

word (*mailbox*). However, since compound words occur much less frequently in Spanish, this particular type of task is much more complex for Spanish-speaking children to understand and to be as engaged in. Thus, unless items for a given task have been simultaneously developed in both English and the other language (or the measurement equivalence has been examined with the Spanish version), as is done with some measures like the Preschool Language Scale-4, there is a much greater risk that the translation process may result in an unintended change in the content, meaning, or linguistic complexity of the desired skill or ability that is being assessed.

5. Many standardized assessment measures (both in English and other languages) contain a very small pool of test items to assess a given skill or ability of interest. Since many existing assessments are designed to assess a number of different skills and abilities, the developers often choose to keep the number of items for any given task to a small number, so as not to end up with an assessment that will be too lengthy and/or frustrating for the shorter attention span of many preschool-age children. However, given the above-noted variability in young children's performance on many such assessments, the inclusion of a greater number of items would be one way to help to offset this inherent variability and improve the precision of the measures.

6. It is not uncommon to see the inclusion of a fairly small number of young children in the normative samples used to develop the standardized assessment measures. Given the expected, normal level of variability in performance for these preschool-age children, one might expect to see the inclusion of larger numbers of children at the younger age levels, even as compared with the number of children included at the older ages for the normative sample. This is especially true with ELLs considering the great within-group variability.

7. Many normative samples have a smaller-than-expected representation of low-income and culturally or linguistically diverse population subgroups, as compared with the composition of the total population of young children. However, information on the specific demographic composition of the normative sample used to develop a given measure may not always be readily available in the published assessment manuals. If the normative sample for a given measure does not match the demographic characteristics of those children who are being assessed, then the resulting norms may not be appropriate for use with such a different group of children.

8. For assessments targeted toward ELL populations, there also is the consideration as to whether the normative samples used were monolingual Spanish-speaking or bilingual children, or some combination of the two. The desirability of different types of normative samples depends upon the nature of the question the user is interested in examining. On the one hand, some users may be most interested in examining a child's performance on a Spanish measure against the performance of monolingual Spanish speakers to assess the child's development against a normative group of children who primarily speak one language, Spanish. However, other users may be interested in examining how a child being raised in a bilingual environment performs in comparison to other, similar bilingual children.

In summary, these are just a few of the considerations that users should understand in order to be better informed when deciding which assessment measure or measures to select from among the different available assessment options, and for what purpose. While some assessments contain adequate descriptions of how the measure was developed, the composition of the normative sample, and the detailed information on the psychometric properties of the measure (e.g., reliability and validity), others provide much less information and, in some cases, contain misleading psychometric information. For example, some assessment manuals present psychometric data, including information on the validity and reliability of the test for the English version of the measure, but don't present similar psychometric information on the specific non-English version. Caution should be exercised by potential users if any assessment does not provide detailed information on all aspects of the test. Despite the many limitations and/or concerns noted above, currently there are some available assessment measures that can be carefully utilized to gain a better understanding of the language development ELL children. Nevertheless there is still need for the continued development of newer and better ELL assessment measures and measurement strategies.

ASSESSMENT OF DEVELOPMENT FOR YOUNG ELL CHILDREN ACROSS LANGUAGE FLUENCY, LITERACY, AND SOCIAL-EMOTIONAL AND COGNITIVE DEVELOPMENT

Language Fluency and Dominance

The first issue facing educators working with dual language learners is to determine the dominant language of the child. Before an assessor can decide on the child's developmental status, educational progress or educational intervention, you need to know in which language the child is more proficient. Young ELL children, whether simultaneous or sequential second language learners, most likely will have a dominant language, which is the one the child has had the most exposure to, uses more fluidly, and, often, prefers to use (Genesee, Paradis, & Crago, 2004; Pearson 2002), even though the differences may be subtle. Typically, the ELL child will have a larger vocabulary, or a specialized vocabulary, along with greater grammatical proficiency and mastery of the linguistic structure of one of the languages. This is the language the child should be assessed in to determine the upper limits of his or her linguistic and cognitive ability.

Although it is important to determine a child's dominant language, there are no individual child assessments specifically designed for this purpose. Genesee and colleagues (2004) have recommended that educators ask the parents/family members about the child's earliest language exposure to determine language dominance. Research indicates that the amount of input, frequency of use, and the parents' estimates of language ability highly relate to the level of proficiency in the language (Gutiérrez-Clellen & Kreiter, 2003). One example of a parent report measure of children's English vocabulary development is the *MacArthur Communicative Development Inventory* (CDI) (Fenson, Pethick, Renda, Dale, & Reznick, 1998). The English version has shown good concurrent validity with other direct measures of English vocabulary (Dale, 1991; Feldman et al., 2000). The CDI has also shown very good reliability and predictive validity with other English-speaking cultures (Reese & Read, 2000). The Spanish-language version of the CDI, the *MacArthur Inventario del Desarrollo de Habilidades Comunicativas: Palabras y Enunciados* (IDHC) (Jackson-Maldonado et al., 2003) has been adapted and validated for Spanish-speaking children from Mexico; however, low-income families were not included in the initial validation sample.

Accurately determining the language proficiency of a monolingual preschooler is not an easy task under the best of circumstances; when the child is learning two languages, the challenge is increased significantly. As was discussed above, the ELL child's dominant language should be used for assessing the child's true abilities across domains. Some researchers have cautioned against standardized vocabulary measures with ELL children because they tend to underestimate ELL children's level of general language development (Genesee et al., 2004; Pearson 1988). During a stage of second language acquisition most preschool ELL children will know fewer words in each language than their monolingual peers, and conclusions from vocabulary test scores could erroneously indicate the child is not developing at an age-appropriate level. Recent data from large-scale studies on low-income preschool-age ELL children suggest that even when the vocabulary scores from both of the child's languages are added together, the vocabulary scores are still significantly below their monolingual peers (Tabors et al., 2004).

Currently there are many standardized language proficiency measures commercially available for ELL children who speak Spanish; however, there are very few for children whose home language is neither Spanish nor English. For these children, it is still recommended that ELL children be assessed in both their home language and English. One reason is that while a child is learning English, he may show greater initial progress in the home language and limited progress in the second language. Another reason is that research shows that when the child's achievements are examined in the home language, teachers can also make fairly accurate predictions about the child's potential for learning in the second language (Gutiérrez-Clellen, 1998). If the ELL child is able to learn age-appropriate concepts in the home language, it is probable he will be able to transfer this knowledge to English language learning.

As there is much variability in the amount and quality of English exposure, as well as home language learning opportunities, ELL children will show uneven progress between the two languages, depending on the language tasks. For example, a child may be proficient in one language for one task (e.g., letter naming, simple vocabulary) but not for another (e.g., listening comprehension) (Valdés & Figueroa, 1994). Another child may be able to hold a simple conversation in English but not be able to answer questions about a story or a sequence of pictures (Gutiérrez-Clellen, 2002). Because of this variability and the fact that knowledge is mediated by language, it is almost impossible to obtain an accurate measure of progress without examining development in the two languages.

Informal, indirect methods of observing ELL children's interactions and language usage can provide important information on the child's level of language proficiency. Research has shown that teachers can be highly reliable in estimating a child's level of proficiency and English usage based on their observations of the child (Gutiérrez-Clellen & Kreiter, 2003). Observations and insights from other staff who speak the child's home language and have contact with the child, such as bus drivers and family or health specialists, also can be collected through the use of standardized forms (Espinosa, 2006; Gutiérrez-Clellen, Restrepo, & Simon-Cereijido, 2006).

In addition to information from parents, staff, and teachers, language proficiency can be assessed directly by asking children to provide spontaneous narrative samples or story retellings. ELL children's retellings can provide information about their ability to produce and comprehend one or more languages. The Renfrew Bus Story (Cowley & Glasgow, 1997) is one example of a standardized language assessment using story retelling. Adults can model a statement about each picture (e.g., "This is John and his frog"; "One day they went to the park.") and then ask the child to retell the story. Through this approach, it is possible to determine if the child has sufficient mastery of the target language to comprehend the parts of the story and use complete sentences to retell it. This type of language assessment can be used in any language by a staff member who is fluent in the child's home language. The results can then be used to compare the child's functioning in English and the home language.

Early Literacy

Although young ELL children are rarely assessed in both their home language and English, it is the only way to determine the child's full language competence. Rarely do studies of preschool-age ELL children assess outcomes in both English and the home language. Most often assessments are conducted only in English, once the child has been judged to be sufficiently fluent in English. Even when the study is addressing the bilingual development of ELL children and assesses children in both their home language and English, the most frequent method is to assess each language separately rather than combining scores from both languages to derive one summary score that represents the child's overall bilingual competence (Gutiérrez-Clellen, Peña, & Quinn, 1995; Winsler, Diaz, Espinosa, & Rodriguez, 1999).

One test that has been designed to assess in both Spanish and English is the *Woodcock-Muñoz Language Survey* (WMLS). The WMLS was developed as a test of language proficiency for ELL children (Woodcock & Muñoz-Sandoval, 1993). It is a picture vocabulary test that measures the child's ability to name pictured objects. The English and Spanish scores can be combined to obtain a total vocabulary score, for example, a child who can produce both "dog" and "perro" is awarded only one point.

While this approach can more accurately capture an ELL child's total vocabulary knowledge and reflect the strengths and variability of bilingual development, it still has notable drawbacks. There are concerns about the standardization samples and whether they represent the full diversity of ELL children in the United States (Laing & Kamhi, 2003). The many language dialects of the children studied may not be fully accounted for in the selection of items, and the sociolinguistic factors that may affect an ELL child's performance are not addressed (Gutiérrez-Clellen et al., 1995). Nevertheless, the information from these types of standardized assessments is an important part of the profile of young ELL children's language abilities. However, caution must be exercised when interpreting the scores, and they should be combined with other assessment information to yield a fuller picture of an ELL child's language competencies.

In 2006, the National Literacy Panel on Language-Minority Children and Youth published their report, *Developing Literacy in Second Language Learners* (August & Shanahan, 2006). The report reviewed and synthesized the research literature on the development of literacy in children whose first language is not English, with an emphasis on Spanish speakers who are learning to read in English. While the National Literacy Panel included a handful of studies that focused on kindergarten children and a few that included pre-kindergarten children, the major focus of their meta-analysis was on the elementary grades. The main findings and conclusions of the report, however, are relevant to this review, because some of the studies included children 5 years of age and younger and the research questions focused on assessment are germane to early childhood (see Chapters 19 & 20, pp. 583–624). A summary of the panel's findings on studies that used language and literacy measures follows.

The panel reviewed a series of studies that examined the use of both the English version of the Peabody Picture Vocabulary Test (PPVT-R) (Dunn & Dunn, 1981) and the Spanish version, Test de Vocabulario en Imágenes Peabody *(TVIP-H)* (Dunn, Padilla, Lugo, & Dunn, 1986) with a sample of language-minority children in the United States and Canada and found major technical and conceptual flaws with the test. They identified test bias due to the administration procedure and incomparable norming samples, resulting in scores that underestimated the vocabulary knowledge of Spanish-speaking children. However, other researchers (Geva, Yaghoub-Zadeh, & Schuster, 2000) have found that the PPVT may "appropriately estimate how well language-minority children's recognition of mainstream English vocabulary matches that of native-English-speaking children" (García, McKoon, & August 2006, p. 607). Earlier researchers also found that using the English version of the PPVT with small samples of Spanish-speaking children showed adequate reliability—however, in this study there were no data reported on the status of the Spanish-speakers' English language development (Argulewicz & Abel, 1984).

Thus, given the difficulty of accurately assessing word knowledge in young ELL children and the technical limitations of most commonly used measures of vocabulary, assessors must use caution when using vocabulary as a central indicator of language development for ELL children. In addition, when standardized measures of vocabulary are used, the scores must be interpreted within the context of the child's particular language history and status as well as with an understanding that vocabulary develops differently for bilingual than for monolingual children.

On tests of variables of demonstrated importance to future literacy in the English-speaking monolingual population (National Early Literacy Panel, 2007)—for example, phonological processing, letter naming, rapid letter naming, letter naming fluency, and phonological awareness—some researchers have found that the assessments administered in English were reliable predictors of future reading disabilities in English for ELL children (Chiappe, Siegel, & Wade-Woolley, 2002; Geva et al., 2000). However, others (Jansky, Hoffman, Layton, Sugar, & Davies, 1989) have found that the typical predictors of later disabilities do not work as well with ELL children because their poor scores reflect low English language abilities and not true reading difficulties.

As has been noted above, there have been serious validity concerns raised about the use of standardized measures in assessing ELL children's English proficiency due to norming samples, complexity of language used, and administration procedures. Alternative approaches to the assessment of English oral proficiency such as cloze tests and curriculum-based measures are showing promise but need more research to verify their educational usefulness (García et al., 2006). To compensate for the psychometric weaknesses of current tests of language proficiency and early reading ability within the ELL population, most researchers have recommended that assessors use multiple measures that may include standardized tests and curriculum-embedded assessments in addition to narrative language samples and observation of children's language usage in natural settings (August & Shanahan, 2006; Gutiérrez-Clellen et al., 2006; Neill, 2005). Table 7.1 provides examples of various types of measures that might be used to serve the different purposes of assessment.

TABLE 7.1. Matrix for the Language/Literacy Assessment of Young ELL Children

Purpose for Assessment	Types of Measures/Procedures Recommended
Determination of Language Dominance	Parent/family survey with questions about language usage, interaction patterns, and language proficiency
	Teacher observation of language usage across multiple contexts
	Possibly English language screener (OLDS)
Language Proficiency	Language samples across multiple settings
	Standardized language measures of receptive and productive capacity used cautiously
	Teacher ratings/observations
Language Outcomes	Informal assessments aligned with curriculum goals in language of instruction
	Language narrative samples in home language and English
	Standardized tests in English and home language

Social-Emotional Development

There is a considerable body of research that underscores the critical nature of children's social and emotional development to their long-term school and life success (Raver & Zigler, 1997; Shonkoff & Phillips, 2000; Wentzel & Asher, 1995). This research points to children's ability to positively build relationships with peers and adults as critical to their academic success. Specifically, current research suggests that preschool children who learn to regulate their emotions in prosocial ways and control negative emotions do better in school (McClelland, Morrison, & Holmes, 2000). If young children can pay attention, follow directions, and get along with others, they are more likely to be accepted by their peers and teachers and succeed academically.

Young ELL children who are learning English in an educational setting have a unique set of social-emotional challenges. "Affective Filter" is the term Krashen and Terrell (1983) have used to refer to the constellation of negative emotional and motivational factors that may interfere with a child's ability to learn a second language efficiently. Researchers have found a consistent relation between various forms of anxiety and language proficiency in all situations, formal and informal, with school-age children. This is an important point when considering the role of social-emotional development for young ELL children because their emotional state as well as their social skills can affect their English language acquisition and ultimate school success.

Due to the strong association of multiple family risk factors, for example, poverty, immigrant status, English language fluency, and limited access to mental and physical health services, Latino ELL children might appear to be at greater risk for social and emotional difficulties compared with their White and non-Hispanic peers. However, when Robert Crosnoe (2005) analyzed data from the ECLS-K on kindergarten teachers' ratings of Mexican immigrant children's level of internalizing symptoms (e.g., anxiety, sadness) and externalizing symptoms (e.g., anger, fighting), he found that children from Mexican immigrant families had lower levels of both sets of symptoms than either their White or their African American peers. In essence, the teachers rated the children of Mexican immigrant families at kindergarten entry as more socially and emotionally competent than their peers from similar backgrounds.

Although these young Hispanic children from low-income families did not appear to be disadvantaged in their social-emotional functioning when using the adapted Social Skills Rating Scale (SSRS; Gresham & Elliot, 1990), it does not mean that the instrument is unbiased for young ELL populations. Other studies have raised concerns about the validity of the SSRS for low-income preschoolers from minority backgrounds (Fantuzzo,

Weiss, Atkins, Meyers, & Noone, 1998). The constructs that are assessed in the SSRS as indicators of social competence, for example, social skills (cooperation, assertion, self-control, responsibility) and problem behaviors (externalizing problems, internalizing problems, hyperactivity) may be expressed in quite different patterns across different subgroups of young ELL children. These important, but difficult-to-measure, social competencies are also reciprocally influential with the process of second language acquisition and so may not follow normal developmental trajectories, just as bilingual preschoolers' language development differs in significant ways from that of monolingual English speakers.

Of the nine most common early childhood social-emotional measures (Berry, Bridges, & Zaslow, 2004) only three have Spanish versions (Behavioral Assessment for Children Parent Rating Scale (BASC), Devereux Early Childhood Assessment (DECA), and Social Competence and Behavior Evaluation (SCBE). The BASC appears to be a direct translation with no psychometric information on the Spanish version; the DECA compared the rating scores of bilingual raters to monolingual raters and found their ratings to be comparable; the SCBE Spanish version was back-translated to ensure accuracy of language, and test-retest reliability for the Spanish version was conducted with a sample of 225 children from Florida.

Clearly, there is a need for improved social-emotional assessment measures for young ELL children. Typically, when ELL children are included in large-scale studies, they are rated on English versions of measures that were developed for monolingual populations. The specific cultural (home cultural norms, values, and practices; circumstances of immigration; SES; etc.) and linguistic (quantity and quality of exposure to English schooling and language, stage of second language acquisition) factors that contribute to their social-emotional functioning are rarely considered when making judgments regarding social-emotional development. In addition, we have almost no studies of the predictive validity of the constructs contained in these measures for young ELL children. There may be significant cultural differences in the areas of assertiveness, cooperation, independence, internalizing and externalizing of problems between ELL and non-ELL populations as well as across language groups within the ELL population.

PROMISING NEW DIRECTIONS IN ASSESSMENT MEASURES AND PROCEDURES FOR YOUNG ENGLISH LANGUAGE LEARNERS

A Compendium of Measures for the Assessment of Young ELLs

A useful review of standardized assessment instruments for children ages 3–5 that have English and Spanish versions is in the final stages of completion (A Compendium of Measures for the Assessment of Young English Language Learners, Barrueco et al., 2007). This review provides detailed information about the 18 direct child assessment measures that met their inclusion criteria. The psychometric characteristics as well as the cultural and linguistic strengths/weaknesses are carefully described in the compendium. Of note is the small number of measures that met their criteria for inclusion (18 out of 150). Of the 150 measures identified that were appropriate for the 3–5 age range and that assessed development in language, literacy, or English language, only 36 had been used with young ELL children and only 18 of those met all the inclusion criteria: is available in English and another language, assesses the child directly, is appropriate for the general child population and not just primarily for children with disabilities, was standardized in the last decade, and is administered by teachers, examiners, and/or researchers.

Of these 18 measures, several important findings emerged. To begin with, the most common procedure used in the development of the Spanish versions of the measures reviewed was to translate the items directly from English to Spanish with some attention to cultural and linguistic appropriateness. Only a few measures actually had standardization information for the Spanish versions with Spanish-speaking norming samples—and these were mostly monolingual Spanish-speaking populations from Mexico or other parts of Latin America. A notable exception to this general finding is the Expressive One-Word Picture Vocabulary Test–Spanish-Bilingual Edition (EOWPVT-SBE) (Brownell, 2000). This is a measure of spoken vocabulary in Spanish and English that was normed on a bilingual sample in the United States. The EOWPVT-SBE yields a total vocabulary score that includes both English and Spanish words—the child is given credit if he or she knows words in either language. This approach provides a profile of the child's total vocabulary competence regardless of language; this method is comparable to the conceptual scoring approach described earlier. The Receptive One Word Picture Vocabulary Test–Spanish-Bilingual Edition (ROWPVT-SBE) was developed at the same time and has similar properties.

The Woodcock-Muñoz Language Survey-Revised (WMLS-R) is a comprehensive test of oral language, language comprehension, reading, and writing that assesses English and/or Spanish language proficiency (Alvarado, Ruef, & Schrank, 2005). This is a broad test of language/literacy abilities and yields scores in the following areas: oral language, reading-writing, broad English ability, listening, oral expression, language comprehension, and applied language proficiency. In addition the test yields two cluster scores: total oral language, and total English ability. Each of the subscales can also be administered and scored in Spanish. Although this measure has comparable English and Spanish versions with good psychometric qualities and content equivalence, the standardization for the Spanish version used a monolingual Spanish-speaking sample again drawn mostly from Mexico and other parts of Latin America. This measure appears to be one of the stronger tools for assessing language development of Spanish-speaking ELL children, although the scores for individual children must be interpreted with caution since the standardization sample may not be equivalent to children in the United States who are dual language learners and there may also be sociocultural influences on the scores of individual children.

Several of the measures reviewed in the *compendium* assessed multiple domains of development in addition to language/literacy. For instance, the *Battelle Developmental Inventory 2nd Edition–Spanish version* (BDI-2) includes five domains: adaptive, personal-social, communication, motor, and cognitive (Newborg, 2005). The test authors claim that most of the constructs being assessed are not culture or language specific, so direct translations from English to Spanish were conducted with only minor adaptations on 20 of the 450 items (Barrueco et al., 2007). While this approach produces a weak overall Spanish version with no psychometric information, it is impossible to know if some of the subscales, for example, motor, personal-social, may be more valid for ELL children. As in the more comprehensive academic tests for elementary school children that Abedi reviewed (2002), it is quite likely that certain domains of development that are less language-dependent may be more adequately assessed with existing instruments.

Parents/Families

Some recent research supports the use of parent reports in determining bilingual children's proficiency in each language. One study (Gutierrez-Clellen & Kreiter, 2003) examined the relationships between parents and teachers' ratings of bilingual children's language use and proficiency in the two languages and the child's actual language performance. These researchers found that amount of language input in the home, frequency of use, and parents' estimates of language ability all are highly related to the child's language proficiency. Based on this research, Gutierrez-Clellen developed the Parent Interview form that is featured in Head Start Bulletin (U.S. Department of Health & Human Services, 2005) Issue 78. The questions on the form are designed to elicit critical information about the child's language background and usage that have been found to be highly correlated with language proficiency. In addition, Hammer and Miccio are developing home language and literacy tools as part of the Bilingual Preschoolers: Precursors to Literacy project. This set of instruments will measure the literacy environment in the home, patterns of language usage and parental beliefs and attitudes about language and literacy (Center for Applied Linguistics, 2007). The team is also developing a Parent Demographic Survey—that captures language practices in the home and at school—as well as teacher descriptors. One of the strengths of this research network is its emphasis on cross-study collaboration with annual sharing of findings and common instruments.

SUMMARY AND RECOMMENDATIONS

In summary, teachers, administrators, and researchers who work with young children in early education settings today urgently need to develop effective instructional and assessment approaches that work for young children from linguistically and culturally diverse backgrounds including how best to assess their abilities and learning needs. Accurate assessments that include information on the child's home language fluency and stage of English acquisition are critical to the educational decision-making process. Early childhood professionals at all levels will need to understand the linguistic, cultural, economical, and social diversity within the ELL population.

It is clear that the current assessment strategies, instruments, and procedures have many psychometric and practical limitations to accurately assessing young ELL populations. Despite the many different limitations and/or concerns noted above, there are currently some available assessment measures and procedures that can be carefully utilized to gain a better understanding of the language development of ELL children, even as we wait for the continued development of newer and better ELL assessment measures and measurement strategies.

RECOMMENDATIONS FOR ASSESSMENT PROCEDURES

Based on this review, I offer the following recommendations. To more accurately document young ELL children's language abilities and overall development, assessors should

1. thoroughly review all psychometric/standardization information provided for any standardized test under consideration and, whenever possible, administer only those that have been standardized/normed with samples that are similar to the children being assessed;
2. assess each ELL child in both home language and English repeatedly over time;

3. use multiple measures that may include standardized tests and curriculum-embedded assessments, in addition to narrative language samples and observation of children's language usage in natural settings;
4. use vocabulary test scores with great caution;
5. include the family as important informants on the assessment team; and
6. provide intensive and sustained professional development to all early childhood professionals on effective instructional and assessment strategies for children from diverse backgrounds.

In addition, it is important to comprehensively assess each ELL child's development in other domains, such as social-emotional functioning, early mathematics, motor development, general knowledge, and conceptual understandings. As described above, many ELL children may be highly competent in areas, such as social-emotional functioning, that are difficult to assess. Young ELL children may also have capacities and abilities that are masked by current testing policies that underestimate their knowledge and potential.

RECOMMENDATIONS FOR FUTURE RESEARCH

Several types of research are needed to continue to advance the field when working with and assessing young ELL children. First, a comprehensive review of all the methodologically sound studies conducted within the last 20 years on ELL infants, toddlers, and preschoolers' language development was beyond the scope of this chapter. However, such a review is highly recommended as it would uncover strengths and weaknesses in the extant databases as well as explicit suggestions for instrument development. It could also serve as a companion volume to *Developing Literacy in Second-Language Learners* (August & Shanahan, 2006) to provide a comprehensive profile of ELL children from birth through the elementary grades.

Second, there is an urgent need to develop formal standardized assessment tools with good psychometric qualities to measure both the status of ELL children's home language and English. In particular, more valid measures are needed in the areas of oral language proficiency, vocabulary, syntax, phonology, and functional competence. Inherent in the development of new measures, new developmental norms that reflect typical development for dual language learners across a broad SES spectrum are critically needed. In addition, new assessment tools that are accessible to practitioners and that will help early childhood teachers and support staff to recognize the language competencies of ELL children are essential.

Third, comprehensive longitudinal studies of ELL children that focus on how the sociocultural context of the child's early home life, the inter-relationships among the child's language/culture, and early education influence language development in both languages are critically needed. The ECLS-B may provide insight into these issues if scholars are funded to complete the necessary secondary analyses. Moreover, the key constructs included in the assessment of social-emotional competence need to be the-oretically and empirically validated across different ELL populations.

Fourth, additional research is needed on the developmental trajecto-ries of ELL children in domains that are less language-dependent—for ex-ample, math, motor, and self-help—and to determine the extent to which existing early childhood measures are adequate or need to be restandard-ized for specific populations of ELL children.

Lastly, additional targeted funding for ongoing large-scale national studies such as those currently funded by NCES, NICHD, and IES, could be used to validate existing measures for ELL subpopulations within these larger samples.

Portions of this chapter were adapted from Espinosa, 2008. *A Review of the Literature on Assessment Issues for Young English Language Learners*. Commissioned paper prepared for the NAS Committee on Developmental Outcomes and Assessments for Young Children.

REFERENCES

Abedi, J. (2002). Measuring instructional quality in accountability systems: Class-room assignment and student achievement. *Educational Assessment, 8*(3), 231–257.

Abedi, J., Leon, S., & Mirocha, J. (2001). *Examining ELL and non-ELL student perfor-mance differences and their relationship to background factors: Continued analyses of extant data.* Los Angeles: University of California, National Center for Research on Evaluation, Standards, and Student Testing.

Alvarado, C., Ruef, M., & Schrank, F. (2005). *Woodcock-Muñoz language survey-Revised* [Comprehensive manual]. Itasca, IL: Riverside Publishing.

American Educational Research Association. (1999). *Laws and regulations, current practice, and research relevant to inclusion and accommodations for students with lim-ited English proficiency in the voluntary national tests.* Washington, DC: Author.

American Psychological Association. (1990). *APA guidelines for providers of psycholog-ical services to ethnic, linguistic, and culturally diverse populations.* Boston: Author.

Argulewicz, E. N., & Abel, R. R. (1984). Internal evidence of bias in the PPVT-R for Anglo-American and Mexican-American children. *Journal of School Psychology, 22*(3), 299–303.

August, D., & Shanahan, T. (2006). *Developing literacy in second-language learners. Report of the National Literacy Panel on Language Minority Children and Youth.* Mahwah, NJ: Erlbaum.

Barrueco, S., López, M., Ong, C., & Lozano, P. (2007). *A compendium of measures for the assessment of young English language learners.* Washington, DC: Pew Task Force on Early Childhood Accountability.

Berry, D. J., Bridges, L. J. & Zaslow, M. J. (2004). *Early childhood measures profiles.* Prepared by Child Trends, Washington, DC. Retrieved May 15, 2009, from http://www.childtrends.org/Files//Child_Trends-2004_09_01_FR_ECMeasures.pdf.

Brooks-Gunn, J., & Markman, L. B. (2005). The contributions of parenting to ethnic and racial gaps in school readiness. *The Future of Children, 15*(1), 139–168.

Brownell, R. (2000). *The Expressive One-Word Picture Vocabulary Test—Spanish-Bilingual version* (EOWPVT-SBE). Novato, CA: Academic Therapy.

Center for Applied Linguistics. (2007). *Development of Literacy in Spanish Speakers (DeLSS).* Retrieved May 15, 2009, from http://www.cal.org/delss/resources/measures.html

Chiappe, P., Siegel, L. S., & Wade-Woolley, L. (2002). Linguistic diversity and the development of reading skills: A longitudinal study. *Scientific Studies of Reading, 6*(4), 369–400.

Cowley, J., & Glasgow, C. (1997). *The Renfrew bus story. Language screening by narrative recall.* Wilmington, DE: Centreville School.

Crosnoe, R. (2005). Double disadvantage or signs of resilience: The elementary school contexts of children from Mexican immigrant families. *American Educational Research Journal, 42,* 269–303.

Dale, P. S. (1991). The validity of a parent report measure of vocabulary and syntax at 24 months. *Journal of Speech and Hearing Research, 34,* 565–571.

Duncan, G. J., & Magnuson, K. A. (2005). Can family socioeconomic resources account for racial and ethnic test score gaps? *Future Child, 15*(1), 35–54.

Dunn, L. M., & Dunn, L. M. (1981). *Peabody picture vocabulary test.* Circle Pines, MN: American Guidance Service.

Dunn, L. M., Padilla, E. R., Lugo, D. E., & Dunn, L. M. (1986). *Test de Vocabulario en Imagines Peabody.* Circle Pines, MN: American Guidance Service.

Espinosa, L. (2006). English-language learners as they enter school. In R. Pianta, M. Cox, & K. Snow (Eds.), *School readiness and the transition to kindergarten in the era of accountability* (pp. 175–196). Baltimore: Paul H. Brookes.

Espinosa, L., Laffey, J., & Whittaker, T. (2006). *Language minority children analysis: Focus on technology use. Final report.* Washington, DC: CREST/NCES.

Espinosa, L., & López, M. (2007). *Assessment considerations for young English language learners across different levels of accountability.* Retrieved May 15, 2009, from http://www.pewtrusts.org/uploadedFiles/wwwpewtrustsorg/Reports/Pre-k_education/Assessment%20for%20Young%20ELLs-Pew%208-11-07-Final.pdf

Fantuzzo, J. W., Weiss, A. D., Atkins, M., Meyers, R., & Noone, M. (1998). A contextually relevant assessment of the impact of child maltreatment on the social competencies of low-income urban children. *Journal of the American Academy of Child and Adolescent Psychiatry, 37*(11), 1201–1208.

Farver, J., Nakamoto, J., & Lonigan, C. (2007). Assessing preschoolers emergent literacy skills in English and Spanish with the Get Ready to Read! screening tool. *Annals of Dyslexia, 57*(2), 161–178.

Feldman, H. M., Dollaghan, C. A., Campbell, T. F., Kurs-Lasky, M., Janosky, J. E., & Paradise, J. L. (2000). Measurement properties of the MacArthur Communicative Development Inventories at ages one and two years. *Child Development, 71*(2), 310–322.

Fenson, L., Pethick, S., Renda, C., Dale, P., & Reznick, S. (1998). Normative data for the short form versions of the MacArthur communicative development inventories. *Infant Behavior and Development, 21,* 404–412.

Gandara, P., Rumberger, R., Maxwell-Jolly, J., & Callahan R. (2003). English learners in California schools: Unequal resources, unequal outcomes, *Education Policy Analysis Archives, 11*(36). Retrieved May 15, 2009, from http://epaa.asu.edu/epaa/v11n36/

García, G., McKoon, G., & August, D. (2006). Language and literacy assessment of language-minority students. In D. August & T. Shanahan (Eds.), *Developing literacy in second-language learners: Report of the National Literacy Panel on Language-Minority Children and Youth* (pp. 597–624). Mahwah, NJ: Lawrence Erlbaum.

Genesee, F., Paradis, J., & Crago, M. (2004). *Dual language development and disorders: A handbook on bilingualism and second language learning.* Baltimore: Paul H. Brookes.

Geva, E., Yaghoub-Zadeh, Z., & Schuster, B. (2000). Part IV: Reading and foreign language learning—Understanding individual differences in word recognition skills of ESL children. *Annals of Dyslexia, 50,* 121–154.

Greshman, F., & Elliot, S. (1990). *Social Skills Rating System.* Bloomington, MN: Pearson Assessments.

Gutiérrez-Clellen, V. F. (1998). Syntactic skills of Spanish-speaking children at risk for academic underachievement. *Language, Speech, and Hearing Services in Schools, 29*(4), 207–215.

Gutiérrez-Clellen, V. F. (2002). Narratives in two languages: Assessing performance of bilingual children. *Linguistics and Education, 13,* 175–197.

Gutiérrez-Clellen, V. F., & Kreiter, J. (2003). Understanding child bilingual acquisition using parent and teacher reports. *Applied Psycholinguistics, 24,* 267–288.

Gutiérrez-Clellen, V. F., Peña, E., & Quinn, R. (1995). Accommodating cultural differences in narrative style: A bilingual perspective. *Topics in Language Disorders, 5*(4), 54–67.

Gutiérrez-Clellen, V. F., Restrepo, M. A., & Simon-Cereijido, G. (2006). Evaluating the discriminate accuracy of a grammatical measure with Spanish-speaking children. *Journal of Speech, Language and Hearing Research, 49,* 1209–1223.

Hart, T. R., & Risley, B. M. (1995). *Meaningful differences in the everyday experience of young American children.* Baltimore: Paul H. Brookes.

Jackson-Maldonado, D., Thal, D. J., Fenson, L., Marchman, V. A., Newton, T., & Conboy, B. (2003). *MacArthur Inventarios del Desarrollo de Habilidades Communicatavitivas: Users guide and technical manual.* Baltimore: Paul H. Brookes.

Jansky, J. J., Hoffman, M. J., Layton, J., Sugar, F., & Davies, M. (1989). Prediction: A six year follow-up. *Annals of Dyslexia, 39*(4), 227–246.

Krashen, S., & Terrell, T. (1983). *The natural approach: Language acquisition in the classroom.* New York: Prentice-Hall.

Laing, S. P., & Kamhi, A. (2003). Alternative assessment of language and literacy in culturally and linguistically diverse populations. *Language, Speech, and Hearing Services in Schools, 34,* 44–55.

Lee, V., & Burkam, D. (2002). *Inequality at the starting gate: Social background differences in achievement as children begin school.* Washington, DC: Economic Policy Institute.

Maxwell, K., & Clifford, R. M. (2004). School readiness assessment. *Young Children, 59*(1), 42–46.

McClelland, M. M., Morrison, F. J., & Holmes, D. L. (2000). Children at risk for early academic problems: The role of learning-related social skills. *Early Childhood Research Quarterly, 15*(3), 307–329.

Meisels, S. (2007). Accountability in early childhood: No easy answers. In R. C. Pianta, M. J. Cox, & K. Snow (Eds.), *School readiness, early learning and the transition to kindergarten* (pp. 38–41). Baltimore: Paul H. Brookes.

National Association for the Education of Young Children (NAEYC) & National Association of Early Childhood Specialists in State Departments of Education (NAECS/SDE). (2003). *Early childhood curriculum, assessment, and program evaluation: Building an effective, accountable system in programs for children birth through age 8.* Retrieved May 15, 2009, from http://www.naeyc.org/about/positions/pdf/CAPEexpand.pdf

National Center for Education Statistics (NCES). (2001). *Early childhood longitudinal study, kindergarten class of 1998–99: Base year restricted-use Head Start data files and electronic codebook* (NCES 2000-097). Washington, DC: National Center for Education Statistics.

National Early Literacy Panel. (2007, March). *Findings from the National Early Literacy Panel: Providing a focus for early language and literacy development.* Presentation to the 10th annual National Conference on Family Literacy, Orlando, FL.

Neill, M. (2005). *Assessment of ELL students under NCLB: Problems and solutions.* Paper prepared for the Iowa State Department of Education. Retrieved May 15, 2009, from http://www.fairtest.org/files/NCLB_assessing_bilingual_students_0.pdf

Newborg, J. (2005). *Battelle Developmental Inventory* (2nd ed.). Itasca, IL: Riverside.

Niemeyer, J., & Scott-Little, C. (2001). *Assessing kindergarten children: A compendium of assessment instruments.* Retrieved May 15, 2009, from http://www.serve.org/_downloads/publications/rdakcc.pdf

Pearson, B. Z. (2002). Narrative competence in bilingual children in Miami. In D. K. Oller & R. E. Eilers (Eds.), *Child language and child development* (pp. 135–174). Tonawanda, NY: Multilingual Matters.

Pearson, J. (1988). Word-internal code-switching constraints in a bilingual child's grammar. *Linguistics, 26,* 479–493.

Raver, C. C., & Zigler, E. F. (1997). Social competence: An untapped dimension in evaluating Head Start's success. *Early Childhood Research Quarterly, 12,* 363–385.

Ray, A., Bowman, B., & Robbins, J. (2006). *Preparing early childhood teachers to successfully educate all children* (Foundation for Child Development Policy Report, September 2006). Retrieved May 15, 2009, from http://www.fcd-us.org/resources/resources_show.htm?doc_id = 463599

Reese, E., & Read, S. (2000). Predictive validity of the New Zealand MacArthur communicative development inventory: Words and sentences. *Journal of Child Language, 27*(2), 255–266.

Rumberger, R., & Anguiano, A. (2004). *Understanding and addressing the California Latino achievement gap in early elementary school* (Working paper 2004-01). Santa Barbara: University of California, Santa Barbara.

Scott-Little, C., Kagan, S. L., & Frelow, V. S. (2005). *Inside the content: The breadth and depth of early learning standards.* Greensboro, NC: SERVE.

Shonkoff, J. P., & Phillips, D. A. (Eds.). (2000). *From neurons to neighborhoods: The science of early childhood development.* Washington, DC: National Academy Press.

Tabors, P., Paez, M., & López, L. (June, 2004). *Dual language and literacy development of Spanish-speaking preschool children.* Paper presented at the Head Start Research to Practice Conference, Washington, DC.

U.S. Department of Health & Human Services, Head Start Bureau. (2005). English language learners. *Head Start Bulletin.* Retrieved May 15, 2009, from http://www.headstartinfo.org/publications/hsbulletin78/cont_78.htm

Valdés, G., & Figueroa, R. A. (1994). *Bilingualism and testing: A special case of bias.* Norwood, NJ: Ablex.

Wentzel, K. R., & Asher, S. R. (1995). Academic lives of neglected, rejected, popular, and controversial children. *Child Development, 62,* 1066–1078.

Winsler, A., Diaz, R. M., Espinosa, L., & Rodríguez, J. L. (1999). When learning a second language does not mean losing the first: Bilingual language development in low-income, Spanish-speaking children attending bilingual preschool. *Child Development, 70*(2), 349–362.

Woodcock, R. W., & Muñoz-Sandoval, A. F. (1993). *Comprehensive manual: Woodcock-Muñoz language survey.* Itasca, IL: Riverside.

CHAPTER 8

Classroom Teaching and Instruction "Best Practices" for Young English Language Learners

Linda M. Espinosa

The number of families who speak a language other than English in the home has been steadily increasing during the past 2 decades according to U.S. preschool population demographics, and projections have been carefully described by D. Hernandez (Chapter 2) in this volume. Clearly, early childhood educators are increasingly challenged by diverse groups of learners who are highly vulnerable to low school achievement (Galindo, Chapter 3, this volume), particularly young children who speak a language other than English in the home and who are not fully fluent in English (ELL). As a group, ELL students have struggled to become proficient in English, lagged well behind in terms of academic achievement, and had school dropout rates almost twice those of native English speakers (Genesee, Linholm-Leary, Saunders, & Christian, 2006).

These demographic shifts and achievement trends are important to the early childhood field for multiple reasons: (a) the proportion of the population that enters early education programs speaking a language other than English is increasing and is projected to grow at even greater rates; (b) the educational success of ELL children is critical to the overall effectiveness of our educational system; (c) increased risk factors associated with poorer school performance have been identified within the ELL population—particularly ELL children from low SES homes; and (d) specific educational approaches that are well implemented during the early years of schooling have the potential to improve the academic achievement of a large and growing group of diverse learners.

The confluence of these factors has created an urgent need to design and implement instructional and assessment approaches that ensure ELL students thrive and achieve at high levels. The issue of how to best educate our non-English-speaking preschool children to full English fluency and prepare them for K–12 school success has suffered from the lack of a deep, comprehensive research base. Fortunately, in the past 2 decades there have been advances in neuroscience, rigorous research on dual language development, early childhood program evaluations, and international research on multilingual development that can provide some guidance on best classroom practices for young ELL children. In this Chapter, I review the research on best classroom practices for young ELLs, beginning with an overview of the central issue of early childhood language and literacy development that provides a base for a summary of research on the following topics: program variations such as English immersion, dual language and bilingual classrooms; language of instruction; transfer of literacy skills across languages; quantity of home language relative to English; culturally responsive pedagogy; and specific instructional approaches focusing on language and early literacy. Drawing from this review, I conclude with recommendations for further research.

EARLY CHILDHOOD LANGUAGE AND LITERACY

In the past 2 decades, a considerable body of research has revealed a great deal about which language and literacy skills learned during the early childhood years are associated with later reading success (Dickinson & Neuman, 2006; National Early Literacy Panel, 2007). These skills—for example, alphabetic knowledge, phonological awareness, vocabulary knowledge, book and print concepts—and discourse skills have become important elements of all early childhood classrooms. However, for the most part, the research conducted that identified the impact of these early skills on long-term literacy was conducted on native English-speaking children. The comparable research literature for children whose primary language is not English is much less robust. We are just beginning to understand the complexities of dual language development, the social and cultural influences on first and second language development, the role of first language on second language fluency and achievement, and the impact of different pedagogies on the short- and long-term achievement of ELL children (August & Shanahan, 2006; Bowman, Donovan, & Burns, 2001; García, 2005; Genesee, Paradis, & Crago, 2004; Genesee et al., 2006).

A common thread that unifies the research on ELL children and monolingual English-speaking children is the emphasis on the development of oral language proficiency as a necessary prerequisite for later literacy (Snow, Burns, & Griffin, 1998). For ELL children, the relationships between oral language abilities in their home language (L1), oral language abilities in English (L2), and English reading achievement are not well understood and often debated. However, most researchers agree that oral language proficiency in English is an important foundation for later English literacy and particularly for English reading comprehension (Carlo et al., 2004; Collins, 2008; Tabors, Páez, & López, 2003).

Oral language development is a central goal for almost all early childhood classrooms and has been linked to later measures of conventional literacy (National Early Literacy Panel, 2007). Oral language research has typically focused on vocabulary, grammar, semantics, and occasionally the pragmatics of language usage (Genesee et al., 2006; Genishi, 1998; National Early Literacy Panel, 2007). In early childhood studies of oral language development the most common variables have been measures of children's expressive and receptive vocabulary, definitional vocabulary, grammar, and listening comprehension. Some researchers also include phonological awareness since it involves the ability to hear and distinguish the sounds of language (any language) as part of oral language skills. Emergent literacy skills, while including oral language abilities, also encompass alphabetic knowledge, concepts about print, phonological processing skills, and visual-perceptual skills (National Early literacy Panel, 2007).

SUMMARY OF RESEARCH ON
INSTRUCTIONAL AND CLASSROOM PRACTICES

While there are many influential studies and policy reports that have documented the long-term benefits of well-designed preschool on children's development and achievement (Barnett, 2008), there are very few empirical, experimental, or quasiexperimental studies that comprehensively address the question of how to best teach young ELL children (August & Shanahan, 2006; Espinosa, 2007, 2008; Genesee et al., 2006). An enduring debate for this population has been the role of the child's home language (L1) on the acquisition of English (L2) and high academic achievement in English. As the accountability demands of No Child Left Behind (NCLB) require that all ELL children be assessed annually (beginning in kindergarten) to determine English proficiency levels and that these children show academic progress in English Language Arts and Mathematics beginning in 3rd grade, it is imperative that we know which approaches best achieve these goals. The proliferation of multiple languages in early childhood settings has further complicated the challenges inherent in designing effective instruction for preschool ELL children.

While there are no definitive research studies, there are several recent large-scale research syntheses focused mainly on elementary school students (Genesee et al., 2006; Slavin & Cheung, 2005; Thomas & Collier, 2002), one meta-analysis (Developing Literacy in Second Language Learners: Report of the National Literacy Panel on Language-Minority Children and Youth; August & Shanahan, 2006) and one preschool policy analysis (National Task Force on Early Childhood Education for Hispanics, 2007) have converged on similar conclusions and recommendations for ELL children.

Types of Programs: English-Only, Bilingual, Dual Language

In English-only programs, ELL students are expected to learn English from the beginning and any support for the child's home language is intended to merely help the child cope with an all-English classroom. In these classrooms English is used almost exclusively and most print is also in English. In some English preschool classrooms, ELL children are offered home language support by support staff or through translations, multilingual materials, and active family-involvement practices. However, the primary goal of these programs is the rapid acquisition of English and the attainment of learning expectations in English. In practice, there is much variability in how much support and attention is paid to the home language in English-dominant preschool programs (Chang et al., 2007).

Bilingual programs can be transitional, maintenance of home language, or one-way or two-way dual language bilingual programs. In all bilingual classrooms, instruction is divided between English and the child's home language; however, the goals in a transitional program focus on using the home language to "bridge" into English, while in a two-way dual language program a portion of the students are native English speakers and all participants are expected to become bilingual and biliterate in a second language—for ELL students it is English, and for English-speaking students it is usually Spanish. One-way dual language bilingual programs typically include only ELL students although they share the goals of bilingualism and biliteracy for the ELL participants.

Bilingual programs also differ in the amount of classroom time spent using English and the non-English language for instructional purposes. The two most common approaches are 90-10 and 50-50. In 90-10 models, students receive 90% of their instruction in a language other than English (usually Spanish) and 10% of their instruction in English, initially, while gradually increasing the amount of English over several years. In 50-50 models the classroom time is divided roughly equally between English and the non-English language throughout the duration of the program (Center for Applied Linguistics, 2003).

Currently, it is difficult to determine with any precision the most common type of program model available for preschool ELL children. There are several published studies of carefully implemented dual language programs and a growing literature on English language preschool approaches for ELL children. However, when one reviews the state early childhood standards and the state and national preschool program evaluations, it appears that most programs do not implement a systematic approach to English acquisition with careful attention to home language proficiency and development (Chang et al., 2007; Gormley, Gayer, Phillips, & Dawson, 2005; Love et al., 2004; Rodríguez, Diaz, Duran, & Espinosa, 1995; Winsler, Diaz, Espinosa, & Rodríguez, 1999; Zill et al., 2003).

Language of Instruction Research

The Report of the National Literacy Panel on Language Minority Children and Youth (August & Shanahan, 2006) reports on a meta-analysis of 15 studies that met their inclusion criteria, 13 of which focused on elementary-school-age students. They found that "for all studies, positive effect sizes indicate a difference favoring bilingual education, whereas negative effects indicate a difference favoring English-only instruction" (p. 387). Taken together, these 15 studies found that bilingual education had a small-to-moderate positive effect on English reading outcomes with the largest effect sizes from the studies that were the most scientifically rigorous, that is, had random assignment. Although the panel cautioned the readers that the findings do not identify potentially moderating variables—such as quality of instruction—that most likely are influential in making bilingual instruction maximally effective for all students, they nonetheless conclude,

> English language learners may learn to read best if taught both in their native language and English from early in the process of formal schooling. Rather than confusing children, as some have feared, reading instruction in a familiar language may serve as a bridge to success in English because decoding, sound blending, and generic comprehension strategies clearly transfer between languages that use phonetic orthographies, such as Spanish, French, and English (August, 2002; August & Hakuta, 1997; Fitzgerald, 1995a, 1995b; García, 2000). (August & Shanahan, 2006, p. 397)

This conclusion is important for several reasons: first, the panel included in the meta-analysis only studies that met their rigorous methodological criteria, meaning that the findings have a high degree of validity; second, they specifically focused on the language of instruction, comparing children taught in English-only classes with those taught in bilingual classes; third, they consistently found differences that favored bilingual instruction; fourth, the dependent variables were standardized quantitative measures of English reading and vocabulary; and finally, they attribute the positive findings to cross-language transfer. Other recent large-scale studies of K–12 grades have also found that those ELL students who receive at least 50% of their instruction in their native language for at least 4 years are the most likely of all ELL students to fully reach the 50th percentile on nationally normed achievement tests in both their home language and English in all subjects; they are also the least likely to drop out of high school (Thomas & Collier, 2002).

A recent, smaller randomized control trial comparing the effects of dual language instruction to the effects of English immersion on preschool children's growth in language, emergent literacy, and mathematics also found that a dual language approach "supported stronger Spanish language gains at no expense to English language development in both native English and native Spanish speakers" (Barnett, Yarosz, Thomas, Jung, & Blanco, 2007, p. 290). This study tested preschoolers' language, literacy, and mathematical skills in the fall and again in the spring, testing the ELL children in both Spanish and English. Those children in the dual language program received all instruction in Spanish one week, then all instruction in English the next week, resulting in a 50-50 model; however, there was some support for Spanish in the English immersion program depending on staff ability and child needs. All the ELL children in the dual language program made greater gains in their Spanish vocabulary, while their peers in the English immersion program lost ground in their native language. This study concludes that ELL preschool children in a two-way immersion program can maintain and continue to develop their home language while also acquiring English at the same rate as those in an English-only program.

Two earlier studies that compared a bilingual preschool program to a Spanish-only setting also found that young Spanish speakers gained more cognitively—and could achieve to almost age-appropriate norms in English vocabulary and productive ability, while also continuing to grow in their Spanish language abilities—when they participated in a high-quality 50-50 bilingual preschool program than when they were in a monolingual Spanish setting (Rodríguez et al., 1995; Winsler et al., 1999).

These research conclusions demonstrating the benefits of instruction in English and home language led the National Task Force on Early Childhood Education for Hispanics (2007) to recommend English-plus-Spanish Approaches in Early Childhood Classrooms:

> English-plus-Spanish Education (EPS): EPS refers to a wide range of formal and informal approaches to using both English and Spanish in the classroom. An example of an informal approach would be classrooms in which instruction is mainly in English, but teachers routinely use Spanish extensively to clarify points or ask questions when the students' knowledge of English is too limited for the exchange. Students would also use varying amounts of both English and Spanish in their own conversations in the classrooms. Transitional bilingual education is an example of a common formal approach to EPS education. (p. 40)

Transfer of Early Literacy Skills Across Languages

One of the ongoing debates in the education of ELL students is which language to use during early literacy instruction. Some scholars in this area have suggested that young children will be confused and that their acquisition of English proficiency and literacy skills might be delayed (Chiappe & Siegel, 1999) if they are not instructed in English-only programs from the very beginning or that using L1 is unnecessary or impractical in preschool programs (Lonigan, 2008). Others have argued that skills in the first language will aid in developing skills in the second language (Cummins, 1979; Durgunoglu, 2006; López & Greenfield, 2004). The potential for transfer, that is, the ability to apply one's previous learning to a new skill, is critical when deciding on the language of instruction for ELL children. Many proponents of bilingual education have argued that the correlations across languages on particular language and literacy skills are evidence of transfer from the first language to the second (Durgunoglu, 2006; Durgunoglu, Mir, & Arino-Marti, 2002). Although, as Snow (2006) has pointed out, these cross-linguistic relationships do not prove the transfer hypothesis because they are not causal in nature: "the case remains somewhat circumstantial" (p. 637).

Both theoretical and empirical efforts have focused on the relationships among first language proficiency and literacy skills and second language proficiency and reading achievement (August & Shanahan, 2006; Genesee et al., 2006). Many factors influence whether or not skills learned in one language are transferable to a second language: similarities between the two languages, the specific domain/skills being studied and the assessment methods, the learning conditions and quality of instruction provided, as well as underlying abilities that are not necessarily addressed in the studies. As these are complex processes that interact dynamically across the developmental continuum, Genesee and colleagues (2006) have argued that transfer might better be conceptualized as "preparedness for learning" (p. 161); this new construct would acknowledge the importance of learning in the first language and its potential for "cross-language bootstrapping" (p. 161) while also expanding the research paradigms used to study the construct of transfer.

Recent research on the transfer of preschool literacy skills from Spanish to English has supported the transfer hypothesis as well. Lisa López and her colleagues at Harvard and the University of Miami have conducted a series of studies on Hispanic Head Start children. They found that "oral language skills in Spanish influence phonological awareness in English" (López & Greenfield, 2004, p. 12). Based on their research with 100 Head Start children in the Miami-Dade County Head Start programs, López and Greenfield argued, "Building on a child's language abilities in his or her L1 will not only help the child fully master that language, but provide him or her with the tools to deconstruct the L2. Early development of language skills, such as semantics, syntax, narrative discourse, and morphology, as well as phonological awareness, will provide the child with a 'meta' understanding of language that he or she can apply to language development and literacy skills in the L2" (López & Greenfield, 2004, p. 13).

As stated above, the National Literacy Panel on Language-Minority Children and Youth (August & Shanahan, 2006) concluded that the available evidence supports the transfer of knowledge (or preparedness for learning) from the first language to the second in certain domains: word reading (if both languages have similar orthographies), spelling, vocabulary with the use of cognates, reading comprehension, reading strategies, and some aspects of writing. Additional studies reviewed for this chapter that focused specifically on the transfer of phonological processing skills between Spanish and English among school-age children also reported evidence of cross-linguistic transfer (Leafsted & Gerber, 2005; Oller & Eilers, 2002). At the very least, ELLs appear to draw on their skills and knowledge in L1 to develop complementary literacy skills in L2. Studies have revealed that some L1 emergent literacy proficiencies are highly influential in L2 (English) literacy development (Genesee et al., 2006).

The conclusions from these studies suggest that young children may gain important metalinguistic skills from learning more than one language, that they are quite capable of learning early literacy and language skills in two languages, and that many early language and literacy skills learned in (L1) Spanish contributed positively to the development of English language and literacy. The children who were taught in English-only classrooms or transitioned to English instruction before they demonstrated well-established oral language abilities in their own language and had achieved some degree of English oral proficiency did not fare as well as those who had the opportunity to learn through two languages (Slavin & Cheung, 2005; Thomas & Collier, 2002).

The National Task Force on Early Childhood Education for Hispanics (2007) recently issued the report *Para Nuestros Niños: Expanding and Improving Early Education for Hispanics,* that outlines an ambitious public policy agenda for state governments, the federal government, private foundations, Hispanic organizations, and educational researchers. The task force has focused on identifying strategies that for which there exists empirical evidence of improving educational outcomes for Hispanics in infant/toddler, preschool, and K–3 programs. After a thorough discussion of the composition and school achievement patterns of Hispanic youngsters, the report recommends multiple strategies to accelerate progress for Spanish-speaking English language learners. In addition to recommending that all states need to greatly expand Hispanic access to high-quality pre-K, the task force stated clearly that one of the primary strategies to promote language development for Hispanic Spanish-speaking children is to provide English-plus-Spanish (EPS) education rather than English-only instruction (see definition above).

While this report did not specify the recommended amount of English versus Spanish, it did conclude that "the weight of the evidence now strongly favors EPS over English-only strategies" (National Task Force on Early Childhood Education for Hispanics, 2007, p. 40). In addition, this task force concurred with the other national evaluations of the impact of English versus Spanish instruction on English reading achievement (see Slavin & Cheung, 2005, and Thomas & Collier, 2002), but they could not recommend which specific bilingual approach, transitional or dual-language, would work best with which students. In part, this is due to inadequate evaluation evidence about EPS approaches and, in part, due to the inherent variability of the Hispanic ELL population. A common underlying feature of Hispanic ELL children is the Spanish language; however, the amount of rich language exposure to Spanish, the amount of exposure to English, the extent of their early literacy learning opportunities, their socioeconomic status and, thus, the family resources available to the child and the timing and circumstances of their immigration to the United States can all vary widely and influence the effectiveness of any particular classroom practice (Espinosa, Castro, Crawford, & Gillanders, 2007).

A related question remains under this topic: At what age/developmental level should English be introduced to ELL children? There is considerable evidence that very young infants who are exposed to two languages (simultaneous bilinguals), in fact, reached their early language milestones at age-appropriate times and that early bilingual language exposure did not cause significant delay to the rate and growth of their vocabulary development in either language (see Genesee, this volume; Petito et al., 2001). When infants have sufficient opportunities to learn both languages, they are fully capable of "different but parallel acquisition of two languages from the very onset of language production" (Petito et al., 2001, p. 493). In fact, recent research suggests "that the development of two languages benefits the brain through the development of greater brain tissue density in areas related to language, memory, and attention. Young children learning two languages also have more neural activity in the parts of the brain associated with language processing" (Espinosa, 2008, p. 4). The children are not confused or delayed by dual language environments, which suggests that a second language can be introduced during the pre-K years—especially if the intent is to foster dual language fluency. Chapter 5 by J. Náñez also discusses in detail the research on early bilingualism including recent studies using sophisticated neuroimaging methods.

The danger in introducing English too early has been studied extensively by Lily Wong Fillmore (see Wong Fillmore, 1991, 1996; Wong Fillmore & Snow, 2000). Her analysis concludes:

> An early English-only focus is not necessarily better here. It is true that children in the preschool years can learn a language quickly and with little apparent effort. These are the years of rapid language development and children can acquire a language in a year or two simply by being in a setting where the language is in daily use. However, it is equally true that languages can be lost with equal ease during this period, especially when the language they are learning is more highly valued than the language they already speak. Over the years, I have tracked many young children who, as soon as they learn a little English in the school, put aside the language they already know and speak, and choose to communicate exclusively in English, even at home with family members who do not speak or understand much English. (Wong Fillmore, 1991, p. 337)

Wong Fillmore then goes on to describe the negative consequences when children stop speaking the language of the family: reduced communication, new family tensions, misunderstandings, and sometimes a breakdown of family functioning. This research emphasizes the dangers of introducing English too early because it may lead to loss of the child's home language. Combining this perspective with the evidence that two languages can benefit young children, it suggests that when introducing preschool-age ELL children to English, care must be taken to support ongoing development of the home language while promoting English language acquisition.

How Much Home Language (L1) Instruction?

While there is a small, but growing body of research on the impact of dual language versus English-immersion approaches during the early years, there are very few empirical studies that can offer guidance on how much L1 should be spoken, represented, and emphasized in the preschool classroom when the primary goal is to promote English proficiency and English literacy. Teachers must grapple with the daily challenges of which language to use during which parts of the day and how long to support the child's home language when the child appears to be moving toward fluency in English. Moreover, many programs lack the personnel and/or the resources to fully implement dual language approaches.

A recent study by researchers at the Frank Porter Graham Center at the University of North Carolina (Chang et al., 2007) sheds some light on the question of the impact of English-only versus some support for the child's home language (Spanish). This study examined the relationship between language interactions and Spanish-speaking pre-kindergarten children's social and language development. The children studied and the data examined were from two large-scale studies of state-funded pre-kindergarten programs across 11 states and included more than 700 schools/centers and 345 Spanish-speaking children. The researchers recorded the quantity and quality of language interactions in addition to the language in which the interaction occurred. Over the course of 1 pre-K school year, these Spanish-dominant children received less than 20% (17.3%) of their language interactions with teachers in Spanish, and less than one-quarter (23%) of the children received some interactions in Spanish. The teachers in these classrooms used English two-thirds of the time when they were addressing a Spanish-speaking child; however, Spanish-speaking teachers had significantly more interactions with Spanish speaking children and they tended to have more elaborate conversations.

The amount of Spanish spoken was significantly related to teachers' ratings of children's social competence: the less a child experienced Spanish, the higher he or she was rated on having conduct and learning problems and the lower the child was rated on frustration tolerance. Teachers' perceptions of their relationships with Spanish-speaking children also varied according to the language used in interactions. Spanish-speaking teachers not only spoke more frequently to Spanish-speaking children, they also rated their relationships with these children as closer than teachers who spoke less Spanish. Those teachers who spoke the least amount of Spanish described their relationships with Spanish-speaking children as having more conflict and the children as having more problem behaviors. Neither the amount of Spanish spoken nor the amount of English spoken was related to children's English proficiency. The authors conclude that an English-only approach in early childhood programs is not in the best interests of English language learners and may fuel the achievement gap between different racial, ethnic, and socioeconomic groups rather than reduce the gap.

While this study does not explicitly address the question of how much home language needs to be spoken to ELL children, it clearly reveals that using only English in pre-K classrooms with ELL children affects their opportunities to have rich language interactions and close relationships with their teachers. Other researchers (Pearson, 2001) have found that in order for young children to develop proficiency in any language, they need to use it at least 25% of the time. If we combine the results of the research available, it is plausible to infer that young ELL children need at least 25% of their language interactions and instruction in English to develop English proficiency and 25% in their home language to develop academic mastery in both languages. It is difficult to specify with any accuracy how much of the remaining time should be devoted to which language.

CULTURALLY RESPONSIVE PEDAGOGY

Culturally Responsive Curriculum

A culturally responsive approach includes the students' personal histories, languages, early experiences, and values in classroom activities and instruction that are consistent with the students' family cultures and include academic content (Espinosa & Burns, 2003).

Developmental literature informs us that cultural groups vary with respect to how they socialize their children and that these cultural patterns are very influential in how children respond to and approach specific learning tasks (García, 1991; McNaughton, 2006). There are many definitions of culture; this author views culture as the behavior, values, beliefs, attitudes, and other meaningful systems created and transmitted by a group of people (Goldenberg, Rueda, & August, 2006). Different cultural groups have different expectations and norms for language use and social interaction of their young children. Whether or not children are considered as appropriate conversational partners and engage in, initiate, and sustain interactions with adults can vary greatly among cultures (Genesee et al., 2004). For ELL children from minority households, these variations in cultural values and norms may create a cultural discontinuity between home and school. Some researchers have suggested that this discontinuity creates a vulnerability for children and puts them at greater risk for poor educational outcomes (García, 2005). The question posed here is whether designing and implementing a culturally responsive curriculum has been linked to higher academic achievement and better school outcomes.

Most researchers in this area have advocated for a school curriculum that recognizes and incorporates the cultural and linguistic knowledge that children bring to school with them (Barrera & Jimenez, 2002; Duke & Purcell-Gates, 2003; García, 2002). To some extent, this concept mirrors what John Bransford and his colleagues have identified as a major principle of effective teaching—build on what the child knows (Bransford, Brown, & Cocking, 2000). In a seminal work on the optimal conditions to foster learning, Bransford proposes three principles of learning: (a) engage prior understanding, (b) integrate factual knowledge with conceptual frameworks, and (c) take active control over the learning process. The first principle is roughly analogous to designing a culturally responsive curriculum that builds new understandings on existing knowledge and prior experiences. This also mirrors an axiom of early childhood education: start where the child is and build new concepts from prior knowledge—make it culturally relevant!

Judith Bernhard and her colleagues have designed and evaluated an early literacy intervention for preschool/primary ELL children that is based on these principles. The intervention, the Early Authors Program (EAP) is an approach to early literacy that links the child's home culture (e.g., the important people, customs, and linguistic patterns of the home) with early reading and writing activities (Bernhard et al., 2006). It was designed and tested on over 1,000 children in Miami-Dade County. The children collaborated with family members, friends, caregivers, and teachers to create "identity texts" in which the children themselves were the main characters. By talking about, writing about, reading about, and publicly sharing their personal life histories, the children, authors believed, would develop self-pride, create a positive orientation to literacy, and create meaningful and engaging text. On two standardized measures of language and literacy, the experimental group (a) increased their absolute language skills more than the controls and (b) did not fall further behind in comparison with national age norms—in fact the children in the EAP intervention moved from the "37th percentile nationally to the 46th percentile on language comprehension" (Bernhard et al., 2006, p. 2397).

One of the most well-known studies on this topic is the research on the Kamehameha Early Education Project (KEEP) in Hawaii (Au, 1993; Au & Mason, 1981, 1983). Au and Mason found that when classroom instructional activities reflected the interactional patterns of Hawaiian native children's native culture, the students benefited and demonstrated much higher achievement-related behaviors. When primary grade students were permitted to interact in less restricted ways that were more similar to home patterns (e.g., not waiting to be called on—overlapping speech, students' selection of when to speak), they were more engaged, generated more responses on topic, and made correct logical inferences during reading lessons. These achievement-related behaviors were viewed as important to higher levels of academic achievement by the authors. When Tharp (1982) evaluated the program's impact on reading achievement, he found a positive, but modest, effect on reading. The National Literacy Panel on Language Minority Children and Youth concludes that although there is not much well-designed research on this topic, "the positive effect of accommodative instruction on literacy attainment therefore remains a highly plausible hypothesis" (August & Shanahan, 2006, p. 275).

Theoretically and empirically, there is evidence (although not a lot of it) that ELL children benefit when schools systematically build connections to children's home language, literacy, and social patterns of behavior. By knowing how the family is socializing the child, what aspirations the parents have for the child, common styles of interaction, and family values and customs, the program staff can design instructional activities that capitalize on and extend the strengths and abilities of ELL children.

Specific Instructional Approaches Including
Explicit Teaching of Literacy Skills and Vocabulary

The National Literacy Panel on Language Minority Children and Youth Report (August & Shanahan, 2006) found only 17 studies addressing the effects of explicitly teaching literacy skills for ELLs; this compares with over 400 studies included in the National Reading Panel on this topic for English speakers. They reviewed two studies that examined fluency instruction with ELL students in grades 1 through 3. Similar to the findings with English speakers, ELL students benefited by direct instruction in fluency—however it was mainly related to their oral reading fluency and not their reading comprehension. In grades 1 through 3, ELL students appeared to learn vocabulary words more proficiently when they were presented in meaningful narratives, used in their own writing, and processed at a deeper level. Six studies examined the effects of direct comprehension instruction on reading comprehension with no measurable improvement. They conclude:

> Phonics shows students how to decode, which helps them as long as the words they are trying to decode are in their oral language. English language learners may lack oral counterparts for the words they decode; under such circumstances, the impact of phonics on text comprehension will be more variable and less certain. (August & Shanahan, 2006, p. 436)

After reviewing all of the studies that met their inclusion criteria for reading outcomes, the panel concluded:

> Although language minority students and their native speaking peers perform at similar levels on measures of phonological processing and word reading, their performance on measures of comprehension falls far below their native-speaking peers. . . . It is evident that we can enhance the literacy development of English language learners with better instruction. . . . To provide maximum benefit to language minority students, instruction must do more than develop a complex array of reading skills; these instructional approaches typically had smaller effect sizes with language minority students than with first language learners. This means that providing high quality instruction in these skills alone would be insufficient to support equal academic success for language minority students. (August & Shanahan, 2006, pp. 447–448)

The amount and quality of research on preschool instructional approaches for ELL children is similarly restricted. Although the National Early Literacy Panel that focused on native English speakers had more than 1,700 studies to review of which more than 300 met their inclusion criteria, the number of experimental studies examining the effectiveness of different curriculum models on school achievement of preschool ELLs is dramatically smaller.

Lonigan and his colleagues have recently completed a study of the development of literacy skills of preschool ELL children from lower SES backgrounds (Lonigan & Farver, 2008). This study examined the relationships between measures of language, phonological awareness, and print knowledge in preschool, kindergarten, and 1st grade in both Spanish and English. For the 185 Head Start children in this study, phonological awareness predicted later reading skills, skills measured in Spanish and English overlapped, and emergent literacy skills predicted later reading abilities. When testing the effectiveness of an emergent literacy intervention on ELL children's literacy skills (Farver, Lonigan, & Epps, 2009), these same researchers found that ELL children could achieve English language outcomes in the average range after a 21-week intervention. The intervention included small group activities focused on oral language, phonological awareness, and print knowledge in either English-only or a Spanish-English transitional group. The English outcomes were assessed using the Preschool-CTOPP, which has subtests for receptive and definitional vocabulary, phonological awareness, and print knowledge (Lonigan, 2008). This study did not find evidence for English-to-Spanish transfer of emergent literacy skills, that is, those taught in English-only did not show increased Spanish language emergent literacy skills, however, the authors did not study the potential for Spanish-to-English transfer of skills. The authors recommend that interventions for young ELL children rely on evidence-based practices, individualize instruction through small groups, include active participation by children, and are implemented by teachers who are competent in the language of instruction (Lonigan, 2008).

Collins has conducted a series of studies examining the specific teaching practices that promote sophisticated vocabulary learning by preschool ELL children (Collins, 2008). In these studies, 70 Portuguese-speaking preschool children were assessed on their knowledge of vocabulary words after 4 weeks of highly skilled storybook reading. Target vocabulary outcome measures included 21 nouns, 24 verbs, and 11 adjectives from the books that were read. The results indicated that those children who received book reading combined with elaborations of word meanings made highly significant gains over the children in the control group, which were read the same books but without the elaborations (Collins, 2008). This researcher recommends these specific storybook reading strategies to promote English vocabulary learning for preschool ELL children: provide definitions and synonyms, point to the word and picture in the book, use gestures to reinforce meanings, provide assistance with comprehension, and provide frequent exposure (Collins, 2008). These studies offer some guidance on how to make specific book reading adaptations that promote English vocabulary learning for ELL preschoolers.

The Center for Research on Education, Diversity & Excellence (CREDE) has recently published a synthesis of the research on language, literacy, and academic achievement for ELL students, pre-K to grade 12 in the United States (Genesee et al., 2006). Although almost all of the reports and articles included in the final synthesis focused on K–12 students, many of the findings from the early primary studies are relevant to this chapter. These authors recommend "instruction that combines interactive and direct approaches" (p. 140) but also caution against overreliance on any one set of conclusions because of the fragmented and limited nature of the research. Their review of the literature points to direct instruction on specific early literacy skills, such as word-level and text-level language skills, embedded within interactive learning environments that are meaningful and contextualized to the students' background as being the most effective (Genesee et al., 2006).

In general, many of the findings for native English speakers also apply to ELL children—however, curricular adaptations must be made. Reading books aloud to children is important for later literacy for all children (National Early Literacy Panel, 2007); the procedures used may need to be adjusted for ELL children. For instance, the Nuestros Niños Early Language & Literacy Program developed in North Carolina has suggested the following practices for Spanish-speaking preschoolers:

1. Engage the children in prereading activities that identify key words and phrases that are key to understanding the text; help the ELL children learn the key vocabulary by translating into Spanish and by using multisensory materials to illustrate the book meaning.
2. Use good book-reading strategies including dialogic reading practices that prompt the children to interact and respond to the story. While interacting with the children during reading, the teacher will also need to consider which stage of English acquisition the child is in and adapt expectations accordingly.
3. After reading books to children, provide opportunities for using the core vocabulary in the same book and related extension activities (Castro, Gillanders, Machado-Casas, & Buysse, 2006).

In summary, the research on ELL achievement during the preschool years suggests that recommended instruction is similar to good instruction for English-speaking children. High-quality instruction for all students also benefits ELL students. Like their English-speaking peers, ELL students benefit from active engagement, small group interactions, opportunities to practice and apply new information, frequent reviews and practice, and direct instruction on certain aspects of literacy. The evidence underscores the need to provide special attention to English vocabulary and English oral-language development for ELL children. The research also indicates that ELL students need instructional accommodations to keep pace with their native-English-speaking peers. Goldenberg (2006) has recommended the following instructional supports for ELL students based on his review of three national data sets:

1. strategic use of the primary language
2. consistent expectations, instruction, and routines
3. extended explanations and opportunities for practice
4. physical gestures and visual cues
5. focusing on the similarities/differences (cognates) between English and home language
6. build on home language (L1) language skills
7. target vocabulary and check comprehension frequently
8. paraphrase students' language and encourage them to expand

RECOMMENDED FUTURE RESEARCH

While the extant research and policy reports based on empirical research offer some guidance on the most effective instructional practices for young ELL children, there is a tremendous amount we do not yet know. For instance, the vast majority of the studies discussed in this chapter and included in the reports reviewed focus on the development of Spanish-speaking ELL children. While there are a few studies that have examined the language and literacy development of Asian-American ELL children (Jia, 2008), we know very little about exactly how the features of different home languages influence the acquisition of English. Most researchers would agree that when two languages have similar orthographies and phonologies, the potential for positive cross-language transfer is greater. Although the majority of ELL children have Spanish as their first language, the number and proportion of young ELL children who speak Asian, Middle Eastern, and European languages is growing and needs increased attention from the research community.

In order to provide widespread and practical guidance on effective teaching and successful learning for preschool ELL children, large-scale, sustained research that is conducted longitudinally across settings and populations is urgently needed. We need research that advances our theoretical understanding of how the features of the child's L1 and his or her level of proficiency in that language influence the acquisition of English oral abilities during the preschool years as well as future school achievement. As these processes are complex and dynamic and are influenced by many out-of-school variables, it will most likely mean a wide array of "best practices" for young ELLs.

Specifically, we need additional research that addresses

1. The role of L1 in English acquisition and school achievement. (We also need to better understand the processes that account for the loss of L1 and the consequences of home language loss on future achievement and social participation.)
2. Language of instruction. (How do entering characteristics of ELL children, that is, family SES, amount of exposure to English, language spoken at home, and home language proficiency, influence effectiveness of various language models?)
3. Possible threshold effects. (Are there thresholds for oral language proficiency in L1 and/or L2 necessary for English language and literacy instruction?)
4. Language balance. (Is there an ideal balance of English and home language in preschool settings and, if so, for which children?)
5. Instructional strategies. (Do the same oral language and early skills important for monolingual English-speaking preschoolers predict later achievement for ELL children?)
   a. Can ECE curricula be adapted to be equally effective for all ELL children?
   b. How can we achieve fidelity of program model for preschool teachers of ELLs?
6. Technology. (How can technology be used to promote preschool dual language development and English achievement?

Portions of this chapter were adapted from Espinosa et al., 2007. *Early school success for English language learners: A review of evidence-based instructional practices for pre-K to Grade 3.*

REFERENCES

Au, K. H. (1993). *Literacy instruction in multicultural settings*. New York: Harcourt Brace.

Au, K., & Mason, J. (1981). Social organization factors in learning to read: The balance of rights hypothesis. *Reading Research Quarterly, 17*(1), 115–152.

Au, K., & Mason, J. (1983). Cultural congruence in classroom participation structures: Achieving a balance of rights. *Discourse Processes, 6*(2), 145–167.

August, D. (2002). *Transitional programs for English language learners: Contextual factors and effective programming*. Baltimore: Center for Research on the Education of Students Placed at Risk.

August, D., & Hakuta, K. (Eds.). (1997). *Improving schooling for language-minority children: A research agenda.* Washington, DC: National Academy Press.

August, D., & Shanahan, T. (2006). *Developing literacy in second-language learners. Report of the National Literacy Panel on Language Minority Children and Youth.* Mahwah, NJ: Erlbaum.

Barnett, W. S. (2008). *Preschool education and its lasting effects: Research and policy implications.* Boulder, CO: Education and the Public Interest Center & Tempe, AZ: Education Policy Research Unit. Retrieved April 29, 2009, from http://epicpolicy.org/publication/preschooleducation

Barnett, W. S., Yarosz, D. J., Thomas, J., Jung, K., & Blanco, D. (2007). Two-way and monolingual English immersion in preschool education: An experimental comparison. *Early Childhood Research Quarterly, 22*(3), 277–293.

Barrera, R., & Jimenez, R. (2002). *The role of literacy in culturally and linguistically diverse student learning.* Washington, DC: National Clearinghouse on Bilingual Education, George Washington University.

Bernhard, J. K., Cummins, J., Campoy, F. I., Ada, A. F., Winsler, A., & Bleiker, C. (2006). Identity texts and literacy development among preschool English language learners: Enhancing learning opportunities for children at risk for learning disabilities. *Teachers College Record, 108*(11), 2380–2405.

Bowman, B. T., Donovan, M. S., & Burns, M. S. (Eds.). (2001). *Eager to learn: Educating our preschoolers.* Washington, DC: National Research Council.

Bransford, J. D., Brown, A. L., & Cocking, R. R. (Eds.). (2000). *How people learn: Brain, mind, experience, and school* (expanded ed.). Washington, DC: National Academy of Sciences.

Carlo, M. S., August, D., McLaughlin, B., Snow, C. E., Dressler, C., Lippman, D., et al. (2004). Closing the gap: Addressing the vocabulary needs of English language learners in bilingual and mainstream classrooms. *Reading Research Quarterly, 39*(2), 188–215.

Castro, D. C., Gillanders, C., Machado-Casas, M., & Buysse, V. (2006). *Nuestros Niños Early Language and Literacy Program.* Chapel Hill: Frank Porter Graham Child Development Institute, University of North Carolina, Chapel Hill.

Center for Applied Linguistics. (2003, January). A national study of school effectiveness for language minority students' long-term academic achievement. *Online Research Brief #10.* Retrieved May 13, 2008, from http://www.cal.org/resources/digest/ResBrief10.html

Chang, F., Crawford, G., Early, D., Bryant, D., Howes, C., Burchinal, M. et al. (2007). Spanish-speaking children's social and language development in prekindergarten classrooms. *Early Education and Development, 18*(2), 243–269.

Chiappe, P., & Siegel, L. S. (1999). Phonological awareness and reading acquisition in English- and Punjabi-speaking Canadian children. *Journal of Educational Psychology, 91*(1), 20–28.

Collins, M. F. (2008, February). *The imperative for rich vocabulary development in preschool: Why we cannot wait.* Presentation to the CPIN Regional Networking Meeting, Los Angeles County Office of Education.

Cummins, J. (1979). Linguistic interdependence and the educational development of bilingual children. *Review of Educational Research, 49*(2), 222–251.

Dickinson, D., & Neuman, S. (Eds.). (2006). *Handbook for early literacy research* (Vol. 2). New York: Guilford.

Duke, N. K., & Purcell-Gates, V. (2003). Genres at home and at school: Bridging the known to the new. *Reading Teacher, 57*(1), 30–37.

Durgunoglu, A. Y. (2006). How the language's characteristics influence Turkish literacy development. In M. Joshi & P. G. Aaron (Eds.), *Handbook of orthography and literacy* (pp. 219–230). Mahwah, NJ: Erlbaum.

Durgunoglu, A. Y., Mir, M., & Arino-Marti, S. (2002). The relationship between bilingual children's reading and writing in their two languages. In S. Ransdell & M. L. Barbier (Eds.), *Psycholinguistic approaches to understanding second-language writing* (pp. 81–100). Dordrecht, Netherlands: Kluwer.

Espinosa, L. (2007). English language learners as they enter school. In R. Pianta, M. Cox, & K. Snow (Eds.), *School readiness and the transition to kindergarten in the era of accountability* (pp. 175–196). Baltimore: Paul H. Brookes.

Espinosa, L. (2008). Challenging common myths about young English language learners. *Foundation for Child Development Policy Brief, No. 8.* Retrieved May 19, 2009, from http://www.fcd-us.org/usr_doc/MythsOfTeachingELLsEspinosa.pdf

Espinosa, L. M., & Burns, M. S. (2003). Early literacy for young children and English-language learners. In C. Howes (Ed.), *Teaching 4- to 8-year-olds: Literacy, math, multiculturalism, and classroom community.* Baltimore, MD: Paul H. Brookes.

Espinosa, L., Castro, D. C., Crawford, G., & Gillanders, C. (2007, May). *Early school success for English language learners: A review of evidence-based instructional practices for preK to grade three.* Paper presented at the First School Symposium, Early School Success: Equity and Access for Diverse Learners, Chapel Hill, NC.

Farver, J. M., Lonigan, C. J., & Epps, S. (2009, May-June). Effective early literacy skill development for young English language learners: An experimental study of two methods. *Child Development, 80*(3), 703–719.

Fitzgerald, J. (1995a). English-as-a-second-language reading instruction in the United States: A research review. *Journal of Reading Behavior, 27*(2), 115–152.

Fitzgerald, J. (1995b). English-as-a-second-language learners' cognitive reading processes: A review of research in the United States. *Review of Educational Research, 65*(2), 145–190.

García, E. E. (1991). Caring for infants in a bilingual child care setting. *Journal of Education Issues of Language Minority Students, 9,* 1–10.

García. E. E. (2000). Treating linguistic and cultural linguistic and cultural diversity as a resource: The research response to the challenges inherent in the Improving America's School Act and California's Proposition 227. In R. D. González and I. Melis (Eds.), *Language ideologies* (pp. 90–113). Mahwah, NJ: Erlbaum.

García, E. E. (2002). Bilingualism and schooling in the United States. *International Journal of the Sociology of Language, 134*(1), 1–123.

García, E. E. (2005). *Teaching and learning in two languages: Bilingualism and schooling in the United States.* New York: Teachers College Press.

Genesee, F., Lindholm-Leary, K., Saunders, W. M., & Christian, D. (2006). *Educating English language learners: A synthesis of research evidence.* New York: Cambridge University Press.

Genesee, F., Paradis, J., & Crago, M. B. (2004). *Dual language development and disorders: A handbook on bilingualism and second language learning.* Baltimore: Paul H. Brookes.

Genishi, C. (1998). *Young children's oral language development* [ERIC Digest No. ED301361]. ERIC Clearinghouse on Elementary and Early Childhood Education.

Goldenberg, C. (2006). Improving achievement for English learners: What research tells us. *Education Week, 25*(43), 34–36.

Goldenberg, C., Rueda, R. S., & August, D. (2006). Social and cultural influences on the literacy attainment of language-minority children and youth. In D. August & T. Shanahan (Eds.), *Developing literacy in second-language learners: Report of the national literacy panel on language minority children and youth* (pp. 269–318). Mahwah, NJ: Lawrence Erlbaum.

Gormley, W., Gayer, T., Phillips, D., & Dawson, B. (2005). The effects of universal pre-K on cognitive development. *Developmental Psychology, 41*(6), 872–884.

Jia, G. (2008). Heritage language development, maintenance, and attrition among recent Chinese immigrants in New York City. In A. W. He & Y. Xiao (Eds.), *Chinese as a heritage language: Fostering rooted world citizenry* (pp. 189–203). Honolulu: University of Hawaii, National Foreign Language Resource Center.

Leafsted, J., & Gerber, M. (2005). Crossover of phonological skills: A study of Spanish speaking students in two instructional settings. *Remedial and Special Education, 26*(4), 226–235.

Lonigan, C. J. (2008, February). *Early literacy skills in Spanish-speaking ELL preschool children.* Presentation made to the Region 9 CPIN Networking Meeting, Los Angeles.

Lonigan, C. J., & Farver, J. M. (2008, July). *Development of reading and reading-related skills in preschoolers who are Spanish-speaking English language learners.* Paper presented at the annual meeting of the Scientific Study of Reading, Asheville, NC.

López, L. M., & Greenfield, D. B. (2004). Cross-language transfer of phonological skills of Hispanic Head Start children. *Bilingual Research Journal, 28*(1), 1–18.

Love, J. M., Kisker, E. E., Ross, C. M., Schochet, P. Z., Brooks-Gunn, J., & Pausell, D. (2004). *Early Head Start research: Making a difference in the lives of infants and toddlers and their families—The impact of Early Head Start* (Vol. 1: Final Technical Report). Retrieved May 13, 2008, from http://www.mathematica-mpr.com/earlycare/ehstoc.asp

McNaughton, S. (2006). Considering culture in research-based interventions to support literacy. In D. Dickinson & S. Neuman (Eds.), *Handbook of early literacy research* (Vol. 2, pp. 229–240). New York: Guilford Press.

National Early Literacy Panel. (2007, March). *Findings from the National Early Literacy Panel: Providing a focus for early language and literacy development.* Presentation to the 10th annual National Conference on Family Literacy, Orlando, FL.

National Task Force on Early Childhood Education for Hispanics. (2007). *Para nuestros niños: Expanding and improving early education for Hispanics* [Main report]. Tempe: Arizona State University.

Oller, K. D., & Eilers, R. E. (Eds.). (2002). *Language and literacy in bilingual children.* Clevedon, UK: Multilingual Matters.

Pearson, B. Z. (2001). Narrative competence in bilingual children in Miami. In D. K. Oller & R. E. Eilers (Eds.), *Language and literacy development in bilingual children* (pp. 135–174). Clevedon, UK: Multilingual Matters.

Petito, L. A., Katerelos, M., Levy, B. G., Guana, K., Tetreault, K., & Ferraro, V. (2001). Bilingual signed and spoken language acquisition from birth. *Journal of Child Language, 28,* 453–496.

Rodríguez, J. L., Diaz, R. M., Duran, D., & Espinosa, L. (1995). The impact of bilingual preschool education of the language development of Spanish-speaking children. *Early Childhood Research Quarterly, 10*(4), 475–490.

Slavin, R. E., & Cheung, A. (2005). A synthesis of research on language of reading instruction for English language learners. *Review of Educational Research, 75*(2), 247–281.

Snow, C. (2006). Cross-cutting themes and future research directions. In D. August & T. Shanahan (Eds.), *Developing literacy in second language learners: Report of the National Literacy Panel on language-minority children and youth* (pp. 631–651). Mahwah, NJ: Erlbaum.

Snow, C. E., Burns, M. S., & Griffin, P. (Eds.). (1998). *Preventing reading difficulties in young children.* Washington, DC: National Academy Press.

Tabors, P., Páez, M., & López, L. (2003). Dual language abilities of bilingual four-year-olds: Initial findings from the early childhood study of language and literacy development of Spanish-speaking children. *NABE Journal of Research and Practice* (Winter), 70–91.

Tharp, R. G. (1982). The effective instruction of comprehension: Results and description of the Kamehameha Early Education Program. *Reading Research Quarterly, 17*(4), 503–527.

Thomas, W., & Collier, V. (2002). *A national study of school effectiveness for language minority students' long-term academic achievement.* Santa Cruz, CA: Center for Research on Education, Diversity & Excellence. Retrieved March 3, 2009 from http://crede.berkeley.edu/research/crede/products/print/research_briefs/rb10.shtml

Winsler, A., Díaz, R., Espinosa, L., & Rodríguez, J. (1999). When learning a second language does not mean losing the first: Bilingual language development in low-income, Spanish-speaking children, attending bilingual preschool. *Child Development, 70*(2), 349–362.

Wong Fillmore, L. (1991). When learning a second language means losing the first. *Early Childhood Research Quarterly, 6*(3), 323–346.

Wong Fillmore, L. (1996). What happens when languages are lost? An essay on language assimilation and cultural identity. In D. Slobin, J. Gerhardt, A. Kyratzis & J. Guo (Eds.), *Social interaction, social context, and language: Essays in honor of Susan Ervin-Tripp* (pp. 435–446). Mahwah, NJ: Lawrence Erlbaum.

Wong Fillmore, L., & Snow, C. (2000). *What teachers need to know about language.* Washington, DC: Center for Applied Linguistics.

Zill, N., Resnick, G., Kim, K., O'Donnell, K., Sorongon, A., McKey, R. H., et al. (2003). *Head Start FACES 2000—A whole-child perspective on program performance.* Retrieved May 19, 2009, from, http://www.acf.hhs.gov/programs/opre/hs/faces/index.html#reports

CHAPTER 9

Educating Preschool Teachers to Support English Language Learners

Margaret Freedson

The quality of preschool services for culturally and linguistically diverse children depends, first and foremost, on the knowledge and classroom practices of teachers. This chapter examines the existing research base on the preparation of preschool teachers to serve the growing population of English language learners (ELLs) in U.S. preschools. The chapter begins by examining characteristics of the current preschool teacher workforce by language ability and competence in bilingual teaching practices. The chapter then discusses limitations in the preparation of early childhood teachers at U.S. colleges and universities and explores the potential impact of more stringent credentialing requirements on the recruitment and retention of bilingual preschool educators. The chapter concludes with a review of the limited body of research that explores how higher education and professional development can increase preschool teachers' competence in working with English learners and an overview of research needs that remain unmet.

EARLY CHILDHOOD TEACHER CHARACTERISTICS

Cultural and Linguistic Diversity in the Workforce

Systematically collected data on the characteristics of the preschool workforce by cultural or linguistic background, language ability, and competence in bilingual practices are scarce. With the exception of the Head Start Program Information Reports (PIRs), there have been no studies nor are there databases at the national level that collect or report such data, and the PIR data are of limited scope. According to the most recent analysis (Hamm, 2006), in 2005, 29% of Head Start children were from homes where English was not the primary language spoken, while 27% of staff were reported to be proficient in a language other than English. Information on the specific language spoken by program staff is not included in the annual PIRs. Based on ethnic background data reported, we might assume there to be a relatively close cultural match between students and teachers: 33% of Head Start enrollees were Hispanic compared with 27% of Head Start staff; 5% of Head Start children were of American Indian or Alaska Native backgrounds compared with 4% of Head Start staff, and 2% of both participants and staff were Asian. These data tell us nothing of teachers' language abilities, however, nor do they link teachers and students at the classroom level, and in failing on these counts, they tell us little about the linguistic or cultural compatibility of teachers and students in actual practice.

An increasing proportion of the country's English-learning preschoolers attend state-funded pre-K programs. Here again, however, there is wide variation across states in the collection of data on teacher language proficiencies and competency in bilingual practices. The New Jersey Department of Education, referring to its Abbott preschool program—recognized for its generally high quality and relatively high level of teacher qualifications (Barnett, Hustedt, Hawkinson, & Robin, 2006)—reports that for the 2009–2010 school year, 18.4% (509) of its 2,769 preschool teachers were proficient in a language other than English, with Spanish by far the most commonly spoken language, followed by Arabic, Portuguese, and Haitian Creole (K. Garver, New Jersey Department of Education, Office of Early Childhood, personal communication, June 6, 2009). A study of classroom quality in a representative sample of 316 of New Jersey's Abbott preschool classrooms found that 50% of the teachers who have Spanish-speaking children speak Spanish themselves, though a significantly higher percentage of all teachers in community-based child care centers reported being fluent in Spanish (28.4%) compared with those in public preschool classrooms (15.4%) (Frede, Jung, Barnett, Lamy, & Figueras, 2007). Nevertheless, just 6.8% of Abbott teachers were certified in bilingual education or English as a Second Language in a program in which more than a third of all 3- and 4-year-old children speak a primary language other than English. Texas and Florida, on the other hand, do not track this information for pre-K specifically, though these two state-run programs serve by far the greatest number of ELL children of any state in the country (K. Dresser, Florida Agency for Workforce Innovation, Office of Early Learning, personal communication, August 24, 2009; M. Ramsay, Texas Education Agency, personal communication, August 18, 2009).

A recent study by the New York City Early Childhood Professional Development Institute and Cornell University (Ochshorn & García, 2007) provides an in-depth snapshot of preschool teacher characteristics in the country's largest and most diverse urban area. Approximately 90%

of the community-based teachers and 80% of school-based teachers sur-
veyed in the New York City study report serving one English learner or
more, with an average of seven per class. Again, Spanish is by far the most
common home language of the ELL population. On the other hand, just
20% of teachers identified themselves as fluent speakers of Spanish, with
foreign language speakers more common in community-based than in
school-based settings. Among assistant teachers, half claimed fluency in
a language other than English, with 40% speaking Spanish. Among both
teachers and community-based assistant teachers, Chinese was the next
most widely spoken language. Just 3% of lead teachers were certified in
bilingual or English as a Second Language teaching practices.

Clearly there remains a great unmet demand for bilingual staff in early
childhood programs, a need acknowledged by state-level program administrators across the country (Buysse, Castro, West, & Skinner, 2004).
In New Jersey, center directors at preschools in many of the state's high-
poverty districts report a particularly urgent need for staff who speak
languages other than Spanish, such as Haitian Creole and Chinese (Whitebook, Ryan, Kipnis, & Sakai, 2008). This need is likely echoed in programs
across the country since preschool-age children living with parents who
speak little or no English at home come from an extraordinary diversity
of language backgrounds (see Hernandez, Chapter 2, this volume). Systematic collection of data on teacher language background will help state
and federal programs structure efforts to recruit bilingual personnel in
response to student demographics.

Teacher Bilingual Proficiencies and Classroom Practices

In considering such measures, however, it should be noted that teachers who self-report as speakers of a language other than English present a
wide spectrum of dual language competencies. Among teachers who are
native speakers of any particular heritage language, some may be fully
bilingual—that is, they have mastery of standard, academic language in
both their home language and English—while others may speak either
a non-standard variety of the heritage language or lack proficiency in
English, or both. Similarly, native-English-speaking teachers who identify as bilingual are likely to present a wide range of second language
competencies. Researchers have only recently begun to investigate the
role of bilingual teachers' actual language proficiencies in preschool
classroom quality, and published findings were not available when this
volume went to press. There is some evidence at the elementary level
that many teachers and teacher assistants who identify themselves as bilingual in Spanish do not speak a level of grammatically and lexically
complex Spanish comparable to the language proficiencies that would be

expected of native English speakers in English (Guerrero, 2003). Guerrero attributes this shortcoming to the "few meaningful educational opportunities prospective teachers have to develop academic Spanish-language proficiency" (p. 174) and the fact that the relatively low status of Spanish in U.S. society tends to impede Spanish-language development.

Further, while it is laudable that early childhood programs have strived to hire staff who share their students' linguistic and cultural backgrounds, and have done so with some success, particularly in Head Start and community-based centers, it is also important to keep in mind that teachers' proficiency in a language other than English tells us little about teachers' knowledge or implementation of bilingual and culturally responsive instructional practices and, thus, may be of limited value as an indicator of high-quality ELL supports. In both the New Jersey and New York City data, we see wide discrepancies between the percentage of language-minority teachers, and the percentage of teachers who have certification in bilingual education. The Health and Human Services report *Celebrating Cultural and Linguistic Diversity in Head Start* (Joseph & Cohen, 2000), suggests that for the most part Head Start teachers do not integrate bilingual or multicultural materials into their classroom curriculum despite the increasing availability of such materials. How bilingual staff actually use their dual language proficiencies in communication with children and families, and in their organization of classroom learning environments and activities is, thus, an important research question for which we have few answers.

HOW HIGHER EDUCATION AND PROFESSIONAL DEVELOPMENT CAN INCREASE TEACHER COMPETENCE

Raising Qualifications for Early Childhood Teachers

Current federal and state policies are rapidly pushing to increase the educational qualifications of the early childhood workforce. Research studies have demonstrated links between higher levels of teacher education, higher overall classroom quality, and improved child outcomes (Barnett, 2004), particularly when teacher qualifications include a bachelor's degree (Kelley & Camilli, 2007) and training specific to the early care and education of young children (Bowman, Donovan, & Burns, 2001). Teachers who possess a bachelor's or higher degree in early childhood education (ECE) have been found to be more sensitive and responsive in their interactions with children than teachers with fewer qualifications (Phillipsen, Burchinal, Howes, & Cryer, 1997), while teachers with Associate's degrees in ECE have been found to be more responsive and less harsh than teachers with only a high school diploma (Howes, 1997). These teacher behaviors are particularly important in classrooms serving ELLs, where teachers must adapt communication to the language needs of children with varying degrees of English proficiency and address the social-emotional challenges faced by children unfamiliar with the language and culture of the classroom.

Eighteen states now require that all pre-K teachers possess a bachelor's degree, up from 13 states just 3 years ago; 20 states with pre-K programs still have no such universal requirement (Barnett, Hustedt, Friedman, Boyd, & Ainsworth, 2007). Further, the Head Start Reauthorization of 2007 (Improving Head Start for School Readiness Act of 2007; H.R. 1429, 2007) sets its benchmark at 2013, by which time at least 50% of Head Start teachers and education coordinators will have a baccalaureate or advanced degree in childhood education (just 31% of Head Start teachers have a bachelor's degree or higher presently) and all teaching assistants will have an associate's degree (Sec. 15, Sec. 19). The reauthorization also requires that all Head Start teachers attend 15 hours of professional development training per year (Sec. 19). Twenty-three states require a similar commitment to professional development for all pre-K teachers (Barnett et al., 2007).

National Accreditation Standards:
Preparing Teachers for Linguistic Diversity

The National Council for Accreditation of Teacher Education (NCATE) requires that accredited professional programs offering initial licensure in early childhood education prepare all teaching candidates with competencies set out by the National Association for the Education of Young Children (NAEYC, 2001). In the domain of language and literacy, these include the following:

Sub-Standard 4c: Understanding Content Knowledge in Early Education

Candidates—including those who are not currently teaching linguistically diverse young children—demonstrate knowledge of second-language acquisition and of bilingualism. They know the home language environments of the children they teach and the possible effects on children when their classroom environment does not reflect the home language. Candidates know the sociopolitical contexts of major language groups and how those may affect children's motivation to learn English. Candidates understand the benefits of bilingualism and the special needs of young English language learners (ELLs), building on the home language systems that children already have developed and assisting them to add a second language to their repertoire. For young ELLs who are learning to read, candidates use, adapt, and assess research-based literacy activities and teaching methods that build on prior knowledge and support successful transitions for those learners (NAEYC, 2001, p. 20).

This NAEYC standard has been in place since 2001. While the standard does not address issues of teacher language proficiency nor does it articulate specific teaching practices known to support dual language learning, it does provide teacher educators with guidance as to the broad competencies early childhood professionals need to effectively serve English language learners.

Coursework and Content on Teaching ELLs

To what degree are institutions of higher education heeding this call and integrating relevant content into their programs? A 2005 study by the National Center for Early Development and Learning surveying early childhood programs at colleges and universities across the country (Maxwell, Lim, & Early, 2006) suggests that there are both signs of progress and severe deficiencies in the preparation of early childhood teachers to serve ELLs. Of the 1,179 Institutions of Higher Education (IHE) that participated in the study (representing 87% of all degree-granting IHEs with early childhood programs of some type), nearly 41% of programs offering an associate degree and more than 46% of those offering a bachelor's degree required at least one entire course in working with children and families from diverse ethnic and cultural backgrounds. However, just 12.7% of AA programs and less than 15% of bachelor's and master's degree programs required students to take an entire course in working with bilingual children learning English as a second language. About 20% of child development associate (CDA) and associate degree programs and about 10% of bachelor's and master's programs did not require *any* coursework in working with ELL children.

Supervised Practical Experience with ELLs

One of the key experiences in early childhood teachers' pre-service preparation is the field practicum-supervised work in a care or education setting with children from birth to age 4. Relative to other content areas covered by students' practica requirements (e.g., working with infants and toddlers, working with families, working with children with disabilities), working with bilingual children learning English as a second language was "least likely to be required as part of a practicum across any of the degree programs" (Maxwell et al., 2006, p. 17). Though not investigated in the Maxwell, Lim, and Early (2006) study, second language requirements for teaching candidates are also notably absent from all but a select few college and university early childhood programs. Programs that require proficiency in a language other than English are discussed below.

Early Childhood Teachers'
Self-Assessment of Their Preparation to Teach ELLs

Given the complexity of knowledge and skills teachers need to effectively support bilingual children's learning, the dearth of opportunities
for teachers to acquire such training in their teacher preparation programs
is grave indeed. Not surprisingly, several recent studies report that early
childhood teachers feel they have not been adequately prepared to work
with children from cultural and linguistic backgrounds different from
their own and that they need more specific skills—not simply general
coursework in diversity issues—to do so (Ray & Bowman, 2003; Ryan,
Ackerman, & Song, 2005). Program administrators share this conclusion.
In one New Jersey study, more than half of the 98 preschool directors inter-
viewed from a representative sample of centers in high-poverty districts
across the state reported that their "highly qualified" teachers—those who
possess a bachelor's degree and early childhood certification—need better teacher preparation in the areas of bilingualism and second language
learning (Whitebook et al., 2008).

Lack of Diversity of College Teacher Education Faculty

Beyond the limited opportunities students enrolled in early childhood
degree programs have to study or apply content related to the early education of English learners, students' understanding is further hampered
by the lack of diversity among college and university faculty. On average,
in 2005 more than 8 in 10 full-time, early childhood faculty members at
both 2- and 4-year institutions were White and non-Hispanic (Maxwell et
al., 2006), while there was slightly more diversity among part-time faculty.
Just 4% of full-time faculty were Hispanic. For programs at 4-year institutions, which will, increasingly, prepare the majority of early childhood
teachers entering the workforce, two of the largest challenges identified
by program chairs were attracting and retaining ethnically and linguistically diverse faculty. In its most recent standards for early childhood professional preparation, NAEYC affirms the urgent need for institutions of
higher education to "create policies, incentives and resources to recruit
diverse teacher candidates and teacher education faculty, and to provide
ongoing support" (NAEYC, 2001, p. 4).

One consequence of the lack of diversity among ECE program faculty
is the limited responsiveness of such programs to students who are themselves from culturally and linguistically diverse backgrounds. Many early
childhood teachers not yet proficient in English either wish to or are required to take coursework to improve their credentials. For these nontraditional students whose recruitment or retention into the early childhood

profession is one critical step in meeting the needs of English language learners, there are few available options. For example, the Child Development and Family Studies Department at City College of San Francisco reports serving students who require advisement in English, Cantonese, Spanish, and Vietnamese, yet they have great difficulty in both recruiting native-speaking instructors and finding language-appropriate materials for use in their early childhood curriculum (Santos Rico, Villazana-Price, Donovan, & Cheng, 2003). A study of early childhood teacher preparation in New Jersey (Ryan et al., 2005) reports that there is so much demand for child development associate (CDA) coursework in Spanish that several child care agencies and community colleges offer such training. However, no 4-year college or university early childhood teacher preparation programs in the state offers required coursework in Spanish.

Raising Preschool Teacher Qualifications: The Double-Edged Sword

The limited number of Hispanic faculty and faculty from other cultural and linguistic-minority groups represented in early childhood teacher preparation programs points to a more deeply entrenched problem in the U.S. education system—the so-called leaky pipeline for minority students (Hill, Carduzaa, Aramburo, & Baca, 1993) and the resulting underrepresentation of Hispanics at all levels of U.S. higher education. Despite the improvement in high school completion rates for Hispanic women between 1994 and 2004 of nearly 6%, in 2004, just 82% of Hispanic women completed high school compared with 94% of non-Hispanic white women (Mishel & Roy, 2006). Low high school completion rates obviously limit the number of Hispanic students eligible to go on to college and ultimately into teacher education. This trend can be observed in the results of a recent study of ECE teacher qualifications in California, which found a spread of at least 10 points between the percentage of White and Latino providers with associate degrees or higher (Whitebook, Bellm, Sakai, Kipnis, Voisin, & Young, 2004).

The majority of Hispanics who do complete high school and pursue postsecondary education first enroll in 2-year colleges (Fry, 2005). Data on early childhood teacher education programs show that Hispanics represent 13% of students enrolled in associate degree programs but just around 10% of students in bachelor's and master's degree programs (Maxwell et al., 2006). Students from American Indian or Alaska Native backgrounds are also underrepresented in 4-year degree programs. This portends future problems as the educational requirements for entry into early childhood teaching are raised. Throughout the country, articulation agreements between 2- and 4-year institutions are weak if they exist at all, resulting in a low transfer rate of Hispanic and other minority teacher education candidates to 4-year institutions and further constraining the pool of potential educators from these groups (Villegas & Clewell, 1998). The rising cost of education at 4-year institutions along with cutbacks in federal financing of postsecondary education further impede language-minority students from entering teaching (Santiago & Brown, 2004). Finally, the teacher testing movement has resulted in the exclusion from teaching of disproportionately large numbers of Hispanics and other minorities (Villegas & Davis, 2008) due to their lower passing rates relative to White candidates.

There is some indication that, all told, demands for increased teacher qualifications may be negatively impacting the diversity of the early childhood workforce and, thus, its capacity to meet the needs of English learners. Anecdotal evidence reported by the National Council of La Raza's network of community-based providers suggests that few limited-English-speaking staff employed by Head Start are able to complete a college degree and, as a result, remain in the program as teaching assistants rather than as lead classroom teachers (Calderón, 2005a). Preschool center directors in New Jersey also report that some teachers may have left the Abbott program or been demoted to assistant teacher because they were unable to meet the new bachelor's degree and certification requirements, though the authors of this study caution that "existing data do not provide an accurate account of such staff, fully explain why they did not pursue further education, or measure any resulting loss or gain in the diversity of the teaching workforce" (Whitebook et al., 2008, p. 47). The evidence does suggest, however, that as state pre-K and Head Start policies shift toward requiring preschool teachers to possess a bachelor's degree—a potentially important step toward improving program quality for ELLs—the pool of Hispanic and other minority teaching candidates who may possess much-needed language skills is likely to shrink unless measures are taken to increase opportunities for these individuals to meet new credentialing requirements. Research on this topic is critical to the formulation of state and federal policies that support language diversity in the preschool workforce.

PROMISING PROGRAMS IN HIGHER EDUCATION

The research literature on early childhood teacher preparation for ELLs is too limited to offer any definitive guidance on how institutions of higher education can infuse the enormous amount of specialized content related to teaching young English learners into a teacher preparation curriculum and also support successful outcomes for bilingual teacher candidates. Bilingual education teacher preparation programs obviously have the greatest capacity for preparing teachers to work effectively with young English learners. Kushner and Ortiz (2000) point out that, unfortunately, bilingual education programs have suffered from a lack of support within universities, inconsistent federal funding, and limited student enrollments due to the leaky pipeline of language-minority students in higher education. As a result of these many challenges, bilingual education teacher training programs with a specific early childhood focus are most rare.

In the selection of promising programs described below, then, I draw on research examining both early childhood and elementary teacher education to highlight programs that have addressed some of the challenges for early childhood teacher preparation described above. Several of the programs have been profiled in policy reports and practitioner briefs but have not been the subject of systematic study. They are included, nonetheless, because they demonstrate how federal and state governments, IHEs, and the nonprofit sector may work collaboratively to support linguistic diversity in the early childhood workforce.

Infusing Content on Cultural and Linguistic Diversity Across the Curriculum

One approach to linguistic diversity taken by some teacher preparation programs is to infuse relevant content across the early childhood education curriculum. At George Mason University, the Unified Transformative Early Education Model (UTEEM) makes diversity its central focus in preparing students to teach children from birth through age 8 in inclusive multicultural settings (Miller, Fader, & Vincent, 2000). A blend of master's programs in early childhood education, early childhood special education, and English as a Second Language, the program embeds into every course content and experiences focused on the linguistic and cultural dimensions of learning. The Crosswalks Project of the University of North Carolina's FPG Child Development Institute has developed a framework to help early childhood faculty at 20 public and private colleges and universities across the state to integrate strategies that address linguistic and cultural diversity into all of their courses, field experiences, and higher education practices. It should be noted, however, that some experts in ELL teacher preparation caution strongly against the adoption of this type of infusion approach given the "lack of experience with the education of ELL by most teacher educators and the time that it takes to build substantial knowledge among them" (Lucas, Villegas, & Freedson-Gonzalez, 2008, p. 370), arguing instead for a separate required course devoted to teaching ELLs.

Special Coursework, Practica, and Supplemental Programs on Teaching ELLs

Available faculty expertise in English learner issues is often best provided through special coursework, practicum requirements, or supplemental programs. At the University of Minnesota, a one-credit course was added to the preservice curriculum in response to preservice teachers' expressed need for better preparation to teach ELLs (Walker, Ranney, & Fortune, 2005). The course engages participants in working with ELLs in schools and addresses topics that include principles of second language learning, information about immigrant groups in the local area, and curricular and instructional practices for successfully teaching ELLs. Wheelock College insists that all students are placed in a practicum setting where they will learn to address the issues teachers face each day in working with children who do not speak English (Daniel & Friedman, 2005). Other institutions have made coursework on teaching ELL students available through minors and certificate programs. At Boston College, Early Childhood Education candidates can add a minor in English as a Second Language (ESL) Education by taking two required courses—(1) Teaching Bilingual Students and (2) Bilingualism, Second Language and Literacy Development—and completing a field experience with bilingual learners (Friedman, 2002).

Faculty Professional Development

Most teacher educators do not have the knowledge and skills to prepare teachers to teach young English language learners. It is important, therefore, that all teacher education faculty begin to educate themselves on ELL issues. Two examples of faculty professional development initiatives are worthy of note. The first took place in the early 1990s at San Diego State University, where nine faculty members with different disciplinary specialties spent 1 year developing their own capacity to prepare teachers to teach ELLs (Gonzalez & Darling-Hammond, 1997). More recently, teacher education faculty at Temple University participated in a 1-year Faculty Linguistic Diversity Academy (Nevárez-La Torre, Sanford-De Shields, Soundy, Leonard, & Woyshner, 2005). During the year, faculty volunteers attended monthly meetings and seminars at which they discussed relevant literature, developed individual projects for their courses, and infused issues of linguistic diversity into the content of at least one course.

Support for Language-Minority Teaching Candidates and Spanish Language Acquisition

For many early childhood educators who speak a language other than English, the requirement that they pass an English language competency test in order to enroll in a bachelor's or associate degree program represents a significant hurdle. Several programs have been designed to help ensure that native Spanish speakers enter the teacher/practitioner pipeline despite language limitations. In Portland, Oregon, both Pacific Oaks College Northwest and the Portland Community College offer early childhood courses with Spanish language support (Calderón, 2005b; Daniel & Friedman, 2005), allowing students to learn early childhood content while they learn English. Similar to two-way immersion programs for young children, the Pacific Oaks program enrolls approximately equal numbers of native English and native Spanish speakers with the goal that all participants become fluent and literate in both conversational and academic English and Spanish. At Portland Community College, advanced classes are offered only in English but with extensive scaffolding for English learners. Arizona State University requires that all early childhood education majors be proficient in Spanish, while the University of Texas at Austin insists that bilingual teaching candidates take some of their teaching methods classes in Spanish to ensure a high level of bilingual academic language proficiency. These programs address just some of the many complex challenges of educating a bilingual early childhood workforce.

Professional Development and Teacher Language Attitudes

For the majority of early childhood teachers already in classrooms, professional development, rather than higher education coursework, will be the principle vehicle for gaining competence in working with English learners. Again, a search of the research literature on effective approaches to professional development for early childhood teachers of ELLs produced no peer-reviewed or published studies. Survey data do indicate, however, that despite the urgent need for increased training in this area (Buysse et al., 2004), working with English learners is among the least commonly offered topics for professional development. In New York City, just 22% of preschool teachers at school-based centers and 6% of teachers at community-based centers reported having attended a workshop on the topic of ELLs in the last 5 years (Ochshorn & García, 2007). This points to the likelihood that preschool educators receive less professional development on teaching ELLs than their K–12 counterparts, who receive little enough as it is (for a review of the K–12 professional development literature, see August et al., 2008), despite the greater representation of English learners in preschool classrooms.

The research literature on professional development for K–12 teachers working with English learners does offer some guidance for planning early childhood professional development opportunities (August et al., 2008). Studies show that effective professional development in bilingual learning contexts must be of sufficient duration—lasting a year or longer—involve ongoing meetings between teachers and professional t providers, include opportunities for classroom practice th mentoring and coaching, and build teacher learning com-Training should emphasize "specific strategies to improve n for language-minority students, the theory that informs the gies, and how to apply the strategies in classrooms" (August et al., 2008, p. 165), for example, improving how teachers read aloud to young bilingual children. This research also suggests the importance of including all staff involved in the education of English learners—including paraprofessionals, early intervention specialists, and classroom teachers—in the same professional development efforts. Findings from the K–12 literature indicate that teacher change to support ELLs is a slow process that may require many meetings, workshops, intensive summer programs, and follow-up in classrooms.

One of the key goals for professional development for early childhood teachers of ELLs is change in teacher beliefs and attitudes (August et al., 2008). K–12 research has shown this to be especially critical for teachers of English learners since teachers' attitudes and beliefs about language-minority children may powerfully influence teacher behaviors, which, in turn, affect educational outcomes for this population of students (Valdes, 2001). Teachers' negative attitudes toward the languages students speak may ultimately lead to negative attitudes toward the students themselves, producing lowered learning expectations that become self-fulfilling. Byrnes, Kiger, and Manning (1997) found that teachers with higher degrees, formal training in working with ELLs, and in locations where they had greater contact with language-minority students had more positive language attitudes. In another study, Shin and Krashen (1996) found that K–12 teachers with some bilingual and ESL training, as well as those who spoke a language other than English, more strongly supported bilingual instruction than monolingual teachers and teachers without special language certification. A more recent study of Arizona elementary teachers' attitudes toward ELLs' languages and bilingual instruction (García-Nevarez, Stafford, & Arias, 2005) found more positive attitudes among bilingual certified teachers than either ESL-certified or traditional teachers. Latino teachers were also more supportive of using students' native languages in the classroom compared with non-Latino teachers, as were teachers with fewer years of teaching experience. Importantly, Ruiz, Rueda, Figueroa, and Boothroyd (1995) noted that change in teacher attitudes toward bilingualism and young English learners may come only after changes in classroom practice produce observable improvements in student outcomes, rather than the change in attitude being a prerequisite to changes in classroom practice.

The K–12 research literature on teacher attitudes and beliefs about English learners, minority languages, and bilingual instruction points to important areas of need for early childhood research. As investments are made to improve early childhood teacher education and professional development, it is critical that researchers examine the impact of these efforts on teachers' attitudes and beliefs about language diversity, their actual practices with English learners in preschool classrooms, and, ultimately, the bilingual learning outcomes of their young students.

RESEARCH NEEDS

As the above review makes clear, there are many gaps in the research base on the preparation of early childhood teachers to work effectively with young English language learners. The following are general topics for which research is needed, as well as specific research questions that may guide future research efforts.

1. There is a need for more systematic collection of data on preschool teacher and assistant teacher background characteristics in Head Start and pre-kindergarten programs across the country. To facilitate policy research on program quality for English language learners, data should be collected on teacher racial/ethnic background, bilingual proficiency and languages spoken, education level, and special language training including bilingual and/or ESL certification. Ideally, teacher background information should be linked to annual classroom/ student profiles.

2. Policy research is needed to examine which teacher background characteristics are the best predictors of classroom quality and enhanced student outcomes for ELLs. For example, how does teacher proficiency in Spanish versus a bachelor's degree contribute to classroom quality? Do ELL students in preschool classrooms with bilingual certified teachers outperform students with ESL certified teachers or teachers with no special language certification? Do ELL students in classrooms with bilingual paraprofessionals and monolingual teachers make greater learning gains than students in classrooms with bilingual teachers?

3. As Head Start and pre-kindergarten teachers across the country scramble to meet the new credentialing mandates, is the early childhood workforce maintaining its cultural and linguistic diversity? Are all subgroups of teachers keeping equal pace with these requirements or are some ethnic and linguistic-minority groups being disproportionately squeezed from the preschool teacher corps?

4. Among Latino teachers, what kind of variation exists in teachers' actual bilingual language proficiencies in Spanish and English (including biliteracy), and how does this variation impact students' learning in English and Spanish? How are college and university early childhood programs helping Latino preschool teachers strengthen their academic Spanish language skills?

5. How are the preschool teachers who are implementing some of the more innovative and possibly effective models of bilingual preschool instruction, such as home language maintenance models and two-way immersion, being prepared to implement these programs effectively and to counter the prevailing trends toward quick transitioning of children into an English-only curriculum?

6. Are there exemplary college and/or university programs that demonstrate how specialized content related to teaching young English learners can best be incorporated into a teacher preparation curriculum for early childhood teachers? What are the characteristics of these programs? What preservice courses or course content are most strongly related to teacher learning and to effective teaching practices for ELLs? Ideally, universities will evaluate the effectiveness of their teacher preparation programs and/or courses by following students into classrooms and measuring both classroom quality for ELLs and ELL student learning.

7. Research is needed to identify how 2- and 4-year teacher preparation programs can best recruit language-minority teacher candidates and provide the array of supports that will help these students successfully complete the program, including the successful completion of any teacher competency testing requirements. Institutions of higher education must also examine how they can address the shortage of bilingual and ESL certified teachers in early childhood classrooms.

8. How can faculty at institutions of higher education expand their knowledge base and thereby improve their capacity to infuse content on working effectively with young English language learners into all early childhood courses?

9. There is great need for research on effective approaches to professional development for early childhood teachers of ELLs. Intervention studies that investigate the impact of particular approaches to professional development, in terms of both content and process, on teacher behaviors vis-à-vis bilingual learners will be particularly valuable.

10. Research on preschool teachers' attitudes and beliefs about language-minority children, their home languages, and bilingual instructional practices is critically important. Given the existing

knowledge base and NCATE accreditation standards calling on preschool teachers to embrace children's home languages and cultures along with English, we must better understand how teacher language attitudes impact classroom language use practices, interactions with ELLs, and, ultimately, child outcomes. Are some teacher background variables associated with more positive attitudes toward ELL students and dual language learning in the preschool context, and what kinds of teacher learning experiences—in both preservice and in-service settings— can best foster positive attitudes toward bilingualism among all teachers?

CONCLUSIONS

Preschool education sits at a crossroads in efforts to meet the needs of English language learners. As the population of English learners in U.S. preschools rapidly expands, policies mandating a more highly qualified workforce will result in a growing proportion of early childhood teachers across the country with 2- and 4-year college degrees. As these more educated teachers become more reflective practitioners, they will have greater capacity to meet the myriad challenges of supporting the development of bilingual learners in their classrooms. Institutions of higher education have a great opportunity to engage teachers in the very specific kinds of inquiry and learning experiences that will prepare them to work effectively with young ELLs, yet our colleges and universities are currently ill-equipped to offer such preparation. Nor have we adequately addressed the question of how we can increase teacher qualifications while also increasing the linguistic diversity of the preschool workforce. Ideally, all preschool ELLs should be taught by qualified teachers with bilingual or ESL certifications, since such teachers are best prepared to support children's first and second language development while also supporting their learning of content. Yet teachers without such certifications must also acquire the competencies to use practices that support children's bilingual development. A great deal of research is still needed to address these problems of teacher practice and to inform policies that can offer the best hope for improving the quality of preschool education for all English language learners.

REFERENCES

August, D., Beck, I., Calderón, M., Francis, D., Lesaux, N., Shanahan, T., et al. (2008). Instruction and professional development (pp. 131–250). In D. August

& T. Shanahan (Eds.), *Developing reading and writing in second language learners.* New York: Routledge.

Barnett, W. S. (2004). Better teachers, better preschools. Student achievement linked to teacher qualifications. *NIEER Preschool Policy Matters* (Issue 2). New Brunswick, NJ: National Institute for Early Education Research.

Barnett, W. S., Hustedt, J. T., Friedman, A. H., Boyd, J. S., & Ainsworth, P. (2007). *The state of preschool 2007: State preschool yearbook.* New Brunswick, NJ: National Institute for Early Education Research.

Barnett, W. S., Hustedt, J. T., Hawkinson, L., & Robin, K. (2006). *The state of preschool 2006: State preschool yearbook.* New Brunswick, NJ: National Institute for Early Education Research.

Bowman, B., Donovan, S., & Burns, S. (Eds.). (2001). *Eager to learn: Educating our preschoolers.* Washington, DC: National Academy Press.

Buysse, V., Castro, D. C., West, T. & Skinner, M. L. (2004). *Addressing the needs of Latino children: A national survey of state administrators of early childhood programs* [Executive summary]. Chapel Hill: Frank Porter Graham Child Development Institute, University of North Carolina, Chapel Hill.

Byrnes, D., Kiger, G., & Manning, M. (1997). Teachers' attitudes about language diversity. *Teaching and Teacher Education, 13*(6), 637–644.

Calderón, M. (2005a). *Head Start reauthorization: Enhancing school readiness for Latino children.* Washington, DC: National Council of La Raza.

Calderón, M. (2005b). *Achieving a high-quality preschool teaching corps: A focus on California.* Washington, DC: National Council of La Raza.

Daniel, J., & Friedman, S. (2005). Preparing teachers to work with culturally and linguistically diverse children. *Beyond the Journal.* Retrieved May 15, 2009, from www.journal.naeyc.org/btj/200511/DanielFriedmanBTJ1105.asp

Frede, E., Jung, K., Barnett, W. S., Lamy, C. E., & Figueras, A. (2007). *The Abbott Preschool Program Longitudinal Effects Study (APPLES).* New Brunswick, NJ: National Institute for Early Education Research.

Friedman, A. A. (2002). What we would have liked to know: Pre-service teachers' perspectives on effective teacher preparation. In Z. F. Beykont (Ed.), *The power of culture: Teaching across language difference* (pp. 193–217). Cambridge, MA: Harvard Education Publishing Group.

Fry, R. (2005). *Recent changes in the entry of Hispanic and White youth into college.* Washington, DC: Pew Hispanic Center.

García-Nevarez, A., Stafford, M., & Arias, B. (2005). Arizona elementary teachers attitudes toward English language learners and the use of Spanish in classroom instruction, *Bilingual Research Journal, 29*(2), 295–317.

Gonzalez, J. M., & Darling-Hammond, L. (1997). *New concepts for new challenges: Professional development for teachers of immigrant youth.* Washington, DC: Center for Applied Linguistics.

Guerrero, M. (2003). We have correct English teachers. Why can't we have correct Spanish teachers? It's not acceptable. *International Journal of Qualitative Studies in Education, 16*(5), 647–668.

Hamm, K. (2006). More than meets the eye: Head Start programs, participants, families and staff in 2005. *CLASP Policy Brief, Head Start Series No. 8.* Washington, DC: Center for Law and Social Policy.

Hill, R., Carduzaa, J., Aramburo, D., & Baca, L. (1993). Culturally and linguistically diverse teachers in special education: Repairing or redesigning the leaky pipeline. *Teacher Education and Special Education, 16*(3), 258–269.

Howes, C. (1997). Children's experiences in center-based child care as a function of teacher background and adult:child ratio. *Merrill-Palmer Quarterly, 43,* 404–425.

Improving Head Start for School Readiness Act of 2007, H.R. 1429, 110 Cong. (2007). Retrieved on March 8, 2010 from http://eclkc.ohs.acf.hhs.gov/hslc/Program%20Design%20and%20Management/Head%20Start%20Requirements/Head%20Start%20Act/2007HeadStartA.htm

Joseph, G., & Cohen, R. (2000). *Celebrating cultural and linguistic diversity in Head Start.* Washington, DC: Department of Health and Human Services.

Kelley, P. J., & Camilli, G. (2007). *The impact of teacher education on outcomes in center-based early childhood education programs: A meta-analysis* (NIEER Working Paper). Retrieved May 15, 2009, from http://nieer.org/resources/research/TeacherEd.pdf

Kushner, M. & Ortiz, A. (2000). The preparation of early childhood education teachers to serve English language learners. In D. Horm-Wingerd, M. Hyson, & N. Karp (Eds.), *New teachers for a new century: The future of early childhood professional development* (pp. 123–154).Washington, DC: U.S. Department of Education.

Lucas, T., Villegas, A. M., & Freedson-Gonzalez, M. (2008). Linguistically responsive teacher education: Preparing classroom teachers to teach English language learners. *Journal of Teacher Education, 59*(4), 361–373.

Maxwell, K., Lim, C., & Early, D. (2006). *Early childhood teacher preparation programs in the United States: National Report.* Chapel Hill: Frank Porter Graham Child Development Institute, University of North Carolina, Chapel Hill.

Miller, P., Fader, L., & Vincent, L. (2000). Preparing early childhood educators to work with families who have exceptional needs. In D. Horm-Wingerd, M. Hyson, N. Karp (Eds.), *New teachers for a new century: The future of early childhood professional development* (pp. 93–122). Washington, DC: U.S. Department of Education.

Mishel, L., & Roy, J. (2006). *Rethinking high school graduation rates and trends.* Washington, DC: Economic Policy Institute.

National Association for the Education of Young Children. (2001). *Standards for early childhood professional preparation: Initial licensure standards.* Washington, DC: Author.

Nevárez-La Torre, A. A., Sanford-De Shields, J. S., Soundy, C., Leonard, J., & Woyshner, C. (2005, April). *Faculty perspectives on integrating linguistic diversity issues into a teacher education program.* Paper presented at the annual meeting of the American Educational Research Association, Montreal, Canada.

Ochshorn, S., & García, M. (2007). *Learning about the workforce: A profile of early childhood educators in New York City's community and school-based centers.* New York: NYC Early Childhood Professional Development Institute.

Phillipsen, L. C., Burchinal, M. R., Howes C., & Cryer, D. (1997). The predictions of process quality from structural features of childcare. *Early Childhood Research Quarterly, 12*(3), 281–304.

Ray, A., & Bowman, B. (2003). *Learning multicultural competence: Developing early childhood practitioners' effectiveness in working with children from culturally diverse communities* [Final report to the A. L. Mailman Family Foundation. Initiative on Race, Class, and Culture in Early Childhood]. Chicago, IL: Erikson Institute.

Ryan, S., Ackerman, D., & Song, H. (2005). *Getting qualified and becoming knowledgeable: Preschool teachers' perspectives on their professional preparation* [Unpublished manuscript]. Rutgers: State University of New Jersey.

Ruiz, N. T., Rueda, R., Figueroa, R. A., & Boothroyd, M. (1995). Bilingual special education teachers' shifting paradigms: Complex responses to educational reform. *Journal of Learning Disabilities, 28*(10), 622–635.

Santiago, D., & Brown, S. (2004). *Federal policy and Latinos in higher education.* Washington, DC: Pew Hispanic Center.

Santos Rico, S., Villazana-Price, N., Donovan, S., & Cheng, E. (2003, June). *Multilingual coursework, academic counseling and career advising: A menu of service and supports for a diverse early childhood workforce.* Paper presented at the NAEYC National Institute for Early Childhood Professional Development, Portland, OR.

Shin, F., & Krashen, S. (1996). Teacher attitudes towards the principles of bilingual education and toward students' participation in bilingual programs: Same or different? *Bilingual Research Journal, 20*(1), 45–53.

Valdes, G. (2001). *Learning and not learning English in American schools.* New York: Teachers College Press.

Villegas, A. M., & Clewell, B. C. (1998). Increasing the number of teachers of color for urban schools. *Education and Urban Society, 21*(1), 42–61.

Villegas, A. M., & Davis, D. (2008). Preparing teachers of color to confront racial/ethnic disparities in educational outcomes. In M. Cochran-Smith, S. Feiman-Nemser, D. J. McIntyre, & K. Demers (Eds.), *Handbook of research on teacher education* (3rd ed., pp. 583–605). New York: Routledge.

Walker, C. L., Ranney, S., & Fortune, T. W. (2005). Preparing preservice teachers for English language learners: A content-based approach. In D. J. Tedick (Ed.), *Second language teacher education, international perspectives* (pp. 313–333). Mahwah, NJ: Lawrence Erlbaum.

Whitebook, M., Bellm, D., Sakai, L., Kipnis, F., Voisin, I., & Young, M. (2004). *Raising teacher education and training standards for universal preschool in California: Assessing the size of the task.* Berkeley, CA: Center for the Study of Child Care Employment.

Whitebook, M., Ryan, S., Kipnis, F., & Sakai, L. (2008). *Partnering for preschool: A study of center directors in New Jersey's mixed delivery Abbott Program.* Berkeley, CA: Center for the Study of Child Care Employment.

CHAPTER 10

A Policy and Research Agenda for Teaching Young English Language Learners

Ellen Frede
Eugene E. García

As the preceding chapters illustrate, the field of early childhood education is beginning to amass a body of research to inform policy and practice for preschool-age children who are learning two languages. In this concluding chapter, we first summarize the research literature attempting to differentiate conclusions that are solidly confirmed by the research base from those that are suggested by current findings but need more extensive research to be conclusive. Based on this review of the evidence base for young early language learners, we make recommendations for policy at the local, state, and federal levels and for further research. As we discuss, the state of our science is clearly better in some areas than in others. However, there are a few policy and implementation questions where the research is so complete that we can answer with confidence "beyond a reasonable doubt."

WHAT WE KNOW ABOUT YOUNG ENGLISH LANGUAGE LEARNERS

Demographics

The proportion of children under the age of 5 who live in homes where a non-English language is spoken is rapidly increasing. Although the vast majority of minority language children in the United States speak Spanish—close to 80% according to data on school-age children (National Clearinghouse for English Language Acquisition, 2007)—more than 435 other languages are spoken in the United States. The overall child population speaking a non-English native language rose from 6% in 1979 to 14%

in 1999, and the number of language-minority students in K–12 schools has been recently estimated to be more than 14 million (August, 2006). The representation of ELLs in U.S. schools has its highest concentration in early education (García & Jensen, 2009).

The majority of young English language learners are born in this country, and their parents are clearly committed to staying here (Hernandez, Chapter 2, this volume). Only 5% of young children from immigrant families live in homes where no parent speaks English; however, 40% of immigrant parents report that they do not speak English well (Hernandez, Chapter 2, this volume). Lack of exposure to fluent English may be compounded by other limitations, given that parents who speak limited or no English are less likely to read to their children in any language (O'Donnell, 2008). Also, low-income parents have been found to provide less language stimulation of any kind to their children (Hart & Risley, 1995), and young English language learners are likely to be from low-income homes (National Center for Children in Poverty, 2007).

Parental Engagement

Rodríguez-Brown (Chapter 6) reviews the research on barriers to home-school communication and engagement with linguistic-minority parents. In addition to the obvious language impediments that may exist, parental concerns about their own lack of formal education may interfere with engagement in school. Often immigrant families have great respect for teachers and are very interested in their children's schools. At the same time families may view their role in their child's upbringing as different from the school's and, possibly, not valued by teachers. Parents who are not English proficient are less likely to engage their children in activities that are associated with gains in learning such as book reading and playing number games. Some research indicates that they appreciate explicit directions in how to assist their children and participate in the school.

Language Development for Bilingual Emergent Children

Children under the age of 5 are capable of learning two languages simultaneously and the process is as "natural as learning one language" (Genesee, Chapter 4, this volume). Simultaneous bilinguals may have smaller vocabularies in each language and code mix in the two languages, but both of these are normative for dual language learners and do not interfere with development—and may, indeed, enhance it by increasing facility with language structure and thus enhancing children's metalinguistic abilities.

For children who are learning a second language for the first time in preschool (sequential bilinguals), the research findings are less clear; however, studies of older children and a few studies of very young children indicate that supporting dual language learning in contrast to English immersion may improve children's learning in English and certainly does not impede it (Genesee, Chapter 4, this volume).

Neurological and cognitive science research is beginning to show that there are clear cognitive benefits to being bilingual proficient that may be manifested in more efficient brain functioning (Náñez, Chapter 5, this volume). In addition to improved metalinguistic awareness, bilinguals have faster reaction times when there are competing demands for attention, and these are manifested across multiple skill areas including language, phonological awareness, writing, reading, numerical operations, spatial concepts, creativity, and problem solving.

In addition, research on academic trajectories shows that children who are bilingual proficient as they enter kindergarten perform as well or better than those who begin with only English. With some variation by home language and family income level, children who begin with only a language other than English do not catch up with their peers by the end of grade school (Galindo, Chapter 3, this volume).

The Influence of Preschool on Young English Language Learners

The number of children who are English language learners and attend state-funded preschool is also growing but they are still less likely than English speakers and other minority groups to attend any setting outside of the home for care or education (Barnett & Yarosz, 2007). Survey research reveals that these lower attendance rates are more related to lack of knowledge of the programs or lack of access than to the common assumption that the parents do not want their children to attend preschool (García & Gonzalez, 2006). It is clear that there are cognitive and social benefits for children who attend high-quality preschool (see Barnett, 2008, for a review of the research on preschool efficacy), and growing evidence indicates that English language learners benefit more than others from effective preschool education (Gormley, 2007).

Young dual language learners who attend out-of-home programs are more likely to be served in lower-quality settings (Barnett & Yarosz, 2007), and some evidence indicates that their teachers are not likely to speak their home language (Espinosa, Chapter 8, this volume; Frede, Jung, Barnett, Lamy, & Figueras, 2007; Karoly, Ghosh-Dastidar, Zellman, Perlman, & Fernyhough, 2008) nor are they trained in strategies to support dual language acquisition (Freedson, Chapter 9, this volume). Research findings also indicate that English immersion programs for children this age can lead to a loss of the home language especially if the home language base is not strong (Genesee, Chapter 4, this volume).

Looking across the literature, Espinosa (Chapter 8, this volume) concludes that those specific teaching practices that are beneficial for all preschool-age children are clearly of benefit for dual language learners, especially those that require teachers to differentiate instruction for the individual learners through strategies such as using shorter, more explanatory language, narrating their own and the child's actions, and referring to concrete materials and pictures to improve comprehension. Espinosa also concludes that both the content and style of teaching must be responsive to the children's cultural backgrounds and must explicitly focus on support of English language acquisition.

Teacher Preparation for Young English Language Learners

Clearly, having a teacher who is bilingual facilitates dual language instruction (Chang et al., 2007) and may improve learning in English as well as in the home language (Barnett, Yarosz, Thomas, Jung, & Blanco, 2007; Gormley, 2007). Data are spotty on the linguistic ability of teachers and teacher assistants in preschool and whether it matches the languages of children in their classrooms. However, looking across the data sources that are available, it is evident that most children who speak a language other than English at home do not have a teacher who speaks their language or who has specialized knowledge in how to support English as a second language for young children (Freedson, Chapter 9, this volume). This lack of expertise makes it especially surprising that teacher preparation programs rarely offer substantive coursework in linguistic and cultural diversity (Early & Winton, 2001).

Assessment Practices

Assessing children under age 5 poses many difficulties (Snow & Van Hemel, 2008), and they are exacerbated when trying to assess an emergent bilingual child (Espinosa, Chapter 7, this volume). Programs have different purposes for administering assessments including measuring the child's language knowledge in both home language and in English to make placement decisions, measuring development and progress in content knowledge such as math and science to inform instruction, and evaluating child progress to determine the effectiveness of programs overall. Current assessment measures and procedures for all of these purposes for young ELLs are inadequate. Assessments are often unavailable in languages other than English and then, typically, only in Spanish. Test construction rarely takes into account the child's knowledge base across both languages and is often simply a direct translation of English tests which does not account for major structural differences in languages, dialectical variations within languages, or the fact that the order of acquisition of specific vocabulary and grammar may differ across languages. Add to this the difficulty of matching language of assessment to language of instruction and the complexities of this issue become clear.

Obviously, there is much we still need to investigate in determining how best to educate young children who are emergent bilingual. In addition, much of the current research is based on large-scale, cross-sectional databases that often assume that two coexisting factors have a causal relationship, and on small-scale, qualitative methods that make generalizations outside of the specific research context less clear. However, this base of research findings on young ELLs helps illuminate the path to policy decision and further research.

POLICY AND PRACTICE IMPLICATIONS OF CURRENT RESEARCH

It is imperative when setting policy to weigh the costs and benefits of implementing the policy. Doing so becomes especially difficult when different constituencies' needs are in conflict. For example, the cost of providing the most effective education for all competes with the costs of providing for other societal needs such as health care. Thus, when research does not clearly point the way, policymakers must weigh the risks of doing what appears to be the most promising for children—even though it is more costly to society—against implementing a less promising—yet less costly—approach, one that may ultimately be found to provide little benefit. Most recommendations, then, made without a firm research base, should be implemented in an investigative mode designed to determine whether the program or method is effective (Campbell, 1991). The following policy and practice recommendations are derived from the research base presented above but in many cases there is a need for further research to make them imperatives.

Fund and Establish Quality Data Systems

Currently, few states or government programs have databases that report on the language characteristics of preschool ELLs (García & Frede, Chapter 1, this volume). To facilitate decision making, complete information must be collected and accessible at the local, state, and national levels. Data should include information on the characteristics of early learning programs (costs; class size; size of the facility; location; and qualifications of teachers, directors, and other staff, especially academic credentials and language fluency), teaching practices, classroom quality ratings, and family characteristics of children served such as languages spoken at home by whom, socioeconomic status (SES), maternal employment and education, and cultural background. The data must be articulated with K–12 local and state level data and, where possible, linked to health and social services information.

Form Early Learning Councils in States and Local Communities

Because the provision of preschool services is so disparate and immigrant and Latino children are less likely to attend preschool of any kind, collaboration among districts officials, churches, child care, Head Start, and language-minority community groups should be a requirement of any state or federal funding for early childhood education programs. Early childhood councils can be formed to assist with coherent provision of services and recruitment of underserved families.

Increase Provision of High-Quality Dual Language Preschool

Dual language programming is rarely available for young children even though research indicates the benefits of bilingualism. Program and learning standards should be established that enhance dual language acquisition. There is a scarcity of high-quality, affordable programs in many ELL communities. ELLs have language and cognitive development needs in the preschool years that can be effectively harnessed through appropriate programming (Barnett et al., 2007; Gormley, 2007). Language plays a prominent role in the mediation of cognitive and social development, and, in addition, the literature indicates that bilingualism can be developed most effectively during the early years and that children who enter kindergarten proficient in two languages have a much better chance of academic success. Yet dual language programming is rarely available at this or later ages, and opportunities for developing English and enhancing the home language are lost.

Successful methods for dual language programming include systematically introducing and supporting both languages within the classroom in one of the following ways:

1. employ at least one teacher or assistant teacher who is bilingual (and preferably both);
2. implement two-way immersion procedures in which classrooms rotate from English-only instruction to home-language only (Some programs vary different parts of the day such as morning in one language and afternoon in another and others rotate daily or even

weekly. This method is particularly practical where there are not enough qualified bilingual teachers.); and

3. bring in home language teachers on a regular basis, typically daily, to teach in the home language.

Educate and Hire Qualified Bilingual Staff

Preschool programs should employ highly qualified bilingual, bicultural staff who can help students bridge the transition from home to school and who can serve as liaisons with the community. Where adequate numbers of qualified bilingual teachers and staff are not available, scholarships should be provided for underqualified early childhood teachers and members of the language-minority communities to obtain a teaching credential in early childhood education, especially if it specializes in bilingual education. These scholarships should be implemented with support for nontraditional students to successfully negotiate the higher education system. In addition, scholarship and in-service programs should be developed that cater to the current teaching workforce to increase their facility in the languages spoken by the children in their classrooms.

Provide Preservice and In-Service Education
on Dual Language Acquisition and Effective Teaching Practices

Even when teaching staff who speak the language of their children are available, they have rarely been trained in how to support dual language acquisition. Programs should have on staff at least one teacher coach who is a specialist in bilingual or ESL education to provide professional development to teachers in effective services for ELLs and their families. In addition, teacher licensure should require coursework in a foreign language and in linguistic development as well as specific teaching strategies for dual language learners.

Support Language-Minority Family Engagement

Programs should ensure that ELL parents are provided support to understand the importance of maintaining the home language and of their involvement in their children's education from an early age. Programs should have at least one staff member who speaks the language of the parents, and where this is not feasible due to the low incidence of the specific language, find a resource to provide translation to the parents. In addition, parent programs should be responsive to the cultural differences of their families and tailor parent involvement and parent education accordingly.

Develop Transition and Program Continuity Plans

Schools and the preschool programs that feed into them should develop individual transition plans for each child to establish seamless and connected educational programming from preschool through 3rd grade. This begins with appropriate assessment of the child's ability in the home language and in English and includes having a family advocate help the family prepare for and negotiate the transitions.

Implement Appropriate Assessment Measures

Whenever policies are enacted that require assessment of young ELL children, educators must ensure that the purpose of the assessment matches the measure chosen. For example, if the purpose of the assessment is to determine the effectiveness of instruction, then, it is necessary to use an assessment measure that matches the language or languages of instruction. Children in dual language classrooms should be assessed in both languages and children in English-only classrooms should be assessed in English. However, if the child's content knowledge, in addition to language ability, is of interest, then, an assessment of knowledge in both languages should be used. Information from standardized assessments, which have norms established on the appropriate population, should be used only in combination with ongoing curriculum-embedded assessments that include parental input on the child's skills.

Develop and Implement Bilingual Education Program Improvement Plans

Funding and oversight agencies should provide support for preschool programs to develop bilingual education program improvement plans that enhance dual language acquisition for young ELLs, support teachers in learning a second language and acquiring skill in supporting ELLs, and set out strategies to assist parents in supporting the home language.

RECOMMENDATIONS FOR FUTURE RESEARCH

The amount of research, both applied and basic, still needed to understand the development and learning of young children in general is vast, and we know far less about children acquiring more than one language than we do about the general population. The databases we called for in the policy recommendations are the first step in establishing a better research base. A critical component that is missing is information about who attends preschool programs and what their programs are like: who are the teachers of the young children; what do child care and preschool regulations require that is specific to a bilingual population; which, if any, certification requirements relate to this population; and which teaching strategies are used? We derived the following research recommendations primarily from the preceding chapters.

Bilingual Language Acquisition

Although we are beginning to understand the language development of preschool children who are simultaneous bilinguals (learned both languages from birth) and who are provided with adequate language learning environments, as Genesee (Chapter 4) points out, we know much less about sequential bilingual children who are learning English for the first time after the acquisition of their first language. We also know very little about second language acquisition for children from linguistically impoverished environments and the relationship to learning in other domains. Research to help us explicate these relationships and learning trajectories is needed.

Domain Knowledge in the Home Language and Its Relationship to Learning in English

The field would benefit from understanding the impact of different domain knowledge in the home language (literacy, math, science, etc.) on learning in English. This is of interest for the early years but also for later learning. Large-scale studies should be designed to investigate the long-term effects of beginning school bilingual with a strong language and knowledge base in both languages compared with having a strong language and knowledge base only in a language other than English or having an impoverished language and knowledge base.

Effect of English Immersion

Well-designed studies are needed to illuminate the impact of English immersion programs on children's first language development, conceptual development, academic achievement, and social development. In particular, what is the extent and nature of language shift and loss, and is this affected by family and community characteristics.

Preschool Classroom Structural and Instructional Features

Many specific questions regarding preschool classroom practice remain to be answered. How much instruction in the primary language will improve outcomes in dual language learners and what should the duration of that instruction be? What is the ideal proportion of home language to English language instruction, and does this ratio vary with age or language fluency? Is a two-way immersion approach more effective than a transitional bilingual one? What specific instructional accommodations impact the academic and social achievement of dual language learners? To what extent do other features of program quality such as class size, length of day, or mixed-age grouping influence the effectiveness of language instruction approaches and specific instructional practices? To what extent do factors related to the school, family and child moderate the impact of instructional practices on dual language learners' development? Is there a differential effect of primary language instruction for some dual language learners versus others, for example, does this effect vary by language or SES?

The Implications for Teaching of the Effect of Differences in Experience on Brain Structures and Functions

In the field of neuroscience, research should move beyond the broad question of the benefit of bilingualism to general cognitive functioning to using neurological methods that document brain activity and development, in order to more directly inform teaching. Researchers who embark on the studies suggested above should add brain imaging to their procedures to investigate how different experiences impact brain functioning, for example, to answer such questions as (a) Does greater content knowledge in the home language before learning English lead to differences at the neurological or structural level? and (b) Is there a relationship between brain structure and functioning and different approaches to bilingual instruction (age at start, two-way immersion vs. dual language instruction, or varying the proportion of home language instruction vs. English)?

Language Facility and Knowledge of Preschool Teaching Staff

We have only limited knowledge of effective staffing patterns for enhancing learning in dual language learners. Must both the teacher and the assistant be proficient in English and the children's first language? How much does the cultural background of the teacher influence learning, and how important are language facility and quality of teaching? How does teacher knowledge of child development and bilingual language acquisition affect teaching practices and child outcomes?

Professional Development of Preschool Teachers

In addition to understanding how teacher characteristics impact bilingual children, we need much more information on how to assist teachers in delivering effective instructional practices. What skills and knowledge do college faculty, program supervisors, and classroom coaches need to assist teachers, and what are the best mechanisms for effective improvement? Is peer coaching effective if a program has limited bilingual teachers? Can small communities of learners assist in improving practices? Can the use of self-evaluation and structured classroom observation tools improve practice? How should quality of practices be measured?

Rigorous and Appropriate Child Assessment

Better measures of children's language are needed to assist in program decisions and teaching; also needed is research to determine whether knowledge can be validly measured using assessment methods that combine children's demonstration of knowledge and skills in both languages within one test administration. Can this method of bilingual administration be used to accurately capture children's full capabilities? In addition, classroom-based observational assessment systems that explicitly address bilingual development should be investigated to determine if implementation results in better teaching and increased learning.

Parental Attitudes, Home Contributions, and School Engagement

We need a more sophisticated understanding of the role that parental attitudes about English learning and maintenance of home language have in children's learning. In addition, surprisingly little is known about how to affect parental engagement in education in the home or classroom and on how that engagement impacts child learning; even less is known with respect to families who speak Spanish or, especially, other non-English languages in the home.

CONCLUSION

The convergence of a rapid increase in young children who speak a language other than English in the home, the increased access to center-based care and education for this age group, and the growing awareness of our global interdependence together create a critical need to establish a comprehensive knowledge base on young English language learners. This knowledge base must not only describe and catalog, but also must explicate the intricate interrelationships among the characteristics of the children, their families, and the programs available to them, as well as how these factors interact with dual language acquisition and learning trajectories across different minority languages. This is an essential time to invest in the future of our children and, thereby, the economic health of the country, however, this investment must be well-informed by rigorous research.

REFERENCES

August, D. (2006). Demographic overview. In D. August & T. Shanahan (Eds.), *Report of the National Literacy Panel on Language Minority Youth and Children*. Mahwah, NJ: Lawrence Erlbaum.

Barnett, W. S. (2008). *Preschool education and its lasting effects: Research and policy implications*. Boulder, CO: Education and the Public Interest Center & Tempe, AZ: Education Policy Research Unit. Retrieved April 29, 2009, from http://epicpolicy.org/publication/preschooleducation

Barnett, W. S., & Yarosz, D. J. (2007). Who goes to preschool and why does it matter? *Policy Matters, 15*. New Brunswick, NJ: National Institute for Early Education Research.

Barnett, W. S., Yarosz, D. J., Thomas, J., Jung, K., & Blanco, D. (2007). Two-way and monolingual English immersion in preschool education: An experimental comparison. *Early Childhood Research Quarterly, 22*(3), 277–293.

Campbell, D. T. (1991) Methods for an experimenting society. *American Journal of Evaluation, 12*(3), 223–260.

Chang, F., Crawford, G., Early, D., Bryant, D., Howes, C., Burchinal, M., et al. (2007). Spanish-speaking children's social and language development in pre-kindergarten classrooms. *Early Education and Development, 18*(2), 243–269.

Early, D. M., & Winton, P. (2001). Preparing the workforce: Early childhood teacher preparation at 2- and 4-year institutes of higher education. *Early Childhood Research Quarterly, 16*(3), 285–306.

Frede, E., Jung, K., Barnett, W. S., Lamy, C. E., & Figueras, A. (2007). *The Abbott Preschool Program Longitudinal Effects Study (APPLES)*. New Brunswick, NJ: National Institute for Early Education Research.

García, E., & Gonzalez, M. D. (2006). *Pre-K and Latinos: The foundation for America's future*. Washington, DC: Pre-K Now.

García, E., & Jensen, B. (2009). The demographic imperative. *Educational Leadership, 65*(7), 8–13.

Gormley, W. (2007, November). *The effects of Oklahoma's pre-K program on Hispanic children*. Paper presented at the annual meeting of the Association for Public Policy Analysis and Management, Washington, DC.

Hart, B., & Risley, T. (1995). *Meaningful differences in the everyday experiences of young children*. Baltimore: Paul H. Brookes.

Karoly, L., Ghosh-Dastidar, B., Zellman, G., Perlman, M., & Fernyhough, L. (2008). *Prepared to learn: The nature and quality of early care and education for preschool-age children in California*. Retrieved October 9, 2009, from http://www.rand.org/pubs/technical_reports/TR539/

National Center for Children in Poverty. (2007). *Low-income children in the United States: National and state trend data, 1996–2006*. Retrieved June 13, 2008, from http://www.nccp.org/publications/pdf/text_761.pdf

National Clearinghouse for English Language Acquisition. (2007). *The growing numbers of limited English proficient students: 1995/96–2005/06*. Retrieved June 16, 2008, from http://www.ncela.gwu.edu/files/uploads/4/GrowingLEP_0506.pdf

O'Donnell, K. (2008). *Parents' reports of the school readiness of young children from the National Household Education Surveys Program of 2007* (NCES 2008-051). Washington, DC: National Center for Education Statistics, Institute of Education Sciences, U.S. Department of Education.

Snow, C. E., & Van Hemel, S. B. (Eds.). (2008). *Early childhood assessment: Why, what and how*. Washington, DC: The National Academic Press.

About the Contributors

Eugene E. García, vice president for education partnerships at Arizona State University, served as dean of the Mary Lou Fulton College of Education from 2002 to 2006. He joined ASU from the University of California, Berkeley, where he was dean of the Graduate School of Education. He chaired the National Task Force on Early Education for Hispanics primarily funded by the Foundation for Child Development and four additional foundations from 2006 to 2008. His most recent book is Teaching and Learning in Two Languages (2005). His research website address is http://www.ecehispanic.org.

Ellen C. Frede, co-director of the National Institute for Early Education Research at Rutgers University, is a developmental psychologist specializing in early childhood education. Prior to joining NIEER as co-director, she was appointed assistant to the commissioner for Early Childhood Education at the New Jersey Department of Education. Her office oversaw the implementation of high-quality preschool in more than 150 school districts, serving 50,000 children and their families. In addition to her work as a teacher educator and researcher, she is co-author of five classroom practices assessment systems, one of which, the Classroom Assessment of Supports for Emergent Bilingual Acquisition (CASEBA), measures environments and teaching practices that support dual language learning in early childhood classrooms.

Linda M. Espinosa, professor of Early Childhood Education (Ret.) at the University of Missouri, Columbia, has served as the co-director of the National Institute for Early Education Research (NIEER) at Rutgers University and as vice president of Education at Bright Horizons Family Solutions. Her recent research and policy work has focused on effective curriculum and assessment practices for young children from low-income families who are dual language learners. She currently serves as the co-chair of the First Five, Los Angeles County Universal Preschool Research Advisory Committee, and is a member of the National Task Force on Early Childhood Education for Hispanics Technical Advisory Group. Espinosa also served on the Head Start National Reporting System (NRS) Technical Advisory Group. Her latest book, Getting It RIGHT for Young Children from Diverse Backgrounds: Applying Research to Improve Practice, has just been published by Pearson/Merrill. Espinosa is the past treasurer of the NAEYC Governing Board and participated on the National Academy of Sciences Research Roundtable on Head Start.

Margaret Freedson is an assistant professor of Early Childhood, Elementary and Literacy Education at Montclair State University and a research fellow at the National Institute for Early Education Research at Rutgers University. A former bilingual primary grade teacher with the Los Angeles public schools, Freedson has conducted research for the Mexican Ministry of Education and coordinated the design of statewide professional development on language and literacy instruction for pre-kindergarten teachers in Texas. Her current research interests include dual language vocabulary and emergent literacy development, classroom discourse, and preschool teaching practices that support the literacy achievement of low-SES English language learners. She is lead author of the CASEBA, a preschool classroom observation instrument designed to assess classroom supports for emergent bilingual acquisition.

Claudia Galindo is an assistant professor in the Language, Literacy and Culture Ph.D. program at the University of Maryland, Baltimore County, where she teaches courses in quantitative methodology, immigration, and inequality in education. She was a post-doctoral fellow at the Center for Social Organization of Schools at Johns Hopkins University. Her research interests focus on educational inequality and minority students' educational experiences. She has published articles on the education of Latino students and on the effects of family and school connections on students' achievement. Her work integrates the fields of sociology of education, educational policy, and immigration. Galindo is a member of the Spencer Panel on Latino Children and Schooling. She was invited to conduct research studies by the National Task Force on Early Childhood Education for Hispanics at Arizona State University and the National Academies/National Research Council's Panel on Hispanics in the United States.

Fred Genesee is a professor in the Psychology Department at McGill University, Montreal. He has served on the Teachers of English to Speakers of Other Languages Board of Directors for 7 years, and part of that time as president. He has been a member of the Executive Committee of American Association of Applied Linguistics, the Standards Steering Committee of the American Council on the Teaching of Foreign Languages, the TESOL ESL Committee on Performance and Assessment Standards, and the National K–12 Foreign Language Resource Center. He has served as a consultant on second/foreign language and bilingual education in countries around the world, including Japan, Spain, Germany, Estonia, Hong Kong, Latvia, Russia, and Italy. He has conducted extensive research on alternative forms of bilingual and immersion education; his current research interests include language acquisition in preschool bilingual children, cross-language adopted children, and the language and academic development of students at-risk in bilingual programs. He is the author of numerous professional and scientific research reports and books, most recently Dual Language Development and Disorders (with J. Paradis & M. Crago, 2004) and Literacy Instruction for English Language Learners (with N. Cloud & E. Hamayan, 2009).

Donald J. Hernandez is a professor in the Department of Sociology, Hunter College, and the Graduate Center (CUNY), authored America's Children: Resources from Family, Government, and the Economy, the first national research documenting the timing, magnitude, and reasons for revolutionary family changes experienced by children since the Great Depression. He also directed the National Academy of Sciences/Institute of Medicine study on the health and adjustment of immigrant children and families. He recently completed research on 140 indicators of child well-being for race-ethnic/immigrant groups by country of origin for the United States and many local areas (www.albany.edu/csda/children) on an alternative poverty measure, and on socioeconomic disparities versus cultural differences in accounting for low early education enrollment among Hispanics in immigrant and native-born families. He is currently using the Foundation for Child Development's Index of Child Well-Being (CWI) to explore child well-being disparities by race-ethnic and immigrant origins, and by socioeconomic status and is conducting research on linguistic isolation in immigrant families. He recently completed a UNICEF project to develop internationally comparable indicators for children in immigrant and native-born families in eight rich countries.

José E. Náñez Sr. is President's Professor of Psychology & Neuroscience and executive director for Community Outreach, University Student Initiatives, at Arizona State University. His research lies within the broad field of developmental cognitive psychology and, in particular, exploration of the relationship between bilingualism and brain plasticity; early research concerned visual perception and cognitive development in infants. As a research professor at the Hispanic Research Center at Arizona State University, Náñez conducted research on developing alternative measures for identifying gifted Latino children and adolescents. Náñez has published extensively in the area of perceptual learning and brain plasticity/

malleability. This cutting-edge cognitive neuroscience research has been published in top international scientific journals including Nature, Nature Neuroscience, Nature Reviews Nature Neuroscience, Proceedings of the National Academy of Science, PLoS ONE, and Current Biology. Current scholarly projects in the area of bilingualism and brain plasticity include a co-authored volume commissioned by the American Psychological Association.

Flora V. Rodríguez-Brown is a professor in Curriculum and Instruction and in the Literacy, Language and Culture Program at the University of Illinois at Chicago. In addition to teaching courses in Bilingualism and literacy, she has been involved in family literacy with the Latino community in Chicago through Project FLAME (www.uic.edu/educ/flame) since 1989. Her research interests are in literacy and second language learning, learning at home, sociocultural issues in literacy learning, the home-school connection and the training of all teachers to serve the needs of English language learners. This research interest has led to her editing the forthcoming book *The Home-School Connection*, to be published by Taylor and Francis. She served as co-editor with Timothy Shanahan of the NRC Yearbook from 1997 to 2000. Rodríguez-Brown is serving on the Editorial Board of *Reading Research Quarterly, Journal of Literacy, The Reading Teacher, The Bilingual Education Research Journal,* and *The Journal of Early Childhood Literacy.* She served as a member of the NRC Multicultural Issues Committee and on the NRC International Issues Committee.

Index